George Lillie Craik

Spenser and his Poetry

Vol. 2

George Lillie Craik

Spenser and his Poetry
Vol. 2

ISBN/EAN: 9783337778064

Printed in Europe, USA, Canada, Australia, Japan

Cover: Foto ©Thomas Meinert / pixelio.de

More available books at **www.hansebooks.com**

SPENSER,

AND HIS

POETRY.

BY

GEO. L. CRAIK, LL.D.

A New Edition,
REVISED AND CORRECTED.

VOL. II.

LONDON:
CHARLES GRIFFIN AND COMPANY,
STATIONERS' HALL COURT.
1871.

CONTENTS.

SECTION III. *(continued.)*—THE FAIRY QUEEN . . . 5

SPENSER AND HIS POETRY.

THE FAIRY QUEEN.

Book Third.

The Third Book of the Fairy Queen contains the Legend of Britomartis, or of Chastity. Britomartis is one of the names of Diana; but it was no doubt selected by Spenser partly also on account of the sound, by which he designs to intimate that his heroine is a Britoness. As may be supposed, in celebrating " that fairest virtue, far above the rest," full advantage is taken by the poet of so fair an opportunity of complimenting his royal patroness, who was almost as vain of her virginity as of her beauty. In a prelude of five stanzas he asks himself what need he has to fetch foreign examples from Fairy Land of what shines forth with such liveliness and perfection in his sovereign, that ladies, ambitious of distinguishing themselves in a similar manner, have no occasion to look any farther—were it not, he ingeniously adds, that her portraiture can be truly expressed neither by " life-resembling pencil," nor artist's " dædal hand," " all were it Zeuxis or Praxiteles,"—

> Ne poet's wit, that passeth painter far
> In picturing the parts of beauty daint.

He then glides gracefully into a reference to his friend Raleigh's poem written in celebration of Elizabeth, which we have already found noticed in his letter explaining the plan and allegory of the Fairy Queen—

———————— that sweet verse, with nectar sprinkeled,
In which a gracious servant pictured
His Cynthia, his heaven's fairest light.

Only, he concludes, let "that same delicious poet" permit a rustic muse for a little while to appropriate his high theme, and let the fairest Cynthia not refuse to view herself in more mirrors than one—

But either Gloriana let her choose,
Or in Belphœbe fashioned to be;
In the one her rule, in the other her rare chastity.

These introductions to the several Books of the Fairy Queen, we may here observe, have all the appearance of having been written after the poem itself, and inserted, like the Dedicatory Sonnets, by the author when he was preparing it for the press.

Canto I. (67 stanzas).—From what is said at the commencement of this Canto, Guyon and the Palmer must be supposed to have returned, after their capture of Acrasia, to the house of Alma, and there rejoined Prince Arthur. Soon after the Briton Prince and Fairy Knight take leave of their fair hostess and set out again on their way together, the enchantress being at the same time sent forward by another road, and under a strong guard, to Fairy Court. After long wandering and many adventures, they see in an open plain a knight advancing towards them, attended by an aged squire, crouching, as if overladen by the burthen of his years, under his three-square or triangular shield. This shield, "bearing a lion passant in a golden field" (the legendary arms of the old British kings), the stranger knight assumes as soon as he sees the Prince and Guyon approaching, as was customary in such circumstances; but he manifests no hostile intent. Somewhat remarkably, nevertheless, Guyon at once proposes to attack him, beseeching "the prince, of grace, to let him run that turn;" and upon his companion assenting he sharply spurs forward

His foamy steed, whose fiery feet did burn
The verdant grass as he thereon did tread.

The issue, however, is that the Fairy Knight, much to his surprise as well as shame and vexation, is in an instant thrown from his saddle, and

———————————— ere well he was aware,
Nigh a spear's length behind his crouper fell.

although without mischance to life or limb. It is the first time,

———————————— sith warlike arms he bore,
And shivering spear in bloody field first shook,

that he has ever suffered such dishonour. But ah, exclaims the poet,

Ah! gentlest knight, that ever armour bore,
Let not thee grieve dismounted to have been,
And brought to ground, that never wast before,
For not thy fault, but secret power unseen:
That spear enchanted was which laid thee on the green!

His grief and shame, in truth, would be much greater if he knew by whom it is that he has been thus discomfited —if he were aware that it is a woman with whom he has fought: for his successful opponent is indeed the famous Britomart, who has come on strange adventure all the way from Britain—

To seek her lover (love far sought, alas!)
Whose image she had seen in Venus' looking-glass.

Upon all this Upton, the most learned of the commentators on the Fairy Queen, has a curious observation. The poem, he remarks, is full of allusions, either moral or historical. It is singular conduct in a courteous knight, like Guyon, to attack another by whom he has not been defied, and whom he has not himself defied. Some secret history is probably alluded to. "In Britomart," says Upton, "I suppose imaged the Virgin Queen; in Sir Guyon the Earl of Essex. Sir Guyon is dismounted, presuming to match himself against Britomart. If Guyon historically and covertly (now and then) means the Earl of Essex, will it not bear an easy allusion to his presuming to match himself with Queen Elizabeth? And has not the poet with the finest art managed a very dangerous and secret piece of history?"

Guyon, snatching his sword, is about to renew the combat, but the Palmer, knowing that "Death sate on the point of that enchanted spear," hastens to him and counsels him to desist; and, the Prince also joining in the same advice, and laying the blame, not on his own carriage, but on "his starting steed that swarved aside," and on "the ill purveyance of his page," he is at last pacified. On this they all agree to make friends, and to pursue their journey together.

> O, goodly usage of those antique times,
> In which the sword was servant unto right;
> When not for malice and contentious crimes,
> But all for praise and proof of manly might,
> The martial brood accustomed to fight:
> Then honour was the meed of victory,
> And yet the vanquished had no despite.

They travel through many lands, till at last they enter a forest, in whose gloomy shades they ride a long while without seeing tract of any living thing, " save bears, lions, and bulls, which roamed them around."

> All suddenly out of the thickest brush,
> Upon a milk-white palfrey all alone,
> A goodly lady did foreby them rush,
> Whose face did seem as clear as crystal stone,
> And eke, through fear, as white as whale's bone:
> Her garments all were wrought of beaten gold,
> And all her steed with tinsel trappings shone,
> Which fled so fast that nothing mote him hold,
> And scarce them leisure gave her passing to behold.

> Still as she fled her eye she backward threw,
> As fearing evil that pursued her fast;
> And her fair yellow locks behind her flew,
> Loosely dispersed with puff of every blast:
> All as a blazing star doth far outcast
> His hairy beams, and flaming locks dispread,
> At sight whereof the people stand aghast;

But the sage wizard tells, as he has read,
That it importunes death and doleful drearihead.

They soon perceive that she is pursued by "a griesly foster," or forester, mounted on a "tireling* jade," which he fiercely urges on

> Through thick and thin, both over bank and bush,
> In hope her to attain by hook or crook,
> That from his gory sides the blood did gush:
> Large were his limbs, and terrible his look,
> And in his clownish hand a sharp boar-spear he shook.

The two gentle knights, seeing this, we are told, instantly set forth together after the lady,

> ———————— in hope to win thereby
> Most goodly meed, the fairest dame alive—

leaving the Prince's squire, Timias, to manage the foul foster. Meanwhile Britomart,

> ——————— whose constant mind
> Would not so lightly follow beauty's chase,

after waiting for them a short time, sets forward on her way by herself. Having got nearly out of the wood, she perceives fronting her a stately castle, before the gate of which a spacious plain is wide outspread; and there six knights are fighting with one, who, though sore beset, is yet neither dismayed nor driven back, but, on the contrary, keeps them all at bay and forces them to recoil. Britomart immediately runs to his rescue, calling at the same time upon the six to forbear; but they do not heed her till she rushes amongst them and soon compels them to be at peace. The single knight then informs her that he loves a lady, "the truest one on ground"—her name the Errant Damsel—and that the six would force him, "by odds of might," to fix his affections on another dame. Certes, says Britomart, ye six are to blame in thus attempting to accomplish by force a thing by no means to be so gone about:

---

* The editors do not explain or notice this word.

> For knight to leave his lady were great shame
> That faithful is; and better were to die.
> All loss is less, and less the infamy,
> Than loss of love to him that loves but one:
> Ne may love be compelled by maistery;
> For, soon as maistery comes, sweet love anon
> Taketh his nimble wings, and soon away is gone.

[The reader will recognise in these two last fine lines the origin of Pope's couplet in the Epistle of Eloisa:

> Love, free as air, at sight of human ties,
> Spreads his light wings, and in a moment flies.]

But the six now state their case by the mouth of one of their number. In the castle dwells

> ——————— a lady fair,
> Whose sovereign beauty hath no living peer;
> Thereto so bounteous and so debonnaire,
> That never any mote with her compare:

and she has ordained a law, approved by them her servants, that every knight passing this way shall, "in case he have no lady nor no love," devote himself to her service; or, if he have another love, either give her up, or maintain in fight with them that she is fairer than the lady of the castle.

> "Perdy," said Britomart, "the choice is hard!
> But what reward had he that overcame?"
> "He should advanced be to high regard,"
> Said they, "and have our lady's love for his reward.

> "Therefore aread, sir, if thou have a love."
> "Love have I sure," quoth she, "but lady none;
> Yet will I not fro mine own love remove,
> Ne to your lady will I service done,
> But wreak your wrongs wrought to this knight alone,
> And prove his cause." With that, her mortal spear
> She mightily aventred towards one,
> And down him smote ere well aware he were;
> Then to the next she rode, and down the next did bear.

After this she throws a third to the ground, and a fourth is disposed of in like manner by the single knight; upon which the two that remain yield themselves prisoners.

They acknowledge that her's is the damsel, and they her liegemen, without however being aware that it is a woman to whom they thus surrender their swords, themselves, and their lady love. They now conduct Britomart into Castle Joyous, and passing through a long and spacious chamber soon bring her into the presence of its mistress, whom they call the Lady of Delight, but whose true name is Malecasta.

> But for to tell the sumptuous array
> Of that great chamber should be labour lost;
> For living wit, I ween, cannot display
> The royal riches and exceeding cost
> Of every pillar and of every post,
> Which all of purest bullion framed were,
> And with great pearls and precious stones embossed;
> That the bright glister of their beames clear
> Did sparkle forth great light, and glorious did appear.

But the richness and royalty of the inner room, in which the lady sits, are still more wonderful:

> The walls were round about appareled
> With costly cloths of Arras and of Tour;
> In which with cunning hand was pourtrayed
> The love of Venus and her paramour,
> The fair Adonis, turned to a flower;
> A work of rare device and wondrous wit.
> First did it show the bitter baleful stoure,
> Which her essayed with many a fervent fit,
> When first her tender heart was with his beauty smit:

> Then with what sleights and sweet allurements she
> Enticed the boy, as well that art she knew,
> And wooed him her paramour to be;
> Now making girlands of each flower that grew,
> To crown his golden locks with honour due;
> Now leading him into a secret shade
> From his beauperes,[a] and from bright heaven's view,
> Where him to sleep she gently would persuade,
> Or bathe him in a fountain by some covert glade:

> And, whilst he slept, she over him would spread
> Her mantle coloured like the starry skies,

---

[a] Fair companions.

And her soft arm lay underneath his head,
And with ambrosial kisses bathe his eyes;
And, whilst he bathed, with her two crafty spies
She secretly would search each dainty limb,
And throw into the well sweet rosemaries,
And fragrant violets, and pansies trim;
And ever with sweet nectar she did sprinkle him.

So did she steal his heedless heart away,
And joyed his love in secret unespied.

In another picture he lies languishing of his wound, while the goddess weeps and laments by his side;

—————————— and evermore
With her soft garment wipes away the gore
Which stains his snowy skin with hateful hue:
But, when she saw no help might him restore,
Him to a dainty flower she did transmue,[b]
Which in that cloth was wrought, as if it lively grew.

All around the chamber are beds or couches, " as whilome was the antique world's guise," and throngs of squires and damsels fill it continually with dance and revel.

And all the while sweet music did divide
Her looser notes with Lydian harmony;
And all the while sweet birds thereto applied
Their dainty lays and dulcet melody,
Aye carolling of love and jollity.

Britomart and the other knight, who now turn out to be our old acquaintance, the Knight of the Redcross—his Errant Damsel, therefore, being Una—loathe the loose demeanour of the wanton crew, but suffer themselves to be led up to the great lady, whom they find seated on a sumptuous bed, glistering all with gold and glorious show, as was the wont of the proud Persian queens. She is of rare beauty, although her wanton eyes roll somewhat lightly, and are, like Lesbia's in Moore's song, too fond of flashing their beams to right and left. By her order the two strangers are bounteously entertained, and, being taken into a bower to be disarmed, " and cheered well with wine and spicery," the Redcross Knight is soon

[b] Transmute.

stripped, but the brave maid will only vent, or lift up, her umbrier, that is the visor of her helmet, so as to allow her face to appear:—

    As when fair Cynthia, in darksome night,
    Is in a noyous cloud enveloped,
    Where she may find the substance thin and light
    Breaks forth her silver beams, and her bright head
    Discovers to the world discomfited ;
    Of the poor traveller that went astray
    With thousand blessings she is heried :[c]
    Such was the beauty and the shining ray
    With which fair Britomart gave light unto the day.

    And eke those six, which lately with her fought,
    Now were disarmed, and did themselves present
    Unto her view, and company unsought ;
    For they all seemed courteous and gent,
    And all six brethren, born of one parent,
    Which had them trained in all civility,
    And goodly taught to tilt and tournament :
    Now were they liegemen to this lady free,
    And her knight's-service ought,[d] to hold of her in fee.

    The first of them by name Gardante hight,
    A jolly person, and of comely view ;
    The second was Parlante, a bold knight ;
    And next to him Jocante did ensue ;
    Basciante did himself most courteous shew ;
    But fierce Bacchante seemed too fell and keen ;
    And yet in arms Noctante greater grew :
    All were fair knights, and goodly well beseen :
    But to fair Britomart they all but shadows been.

    For she was full of amiable grace,
    And manly terror mixed therewithal ;
    That, as the one stirred up affections base,
    So the other did men's rash desires appal,
    And hold them back that would in error fall :
    As he that hath espied a vermeil rose,
    To which sharp thorns and breres the way forestall,
    Dare not for dread his hardy hand expose,
    But, wishing it far off, his idle wish doth lose.

The " fresh and lusty knight," as Britomart seems, soon

    [c] Praised, blessed.   [d] Owed.

kindles a flame in the bosom of the very combustible lady of the castle, who manifests her passion by sufficiently intelligible signs; but Britomart takes no notice of her crafty glances.

> Supper was shortly dight, and down they sat;
> Where they were served with all sumptuous fare,
> Whiles fruitful Ceres and Lyæus fat
> Poured out their plenty, without spite or spare;
> Nought wanted there that dainty was and rare:
> And aye the cups their banks did overflow:
> And aye between the cups she did prepare
> Way to her love, and secret darts did throw;
> But Britomart would not such guileful message know.

At last she plainly intimates in words what she feels, and Britomart, who, " by self-feeling of her feeble sex," knows what love is, is not so hard-hearted as to receive her confession with discourtesy—though deeming her somewhat light in thus wooing a wandering guest. As the evening advanced every knight and gentle squire

> Gan choose his dame with basciomani gay,

that is, with kissing of hands; and

> Some fell to dance; some fell to hazardry;e
> Some to make love; some to make merriment;
> As diverse wits to diverse things apply:
> And all the while fair Malecasta bent
> Her crafty engines to her close intent.
> By this the eternal lamps, wherewith high Jove
> Doth light the lower world, were half yspent,
> And the moist daughters of huge Atlas strove
> Into the ocean deep to drive their weary drove.

All now retire to rest, guided to their bowers by long waxen torches—the Britoness also now undressing, and committing herself to " her soft-feathered nest," where she soon falls sound asleep. Sometime after, however, she is awakened by finding some one stretched beside her; she starts from her bed, and runs to seize her sword; but Malecasta, for it is she,

. The game of hazard.

———————— half dead
Through sudden fear and ghastly drearihead,
Did shriek aloud, that through the house it rong,
And the whole family therewith adread
Rashly out of their roused couches sprong,
And to the troubled chamber all in arms did throng.

The confusion that ensues may be imagined. Only the Redcross Knight openly stands by Britomart; the others, still remembering the event of their yesterday's encounter, are not disposed too rashly again to draw down her hostility;—

But one of those six knights, Gardante hight,
Drew out a deadly bow and arrow keen,
Which forth he sent, with felonous despite
And fell intent, against the virgin sheen:
The mortal steel stayed not till it was seen
To gore her side; yet was the wound not deep,
But lightly razed her soft silken skin,
That drops of purple blood thereout did weep,
Which did her lily smock with stains of vermeil steep.

Wherewith enraged she fiercely at them flew,
And with her flaming sword about her laid,
That none of them foul mischief could eschew,
But with her dreadful strokes were all dismayed:
Here, there, and every where, about her swayed
Her wrathful steel, that none mote it abide;
And eke the Redcross Knight gave her good aid,
Aye joining foot to foot, and side to side;
That in short space their foes they have quite terrified.

Tho,^f whenas all were put to shameful flight,
The noble Britomartis her arrayed,
And her bright arms about her body dight;
For nothing would she lenger there be stayed,
Where so loose life and so ungentle trade
Was used of knights and ladies seeming gent:
So, early, ere the gross earth's greasy shade
Was all dispersed out of the firmament,
They took their steeds, and forth upon their journey went.

Canto II. (52 stanzas).—The poet begins this Canto by

---

^f Then.

complaining that men have not generally shown themselves "indifferent," that is, impartial, "to womankind;"

> To whom no share in arms and chivalry
> They do impart, ne maken memory
> Of their brave gests and prowess martial:
> Scarce do they spare to one, or two, or three
> Room in their writs; yet the same writing small
> Does all their deeds deface, and dims their glories all.

By record of ancient times, nevertheless, he finds that women were formerly wont in wars to bear the greatest sway, and even in all great exploits to bear away the garland, till envious men began to "coin strait laws to curb their liberty." Yet, he gallantly adds, since they have laid aside warlike weapons and exercises,

> They have excelled in arts and policy,
> That now we foolish men that praise gan eke to envy.

This, of course, is a piece of adulation to Queen Elizabeth.

As Britomart and the Redcross Knight (here called Guyon, by a mistake either of the press, or, more probably, of the author) are journeying on together, the maid, at the fairy's request, and after suffering violent agitation before she begins, relates to him what it is that has induced her to take up the vocation of knight errantry. Ever since her birth she has been trained to arms, and has loathed her life to lead,

> As ladies wont, in pleasure's wanton lap,
> To finger the fine needle and nice thread.

All her delight, on the contrary, has been in warlike adventures; and in quest of praise and fame so to be acquired it is that she has come from her native soil, the Greater Britain, hither to Fairy Land. But can the knight, she asks, give her any tidings of one who has lately done her foul dishonour, and on whom she is now seeking to be revenged, one whose name is Arthegal? She would recall the words, but it is too late: "Fair martial maid," replies the Redcross Knight,

> ——————— of all that ever played
> At tilt or tourney, or like warlike game,
> The noble Arthegal hath ever borne the name.

Britomart is inwardly rejoiced " to hear her love so highly magnified;" but she still professes to be intent on revenge, and requests the knight to direct her where she " that faitor false [false doer or deceiver] may find." He answers that it is not easy to say where or how Sir Arthegal may be found;

> For he ne wonneth in one certain stead,
> But restless walketh all the world around,
> Aye doing thinges that to his fame redound,
> Defending ladies' cause and orphans' right.

His words sink into her " molten heart:"—

> For pleasing words are like to magic art,
> That doth the charmed snake in slumber lay:
> Such secret ease felt gentle Britomart,
> Yet list the same efforce with feigned gainsay;
> (So discord oft in music makes the sweeter lay).

So she goes on to protest that, if she and Arthegal chance to encounter, one of them shall certainly die or surrender; and she gets the Redcross Knight to describe to her his shield, his arms, his horse, his person, that she may know him when she beholds him. Yet all these particulars she is already familiar with, and has had by heart ever since she first fell in love with Arthegal upon seeing his image in Britain revealed in the magician Merlin's wondrous mirror. This looking-glass Merlin had fabricated in Deheubarth, or South Wales, in the days of King Ryence:—

> It virtue had to show in perfect sight
> Whatever thing was in the world contained
> Betwixt the lowest earth and heaven's height,
> So that it to the looker appertained:
> Whatever foe had wrought, or friend had feigned,
> Therein discovered was, ne ought mote pass,
> Ne ought in secret from the same remained;
> Forthy^g it round and hollow shaped was,
> Like to the world itself, and seemed a world of glass.

---

^g Therefore, accordingly.

Who wonders not, that reads so wondrous work?
But who does wonder, that has read the tower
Wherein the Ægyptian Phao[h] long did lurk
From all men's view, that none might her discour,[i]
Yet she might all men view out of her bower?
Great Ptolemy it for his leman's sake
Ybuilded all of glass by magic power,
And also it impregnable did make;
Yet, when his love was false, he with a peaze it brake.
Such was the glassy globe that Merlin made,
And gave unto King Ryence for his guard.
That never foes his kingdom might invade,
But he it knew at home before he heard
Tidings thereof, and so them still debarred:
It was a famous present for a prince,
And worthy work of infinite reward,
That treasons could bewray, and foes convince:
Happy this realm, had it remained ever since!

Britomart, who was King Ryence's only daughter, and the heir of his kingdom, having one day gone into her father's closet, first viewed awhile her fair self in that fair mirror; but then,—

—— as it falleth, in the gentlest hearts
Imperious Love hath highest set his throne,
And tyrannizeth in the bitter smarts
Of them that to him buxom are and prone;—
So thought this maid (as maidens use to done)
Whom fortune for her husband would allot.

Soon there presented himself in the glass a comely knight, in complete armour, with his visor up so as to disclose his manly face; his person was portly and of heroic grace:—

His crest was covered with a couchant hound,
And all his armour seemed of antique mould,
But wondrous massy and assured sound,
And round about yfretted all with gold,
In which there written was, with cyphers old,

---

[h] The mistress of one of the Ptolemies.
[i] Discover.　　　　　　　　　　　　Blow.

Achilles' arms which Arthegal did win:
And on his shield enveloped sevenfold
He bore a crowned little ermilin,
That decked the azure field with her fair pouldred[k] skin.

She both viewed this personage well, and liked him well; but lingered no further over what she saw, and went her way:—

———————— ne her unguilty age
Did ween, unwares, that her unlucky lot
Lay hidden in the bottom of the pot:
Of hurt unwist most danger doth redound.

The "false archer," however, had shot his bolt:—

Thenceforth the feather in her lofty crest,
Ruffed[l] of love, gan lowly to avail;
And her proud portance and her princely gest,[m]
With which she erst triumphed, now did quail.

By day, by night, she cannot escape from the thought of "that fair image written in her heart." At last one night her aged nurse Glauce, who slept with her, extracted her secret and restored to her some measure of peace of mind. "O daughter dear," rejoined the old woman to Britomart's first confession of hopeless affection,

———————— "despair no whit,
For never sore but might a salve obtain;
That blinded god, which hath ye blindly smit,
Another arrow hath your lover's heart to hit."

"But neither god of love nor god of sky
Can do," said she, "that which cannot be done."
"Things oft impossible," quoth she, "seem ere begun."

And then the kind and wise-hearted dame followed up her re-assuring words with caresses that made them irresistible:—

[k] Spotted.   [l] Ruffled.   [m] Carriage.

With that, upleaning on her elbow weak,
Her alabaster breast she oft did kiss,
Which all that while she felt to pant and quake,
As it an earthquake were.

In the end, when Britomart had told her all, her faithful friend vowed, if she could not conquer her passion, that, by wrong or right, she would compass her desire and find for her the object of her love. In the morning they both arose before day, and repaired to church, where, however, we are told, they said their prayers, although with great devotion, yet with little zeal:—

For the fair damsel from the holy herse [n]
Her love-sick heart to other thoughts did steal:
And that old dame said many an idle verse,
Out of her daughter's heart fond fancies to reverse.

Returned home, the royal infant fell
Into her former fit; for why? no power
Nor guidance of herself in her did dwell.
But the aged nurse, her calling to her bower,
Had gathered rue, and savin, and the flower
Of camphora, and calamint, and dill;
All which she in an earthen pot did pour,
And to the brim with coltwood did it fill,
And many drops of milk and blood through it did spill.

Then, taking thrice three hairs from off her head,
Them trebly braided in a threefold lace,
And round about the pot's mouth bound the thread,
And, after having whispered a space
Certain sad words with hollow voice and base,
She to the virgin said, thrice said she it;
"Come, daughter, come; come, spit upon my face;
Spit thrice upon me, thrice upon me spit;
The uneven number for this business is most fit."

That said, her round about she from her turned,
She turned her contrary to the sun;
Thrice she her turned contrary, and returned
All contrary; for she the right did shun;
And ever what she did was straight undone.

---

[n] Rehearsal of the service.

So thought she to undo her daughter's love:
But love, that is in gentle breast begun,
No idle charm so lightly may remove:
That well can witness who by trial it does prove.

The noble maid, in fact,

—— shortly like a pined ghost became
Which long hath waited by the Stygian strand;

and Glauce, utterly baffled, wist not what to do.
Canto III. (62 stanzas).—"Most sacred fire," exclaims the poet, in commencing the continuation of the story of Britomart,

Most sacred fire that burnest mightily
In living breasts, ykindled first above
Amongst the eternal spheres and lamping° sky,
And thence poured into men, which men call Love;
Whence spring all noble deeds and never-dying fame:
Well did Antiquity a god thee deem,
That over mortal minds hast so great might.

He then proceeds to relate how Glauce, finding all her efforts and experiments vain, at last advised that application should be made to Merlin, the fabricator of the mirror; and how thereupon she and Britomart, disguising themselves "in strange and base array," set out together for Maridunum, now Cayr-Merdin (Caermarthen), where

—————— the wise Merlin whilome wont (they say)
To make his won, low underneath the ground,
In a deep delve, far from the view of day,
That of no living wight he mote be found,
Whenso he counseled with his sprites encompassed round.

The place is a hideous cavern under a rock, lying a little space

From the swift Barry, tumbling down apace
Amongst the woody hills of Dynevowre—

that is Dynevor Castle, near Caermarthen, formerly the

° Shining.

chief seat of the Princes of South Wales. But, continues the poet,

> — dare thou not, I charge, in any case
> To enter into that same baleful bower,
> For fear the cruel fiends should thee unwares devour;
>
> But standing high aloft low lay thine ear,
> And there such ghastly noise of iron chains
> And brazen cauldrons thou shalt rumbling hear,
> Which thousand sprites with long enduring pains
> Do toss, that it will stun thy feeble brains;
> And oftentimes great groans, and grievous stounds,
> When too huge toil and labour them constrains;
> And oftentimes loud strokes and ringing sounds
> From under that deep rock most horribly rebounds.

The cause is said to be this: a short time before his death Merlin had set his spirits at work to fabricate a brazen wall which he designed to erect around the city of Caermarthen; meanwhile the Lady of the Lake, whom he had long loved, sending for him in haste, he bound them not to slacken their labour till he should come back. But the luckless magician was destined never to revisit his ancient home :—

> ——————— through that false lady's train [p]
> He was surprised, and buried under bier,
> Ne ever to his work returned again.

Or, as the story is told in the old romance of *La Morte d'Arthur*:—" The Lady of the Lake and Merlin departed; and by the way as they went Merlin showed to her many wonders, and came into Cornwall. And always Merlin hung about the lady, for to have her favour; and she was ever passing weary of him, and fain would have been delivered of him; for she was afraid of him, because he was a devil's son, and she could not put him away by no means. And so upon a time it happened that Merlin shewed to her in a rock wherein was a great wonder, and wrought by enchantment, which went under a stone ; so, by her subtile craft and working,

[p] Deceit.

she made Merlin to go under that stone, to let him wit of the marvels there. But she wrought so there for him that he came never out, for all the craft that he could do." There, accordingly, it is believed that he remains till this hour.

> Natheless those fiends may not their work forbear,
> So greatly his commandëment they fear,
> But there do toil and travail day and night,
> Until that brazen wall they up do rear;
> For Merlin had in magic more insight
> Then ever him before or after living wight:
>
> For he by words could call out of the sky
> Both sun and moon, and make them him obey;
> The land to sea, and sea to mainland dry,
> And darksome night he eke could to turn to day;
> Huge hosts of men he could alone dismay,
> And hosts of men of meanest things could frame,
> When so him list his enemies to fray:
> That to this day, for terror of his fame,
> The fiends do quake when any him to them does name.

It is said that he was no son of mortal sire, but the offspring of "a fair lady nun," Matilda, daughter to Pubidius, Lord of Mathtraval (one of the three provinces into which Wales was divided by Roderic the Great), and cousin to King Ambrosius, conceived in her "by false illusion of a guileful sprite." Britomart and Glauce, after some hesitation, entering (the maid first, made courageous by love) the dread magician's cave, found him deeply intent about one of his wondrous works,

> And writing strange characters in the ground,
> With which the stubborn fiends he to his service bound.

He had been aware both that they were coming and what was their object; and he only smiled at Glauce's attempts to conceal from him who they were, and to dissemble by "womanish guile" her knowledge of Britomart's real ailment. Bursting forth at length into a laugh, he exclaimed—

> " Glauce, what needs this colourable word
> To cloak the cause that hath itself bewrayed?

Ne ye, fair Britomartis, thus arrayed,
More hidden are than sun in cloudy vale."

On this, we are told—

The doubtful maid, seeing herself descried,
Was all abashed, and her pure ivory
Into a clear carnation sudden dyed ;
As fair Aurora, rising hastily,
Doth by her blushing tell that she did lie
All night in old Tithonus' frozen bed,
Whereof she seems ashamed inwardly :

but the old nurse boldly demanded of the prophet, that, seeing he knew all, he would not withhold pity and relief. He paused awhile, and then his spirit broke forth :—

" Most noble virgin, that by fatal lore
Hast learned to love, let no whit thee dismay
The hard begin that meets thee in the door,
And with sharp fits thy tender heart oppresseth sore :

For so must all things excellent begin."

And then he told her that from her womb should spring a famous progeny of the ancient Trojan blood, that should

———————— revive the sleeping memory
Of those same antique peers, the heaven's brood,
Which Greek and Asian rivers stained with their blood ;

and re-establish the power of the Britons, broken and enfeebled by long wars against a foreign foe from a distant land. The man ordained to be the spouse of Britomart, he afterwards informed them, was Arthegal : he dwelt in the Land of Fairy, yet was no fairy's son, nor related at all to the race of the elfs, but of earthly lineage, having only been in infancy stolen from his cradle by the fairies, and imagining himself to be the offspring of an elf and a fay. He was in truth the son of Gorlois, Prince of Cornwall, and brother to Cador, now reigning in that kingdom, and renowned for his warlike feats from the rising to the setting sun. 'It was ordained that Britomart should bring him back to his native soil, and that both he and she should give great proof of their valour, until Arthegal should be cut off too early by the treachery of secret foes. But his son by Britomart (apparently the same who is called Aurelius Conan by the old British historians) should remain the living representation of his sire; and should take from his cousin Constantius (or Constantine, son of Cador) the crown that had of right belonged to his father Arthegal. He, after a reign in which he should fight three great battles with the Saxons, two of them ending in the defeat of the intruders, the third " in fair accordance," that is, apparently, in an agreement or peace on equal terms, should be succeeded by his son Voltipore " in kingdom, but not in felicity." Voltipore's son Malgo, however, should avenge the misfortunes of his father—Malgo, who should reduce to subjection " the six islands, comprovincial in ancient times unto great Britany." namely, Ireland, Iceland, Gothland, the Orkneys, Norway, and Dacia (that is, Denmark); all which his son Careticus should well defend from the Saxon foe; till great Gormond (King of Africa), after having subdued Ireland, " and therein fixed his throne," should come over with a multitude of his Norveyses (or Norwegians) to assist the latter—when their united bands, said Merlin, shall sack and slay, and commit such devastation, that

  —— " the green grass that groweth they shall bren,⁋
  That even the wild beast shall die in starved den."

In the rest of his address he continued the history of the wars between the Saxons and Britons to the time of Cadwallader, and his expulsion, towards the close of the seventh century, to Armorica, or the Lesser Britain " Then," he concluded,

  ——"woe, and woe, and everlasting woe,
  Be to the Briton babe that shall be born
  To live in tharldom of his father's foe!
  Late king, now captive; late lord, now forlorn;

⁋ Burn.

> The world's reproach; the cruel victor's scorn;
> Banished from princely bower to wasteful wood!
> O! who shall help me to lament and mourn
> The royal seed, the antique Trojan blood,
> Whose empire longer here than ever any stood!"

But, he afterwards added, in reply to the further inquiries of Britomart, the thraldom of the Britons was limited to a certain term; after twice four hundred years they should be restored to their former rule and sovereignty; and then he sketched the remainder of the English story through the Danish invasions, the Norman Conquest, the Welsh revolts, to the acquisition of the crown by Henry VII. of the Welsh House of Tudor. From that time henceforth should be peace and eternal union between the two nations;—

> "Then shall a royal virgin reign, which shall
> Stretch her white rod over the Belgic shore,
> And the great Castle smite so sore withal,
> That it shall make him shake, and shortly learn to fall:
> But yet the end is not."

The allusions here are explained as being to Queen Elizabeth's protection of the revolted Netherlanders, and her shaking the power of the Castilian (or Spanish) King. At those last words the Magician paused, "as overcomen of the spirit's power;" but he soon recovered, and dismissed the two women with his usual cheerful looks. When they had returned home, it was suggested by the always ready Glauce, that they should disguise themselves in armour, and go and join King Arthur, now making war upon the Saxon brethren, Octa and Oza (or Eosa, as the name is written by Geoffrey of Monmouth); and this plan they executed by means of a suit of armour belonging to Angela, Queen of the Angles (a fictitious personage), which had a few days before been taken by the Britons, and suspended by King Ryence in his principal church; with this, and with a spear which stood beside it, long before made by King Bladud by magic art, and possessed of wondrous virtues, the old woman arrayed Britomart, and then,

Another harness which did hang thereby
About herself she dight, that the young maid
She might in equal arms accompany,
And as her squire attend her carefully:
Tho to their ready steeds they clomb full light;
And through back ways, that none might them espy,
Covered with secret cloud of silent night,
Themselves they forth conveyed, and passed forward right.

Nor did they rest till they came to Fairy Land, as Merlin had directed them; there Britomart and the Redcross Knight having met, as has already been told, for some time journeyed and held discourse together; till at length, their ways separating, they bid each other affectionately adieu—the Redcross Knight turning off in another direction, Britomart continuing to ride forward.

Arthegal is supposed to be designed for Spenser's patron, Arthur Lord Grey of Wilton.

Canto IV. (61 stanzas).—The glory of all antique heroines, the poet assures us, is eclipsed by that of noble Britomart; "well worthy stock," he exclaims,

—————— from which the branches sprong
That in late years so fair a blossom bare,
As thee, O Queen, the matter of my song,
Whose lineage from this lady I derive along.

She and her companion having parted, as has been told, after binding themselves to each other in "a friendly league of love perpetual,"

— Britomart kept on her former course,
Ne ever doffed her arms; but all the way
Grew pensive through that amorous discourse.
By which the Redcross Knight did erst display
Her lover's shape and chivalrous array:
A thousand thoughts she fashioned in her mind;
And in her feigning fancy did pourtray
Him, such as fittest she for love could find,
Wise, warlike, personable, courteous, and kind.

At last she and her old squire come to the sea-coast.

Here sitting down, she pours out her lament to the waves, not more restless than the billows of passion that toss her heart:—

> "Love, my lewd pilot, hath a restless mind;
> And Fortune, boatswain, no assurance knows;
> But sail withouten stars gainst tide and wind:
> How can they other do, sith both are bold and blind!
>
> Thou god of winds, that reignest in the seas,
> That reignest also in the continent,
> At last blow up some gentle gale of ease."

She is soon roused, however, by the approach of an armed and mounted knight, who when he comes up instantly and sternly demands that she should fly without loss of a moment from a way or road which he claims as his own.

> Ythrilled with deep disdain of his proud threat,
> She shortly thus; "Fly they, that need to fly;
> Words fearen babes: I mean not thee entreat
> To pass; but maugre thee will pass or die."

And with these words, staying for no reply, she dashes against the stranger knight, who at the same time boldly advances and strikes her full in the breast, so as to make her

———————————————— down
Decline her head, and touch her crupper with her crown;

but she, nevertheless, sends her spear through the three-square scutcheon on his shield into his left side, and, pitching him the full length of the shaft from his seat, lays him on the sand tumbled together in a heap and wallowing in his blood.

> Like as the sacred ox, that careless stands
> With gilden horns and flowery girlands crowned,
> Proud of his dying honour and dear bands,
> Whiles the altars fume with frankincense around,
> All suddenly with mortal stroke astound
> Doth grovelling fall, and with his streaming gore
> Distains the pillars and the holy ground,

And the fair flowers that decked him afore:
So fell proud Marinel upon the precious shore.

The meaning of the epithet thus given to the shore appears from the next stanza:—

> The martial maid stayed not him to lament,
> But forward rode, and kept her ready way
> Along the strond; which, as she over-went,
> She saw bestrewed all with rich array
> Of pearls and precious stones of great assay,
> And all the gravel mixt with golden ore:
> Whereat she wondered much, but would not stay
> For gold, or pearls, or precious stones, an hour,
> But them despised all; for all was in her power.

Marinel, who has been thus overthrown, is the son of black-browed Cymoent, daughter of great Nereus, by an earthly father, " the famous Dumarin;" he was brought up by his mother in a rocky cave,

> —————————— till he became
> A mighty man at arms, and mickle fame
> Did get through great adventures by him done.
> For never man he suffered by that same
> Rich strond to travel, whereas he did won,
> But that he must do battle with the sea-nymph's son.

At the request of Cymoent, his grandfather had endowed him with such abundance of wealth as never was possessed by offspring of earthly womb:—

> ——— his heaped waves he did command
> Out of their hollow bosom forth to throw
> All the huge threasure which the sea below
> Had in his greedy gulf devoured deep,
> And him enriched through the overthrow
> And wrecks of many wretches, which did weep
> And often wail their wealth which he from them did keep.
>
> Shortly upon that shore there heaped was
> Exceeding riches and all precious things,
> The spoil of all the world; that it did pass
> The wealth of the East, and pomp of Persian kings:
> Gold, amber, ivory, pearls, owches, rings,

And all that else was precious and dear,
The sea unto him voluntary brings;
That shortly he a great lord did appear,
As was in all the land of Fairy, or elsewhere.

Proteus had ere this alarmed Cymoent by foretelling her, though in the usual deluding language of prophecy, what would be the fate of her son: he,

—— through foresight of his eternal skill,
Bade her from womankind to keep him well;
For of a woman he should have much ill;
A virgin strange and stout him should dismay or kill.

Forthy she gave him warning every day
The love of women not to entertain;
A lesson too too hard for living clay,
From love in course of nature to refrain!
Yet he his mother's lore did well retain,
And ever from fair ladies' love did fly;
Yet many ladies fair did oft complain,
That they for love of him would algates die:
Die whoso list for him, he was love's enemy.

Tidings of what has befallen him are now brought to his mother,

——————— whereas she played
Amongst her watery sisters by a pond,
Gathering sweet daffodillies, to have made
Gay girlands from the sun their foreheads fair to shade.

After she recovers from the swoon into which she is thrown by the news,

—— she bade her chariot to be brought;
And all her sisters, that with her did sit,
Bade eke at once their chariots to be sought:
Tho, full of bitter grief and pensive thought,
She to her waggon clomb; clomb all the rest,
And forth together went, with sorrow fraught:
The waves obedient to their behest
Them yielded ready passage, and their rage surceast.

Great Neptune stood amazed at their sight,
Whilst on his broad round back they softly slid.

And eke himself mourned at their mournful plight,
Yet wist not what their wailing meant, yet did,
For great compassion of their sorrow, bid
His mighty waters to them buxom be:
Eftsoons the roaring billows still abid,ʳ
And all the grisly monsters of the sea
Stood gaping at their gait,ˢ and wondered them to see.

A team of dolphins ranged in array
Drew the smooth chariot of sad Cymoent;
They were all taught by Triton to obey
To the long reins at her commandement:
As swift as swallows on the waves they went,
That their broad flaggy fins no foam did rear,
Ne bubbling roundel they behind them sent;
The rest, of other fishes drawen were,
Which with their finny oars the swelling sea did shear.

Arrived at the rich strand, they leave their chariots,

And let their timid fishes softly swim
Along the margent of the foamy shore.
Lest they their fins should bruise, and surbateᵗ sore
Their tender feet upon the stony ground.

At sight of Marinel, his mother, we are told, made such piteous moan,

That the hard rocks could scarce from tears refrain,

her sister nymphs accompanying her with their sobs and cries. She inveighs against "Fond Proteus, father of false prophecies," and those more fond who believe him, for here, as she says, is evidently no work of woman's hand. Then, softly taking off his armour, and spreading on the ground beneath him their "watchet," or blue, mantles fringed with silver, they bind up the wound, and pour into it

———— sovereign balm and nectar good,
Good both for earthly medicine and for heavenly food.

"The lily-handed Liagore," who had been taught leech-

ʳ Abided, remained.　　　ˢ Going, progress.
　　　ᵗ Weary.

craft by great Apollo, by whom she was the mother of
Pæon, now feels his pulse, and revives some hope in
the heart of Cymoent by assuring her that some little
spark of life still remains. On this they take him up in
their tender hands, and bear him softly to his mother's
chariot :—

> Her team at her commandment quiet stands,
> Whilst they the corse into her waggon rear,
> And strew with flowers the lamentable bier:
> Then all the rest into their coaches climb,
> And through the brackish waves their passage shear;
> Upon great Neptune's neck they softly swim,
> And to her watery chamber swiftly carry him.
>
> Deep in the bottom of the sea her bower
> Is built of hollow billows heaped high,
> Like to thick clouds that threat a stormy shower,
> And vaulted all within like to the sky,
> In which the gods do dwell eternally:
> There they him laid in easy couch well dight;
> And sent in haste for Tryphon, to apply
> Salves to his wounds, and medicines of might:
> For Tryphon of sea-gods the sovereign leech is hight.

The story now returns to Prince Arthur and Guyon,
who, it may be remembered, were left in the First Canto
engaged in the pursuit of Florimel, while Timias, the
Prince's squire, went after the wicked foster from whom
the lady was flying. After chasing " the fearful damsel "
together for some time,

> Through thick and thin, through mountains and through
>   plains,

the two knights had at last separated, each taking one
of two ways into which the road divided. It was the
Prince's fortune to choose that which brought him within
view of the lady, whom, however, he cannot prevail upon
to stop with all his courteous and re-assuring words ; so
that, after riding till clouds have covered the nocturnal
sky and concealed the long risen stars, he is obliged to
give up the hopeless attempt to catch her, and, dis-
mounting, he lays himself down on the grass to sleep.

But no sleep will come; a thousand fancies beat his idle
brain with their light wings; he wishes and half hopes
that the lady fair may be his Fairy Queen herself; and
he pours out his reproaches on the night, which has reft
her from him:—

"Night! thou foul mother of annoyance sad,
Sister of heavy Death, and nurse of Woe,
Which wast begot in heaven, but for thy bad
And brutish shape thrust down to hell below,
Where, by the grim flood of Cocytus slow,
Thy dwelling is in Erebus' black house,
(Black Erebus, thy husband, is the foe
Of all the gods), where thou ungracious
Half of thy days dost lead in horror hideous;

What had the Eternal Maker need of thee
The world in his continual course to keep,
That dost all things deface, ne lettest see
The beauty of his work? Indeed in sleep
The slothful body that doth love to steep
His lustless limbs, and drown his baser mind,
Doth praise thee oft, and oft from Stygian deep
Calls thee his goddess, in his error blind,
And great dame Nature's handmaid cheering every kind

But well I wote that to an heavy heart
Thou art the root and nurse of bitter cares,
Breeder of new, renewer of old smart:
Instead of rest thou lendest railing ᵘ tears:
Instead of sleep thou sendest troublous fears
And dreadful visions, in the which alive
The dreary image of sad Death appears:
So from the weary spirit thou dost drive
Desired rest, and men of happiness deprive.

Under thy mantle black there hidden lie
Light-shunning Theft, and traitorous Intent,
Abhorred Bloodshed, and vile Felony,
Shameful Deceipt, and Danger imminent,
Foul Horror, and eke hellish Dreariment:
All these I wote in thy protection be,
And light do shun, for fear of being shent:

ᵘ Trickling.

> For light alike is loathed of them and thee;
> And all that lewdness love do hate the light to see.
>
> For Day discovers all dishonest ways,
> And sheweth each thing as it is in deed:
> The praises of High God he fair displays,
> And His large bounty rightly doth aread:
> Day's dearest children be the blessed seed
> Which Darkness shall subdue and heaven win:
> Truth is his daughter; he her first did breed
> Most sacred virgin without spot of sin:
> Our life is day; but death with darkness doth begin.
>
> O, when will Day then turn to me again,
> And bring with him his long-expected light!
> O Titan! haste to rear thy joyous wain;
> Speed thee to spread abroad thy beames bright.
> And chase away this too long lingering Night:
> Chase her away, from whence she came, to hell:
> She, she it is, that hath me done despite:
> There let her with the damned spirits dwell,
> And yield her room to Day, that can it govern well."

Thus he spends the time " in restless anguish and unquiet pain," till the re-appearance of the light, when, " half in great disdain," he again mounts his steed, and " with heavy look and lumpish pace," the animal accommodating his steps to his master's mood of mind, pursues his way.

Canto V. (55 stanzas).—The Prince rides long without finding a way out of the forest; but at last meets a dwarf, running along in affright, who, in reply to his inquiry what he flies from or after, intimates in a few hasty words, that he is in pursuit of his mistress, " a lady of great sway and high account throughout all Elfin Land," whom he had long served, and who had lately set out from Fairy Court, and taken this road. Further questioned, he describes her as " royally clad in cloth of gold;" adding,

> " Her fair locks in rich circlet be enrolled,
> A fairer wight did never sun behold;
> And on a palfrey rides more white than snow,
> Yet she herself is whiter manifold·

The surest sign, whereby ye may her know,
Is, that she is the fairest wight alive, I trow."

It is clear that she is the lady whom the Prince had himself been lately pursuing. The Dwarf informs him that she is a virgin renowned for her chastity and virtue; that she is named Florimel the Fair—

Fair Florimel, beloved of many a knight,
Yet she loves none but one, that Marinel is hight.

Marinel, however, warned by his mother against ladies' love, "sets nought at all by Florimel." But it is now reported that he is slain; five days, they say, it is since this happened, and it is four since Florimel left the court of Fairy, vowing never to return till she should have found him alive or dead. On hearing this relation the Prince comforts the Dwarf by vowing never to forsake him till they should learn tidings of his lady. Meanwhile Timias, his faithful squire, the loss of whom he greatly laments, has fallen into evil plight. The foul foster after whom he went in pursuit had escaped him; and had then gone and got his two brothers—

———————————— for they were three
Ungracious children of one graceless sire—

to undertake to revenge him on his assailant, who they swore should never leave the forest alive. They had all three accordingly attacked him at a ford over which they knew he must pass: while the foster stationed on the bank kept him from landing with his long boar-spear, one of the others lurking in a neighbouring thicket let fly at him a shaft "feathered with an unlucky quill," which struck him in the left thigh, and inflicted exquisite pain; yet he fought his way up the bank, and slew one brother with his spear; another (his first enemy, the foster) by cleaving him in twain from the pannicle, or brain-pan, to the chin; and the third by smiting off his head. He himself, however, came off only with his life; the blood continuing to pour from his wound, he fell from his steed in a swoon, and lay without sense or motion:—

Now God thee keep, thou gentlest squire alive!
Else shall thy loving lord thee see no more.

But he is not in this state forgotten by heaven. Belphœbe, the beautiful huntress, by whose bright apparition Braggadoccio was thrown into such a fright in the third Canto of the preceding Book, chanced at this time to be pursuing in the forest some wild beast which she had wounded, and was thus led to the spot where the squire lay drenched in blood and seemingly dead. At first when she saw him,

> All suddenly abashed she changed hue,
> And with stern horror backward gan to start:
> But, when she better him beheld, she grew
> Full of soft passion and unwonted smart:
> The point of pity pierced through her tender heart.

Finding that his pulse still beat, she rubbed his temples, undight his habergeon, or cuirass, and relieved his head of his burganet, or helmet; then, having great skill in herbs, which she had been taught by the nymph who had nursed her in her childhood, she went into the wood to gather such as might prove serviceable in the present case; and

> There, whether it divine tobacco were,
> Or panachæa, or polygony,
> She found, and brought it to her patient dear,
> Who all this while lay bleeding out his heart-blood near.

> The sovereign weed betwixt two marbles plain
> She pounded small, and did in pieces bruise;
> And then atween her lilly handes twain
> Into his wound the juice thereof did scruise;^v
> And round about, as she could well it use,
> The flesh therewith she suppled and did steep,
> To abate all spasm and soak the swelling bruise;
> And, after having searched the intuse ^w deep,
> She with her scarf did bind the wound, from cold to keep. .

He was not long in opening his eyes, when, turning round and seeing "the goodly maid, full of divinities

^v Squeeze.   ^w Contusion.

and gifts of heavenly grace," sitting by him, with her bow and gilded quiver lying on the ground,

> " Mercy ! dear Lord," said he, " what grace is this
> That thou hast shewed to me, sinful wight,
> To send thine angel from her bower of bliss
> To comfort me in my distressed plight !
> Angel, or goddess do I call thee right?
> What service may I do unto thee meet,
> That hast from darkness me returned to light,
> And with thy heavenly salves and medecines sweet
> Hast drest my sinful wounds? I kiss thy blessed feet."

She had but time to tell him, blushing, that she was neither goddess nor angel, but a wood-nymph's daughter, when her damsels, who had been hunting along with her, came up; and now, the squire's horse being soon found, they set him upon it, and took him along with them.

> Into that forest far they thence him led
> Where was their dwelling; in a pleasant glade
> With mountains round about environed
> And mighty woods, which did the valley shade,
> And like a stately theatre it made,
> Spreading itself into a spacious plain;
> And in the midst a little river played
> Amongst the puny stones, which seemed to plain
> With gentle murmur that his course they did restrain.
> Beside the same a dainty place there lay,
> Planted with myrtle trees and laurels green,
> In which the birds sung many a lovely lay
> Of God's high praise, and of their loves' sweet teen,[x]
> As it an earthly paradise had been:
> In whose enclosed shadow there was pight[y]
> A fair pavilion, scarcely to be seen,
> The which was all within most richly dight,
> That greatest princes living it mote well delight.

Timias soon recovered of his wound, but lost his heart.

> Ah God ! what other could he do at least,
> But love so fair a lady that his life releast !

---

[x] Pleasing pain.   [y] Pitched.

He struggles long to subdue his passion. "Fool!" he says to himself,

> —————— " what boots thy service base
> To her, to whom the heavens do serve and sue?
> Thou, a mean squire, of meek and lowly place;
> She, heavenly born and of celestial hue."

But it is all in vain. Yet, while Belphœbe sees him pining away, he never allows her to suspect the true cause.

> She, gracious lady, yet no pains did spare
> To do him ease, or do him remedy:
> Many restoratives of virtues rare
> And costly cordials she did apply,
> To mitigate his stubborn malady:
> But that sweet cordial, which can restore
> A love-sick heart, she did to him envy;
> To him, and all the unworthy world forlore.
> She did envy that sovereign salve in secret store.

> That dainty rose, the daughter of her morn,
> More dear than life she tendered, whose flower
> The girland of her honour did adorn:
> Ne suffered she the mid-day's scorching power,
> Ne the sharp northern wind, thereon to shower;
> But lapped up her silken leaves most chair,[a]
> Whenso the froward sky began to lower;
> But, soon as calmed was the crystal air,
> She did it fair dispread and let to flourish fair.

> Eternal God, in his almighty power,
> To make ensample of his heavenly grace,
> In Paradise whilome did plant this flower;
> Whence he it fetcht out of her native place,
> And did in stock of earthly flesh enrace,
> That mortal men her glory should admire.
> In gentle ladies' breast and bounteous race
> Of womankind it fairest flower doth spire,[a]
> And beareth fruit of honour and all chaste desire.

Timias is understood to stand for Sir Walter Raleigh.

Canto VI. (54 stanzas).—In this Canto the poet pro-

---

[a] Chary, careful.   [a] Shoot forth.

ceeds to satisfy the curiosity which he conceives must
be felt by his lady readers, by relating the story of the
birth and upbringing of the "noble damosel" with
whom poor Timias has been thus smitten. To this fair
Belphœbe, he tells us, "in her birth, the heavens so
favourable were and free,"

> That all the gifts of grace and chastity
> On her they poured forth of plenteous horn :
> Jove laughed on Venus from his sovereign see,[b]
> And Phœbus with fair beams did her adorn,
> And all the Graces rocked her cradle being born.

He goes on to state that

> Her birth was of the womb of morning dew,
> And her conception of the joyous prime;

—as it is said in the old translation of the 110th Psalm,
"The dew of thy birth is of the womb of the morning;"
—that her mother was the fair Chrysogone, the daughter
of Amphisa, a lady of high rank and fairy lineage. Be-
sides Belphœbe, Chrysogone bore another daughter,
"fair Amoretta in the second place :"—

> These two were twins, and twixt them two did share
> The heritage of all celestial grace ;
> That all the rest it seemed they robbed bare
> Of bounty, and of beauty, and all virtues rare.

They were not "enwombed in the sacred throne of her
chaste body" as "other women's common brood;"

> But wondrously they were begot and bred
> Through influence of the heaven's fruitful ray,
> As it in antique books is mentioned.
> It was upon a summer's shiny day,
> When Titan fair his beames did display,
> In a fresh fountain, far from all men's view,
> She bathed her breast the boiling heat to allay;
> She bathed with roses red and violets blue,
> And all the sweetest flowers that in the forest grew.

When faint through weariness, she laid herself down

[b] Seat.

upon the grassy ground and fell asleep; and her conception was the effect of the sun. Ashamed, though conscious of no guilt, she fled with her burthen into the wilderness. There, having one day set herself down to rest after long travel, sleep again fell upon her. Now it so chanced that at this time Venus had left her heavenly house—

> The house of goodly forms and fair aspects,
> Whence all the world derives the glorious
> Features of beauty, and all shapes select,
> With which high God his workmanship hath deckt,—

to look after "her little son, the winged God of Love," who had fled from her "for some light displeasance," as he had often done before, wandering about in the world, and disguising himself in a thousand shapes. She sought him in the court, in cities, and then in the country, where

> ———————— the gentle shepherd swains, which sat
> Keeping their fleecy flocks as they were hired
> She sweetly heard complain both how and what
> Her son had to them done; yet she did smile thereat.

At last she resolved to repair to the woods,

> In which full many lovely nymphs abide;
> Mongst whom might be that he did closely lie,
> Or that the love of some of them him tied.

There she found Diana with her companions seated around a fountain, resting themselves in the cool shade—their mistress herself, with her bow and painted quiver hung on a neighbouring bough, her silver buskins unlaced, all her dress loosened, and her golden locks hanging undight about her shoulders. Ashamed and half angry with her damsels for allowing her to be so surprised, she gathered her garments about her as well as she could, and rising up advanced to meet her sister goddess,

> Whiles all her nymphs did like a girland her enclose.

When Venus informed her what had brought her to the

wilderness, she smiled in scorn " of her vain plaint ;" but the other replied to her contemptuous words, that it ill became her, with her lofty crest,

To scorn the joy that Jove is glad to seek ;

and then proceeded narrowly to inspect each of the nymphs, in the notion that one of them might possibly be her lost boy in disguise.

But Phœbe therewith sore was angered,
And sharply said : " Go, dame ; go, seek your boy
Where you him lately left, in Mars his bed :
He comes not here; we scorn his foolish joy,
Ne lend we leisure to his idle toy :
But, if I catch him in this company,
By Stygian lake I vow, whose sad annoy
The gods do dread, he dearly shall aby :[c]
I'll clip his wanton wings that he no more shall fly."

Whom whenas Venus saw so sore displeased,
She inly sorry was, and gan relent
What she had said : so her she soon appeased
With sugared words and gentle blandishment,
Which as a fountain from her sweet lips went
And welled goodly forth, that in short space
She was well pleased, and forth her damsels sent
Through all the woods, to search from place to place
If any tract of him or tidings they mote trace.

To search the god of love her nymphs she sent
Throughout the wandering forest every where :
And after them herself eke with her went
To seek the fugitive both far and near.

While thus engaged they came to the place where lay Chrysogone, and, wonderful to tell, by her side two new-born babes "as fair as springing day," which she had brought forth, without pain, and unawares, in her slumbrous trance. The goddesses agreed not to awake the mother, but to take the babes from her loving side, each appropriating one. Diana gave her's one of her own names, Belphœbe, and committed her to a nymph " to be upbrought in perfect maidenhead :"

[c] Suffer.

But Venus her's thence far away conveyed,
To be upbrought in goodly womanhead;
And, in her little Love's stead which was strayed,
Her Amoretta called, to comfort her dismayed.

She brought her to her joyous paradise
Where most she wons when she on earth does dwell,
So fair a place as nature can devise:
Whether in Paphos, or Cytheron hill,
Or it in Gnidus be, I wote not well;
But well I wote by trial, that this same
All other pleasant places doth excel,
And called is, by her lost lover's name,
The Garden of Adonis, far renowmed by fame.

From this garden are brought all the goodly flowers wherewith Dame Nature beautifies herself; there is the first seminary of all things born to live and die, according to their kinds; it were an endless work to enumerate "all the weeds that bloom and blossom there." It had two walls, the one of iron, the other of gold; and two gates always standing open, " the one fair and fresh, the other old and dried." Old Genius was the porter at both —" old Genius, the which a double nature has." All who desire to come into the world he lets both in and out:

A thousand thousand naked babes attend
About him day and night, which do require
That he with fleshly weeds would them attire:
Such as him list, such as eternal fate
Ordained hath, he clothes with sinful mire,
And sendeth forth to live in mortal state,
Till they again return back by the hinder gate.

After that they again returned been,
They in that garden planted be again,
And grow afresh, as they had never seen
Fleshly corruption nor mortal pain:
Some thousand years so doen they there remain,
And then of him are clad with other hue,
Or sent into the changeful world again,
Till thither they return where first they grew:
So, like a wheel, around they run from old to new.

Ne needs there gardener to set or sow,
To plant or prune; for of their own accord
All things, as they created were, do grow,
And yet remember well the mighty word
Which first was spoken by the Almighty Lord,
That bade them to *increase and multiply:*
Ne do they need, with water of the ford
Or of the clouds, to moisten their roots dry;
For in themselves eternal moisture they imply.

Infinite shapes of creatures are there bred, both human and bestial; and although some are constantly sent away to replenish the earth, yet is the stock never diminished, for " in the wide womb of the world" lies a huge eternal chaos out of which comes continually a new supply. Besides, nothing is consumed or annihilated, but only changed; that is to say, only the form is altered—the substance remains:

For forms are variable, and decay
By course of kind and by occasion;
And that fair flower of beauty fades away,
As doth the lily fresh before the sunny ray.

'Great enemy to it, and to all the rest
That in the Garden of Adonis springs,
Is wicked Time; who with his scythe addrest
Does mow the flowering herbs and goodly things,
And all their glory to the ground down flings,
Where they do wither and are foully marred:
He flies about, and with his flaggy wings
Beats down both leaves and buds without regard.

. . . . .

But, were it not that Time their troubler is,
All that in this delightful garden grows
Should happy be, and have immortal bliss:
For here all plenty and all pleasure flows;
And sweet Love gentle fits amongst them throws,
Without fell rancour or fond jealousy:
Frankly each paramour his leman knows;
Each bird his mate; ne any does envy
Their goodly merriment and gay felicity.

There is continual spring, and harvest there
Continual, both meeting at one time:

> For both the boughs do laughing blossoms bear,
> And with fresh colours deck the wanton prime,
> And eke at once the heavy trees they climb,
> Which seem to labour under their fruits' load:
> The whiles the joyous birds make their pastime
> Amongst the shady leaves, their sweet abode,
> And their true loves without suspicion tell abroad.
>
> Right in the middest of that paradise
> There stood a stately mount, on whose round top
> A gloomy grove of myrtle trees did rise,
> Whose shady boughs sharp steel did never lop,
> Nor wicked beasts their tender buds did crop,
> But like a girland compassed the height,
> And from their fruitful sides sweet gum did drop,
> That all the ground, with precious dew bedight,
> Threw forth most dainty odours and most sweet delight.
>
> And in the thickest covert of that shade
> There was a pleasant arbour, not by art
> But of the trees' own inclination made,
> Which knitting their rank branches part to part,
> With wanton ivy-twine entrailed athwart,
> And eglantine and caprifole among,
> Fashioned above within their inmost part,
> That neither Phœbus' beams could through them throng
> Nor Æolus' sharp blast could work them any wrong.
>
> And all about grew every sort of flower,
> To which sad lovers were transformed of yore;
> Fresh Hyacinthus, Phœbus' paramour
> And dearest love;
> Foolish Narcisse, that likes the watery shore;
> Sad Amaranthus, made a flower but late,
> Sad Amaranthus, in whose purple gore
> Me seems I see Aminta's wretched fate,
> To whom sweet poet's verse hath given endless date.

There Venus was often wont to enjoy the company of her dear Adonis; and

> There yet, some say, in secret he does lie,
> Lapped in flowers and precious spicery,
> By her hid from the world, and from the skill
> Of Stygian gods, which do her love envy:

but she herself, whenever she wills, still has him all her own. "And sooth it seems they say;" for he, although he be subject to mortality, may not

> For ever die, and ever buried be
> In baleful night, where all things are forgot;

he is eternal in mutability; often transformed, but never destroyed;

> For him the father of all forms they call;
> Therefore needs mote he live, that living gives to all.

This is the doctrine of the ancient philosophical mythology, according to which Venus is ever-fluctuating *form*, Adonis everlasting *matter*. There he lives in eternal bliss and never-ending joy, the boar that wounded him imprisoned by Venus for aye in a strong rocky cave hewn underneath that mount:—

> There now he lives in everlasting joy,
> With many of the gods in company
> Which thither haunt, and with the winged boy,
> Sporting himself in safe felicity:
> Who when he hath with spoils and cruelty
> Ransacked the world, and in the woeful hearts
> Of many wretches set his triumphs high,
> Thither resorts, and, laying his sad darts
> Aside, with fair Adonis plays his wanton parts.
>
> And his true love fair Psyche with him plays,
> Fair Psyche to him lately reconciled,
> After long troubles and unmeet upbrays,[d]
> With which his mother Venus her reviled,
> And eke himself her cruelly exiled:
> But now in stedfast love and happy state
> She with him lives, and hath him borne a child,
> Pleasure, that doth both gods and men aggrate,[e]
> Pleasure, the daughter of Cupid and Psyche late.

Hither, then, Venus brought Amoretta, and gave her in charge to Psyche to be by her "trained up in true femi-

---

[d] Upbraidings   [e] Gratify, please.

nity;" and Psyche "tendered" her no less carefully than her own daughter Pleasure, to whom she

> Made her companion, and her lessoned
> In all the lore of love and goodly womanhead;

in which when she had grown to perfect ripeness, she brought her forth into the world's view to be the example of true love,

> And loadstar of all chaste affection
> To all fair ladies that do live on ground.

Coming to Fairy Court, she there wounded many hearts;

> But she to none of them her love did cast,
> Save to the noble knight Sir Scudamore;

the story of her faithful enduring attachment to whom, however, is deferred for the present, till we have heard what happened to Florimel in her further search for "her lover dear, her dearest Marinel."

We have Spenser's own testimony, in his letter to Raleigh, that by Belphœbe he, partly or occasionally at least, designs to picture Elizabeth; and it is a notion of some of the commentators that Amoretta in this Canto may be intended to shadow forth Mary Stuart. But scarcely any one of these interpretations will be found to hold good throughout.

Canto VII. (61 stanzas).—Florimel, continuing to fly even when no one pursued, rode hard all the night, and then, when her white palfrey could carry her no longer, proceeded on foot till she found herself on the declivity of a hill overlooking a little woody valley, where a thin smoke rising among the trees directed her wearied steps to a little cottage built of sods and thatched with reeds. This proves to be the miserable abode of a malignant witch, who is, however, moved to compassion by the maid's tears and desolate condition; and the latter, invited to enter, seats herself beside the hag on the dusty ground, "as glad of that small rest as bird of tempest gone." When she has put in such order as she can her torn garments and dishevelled hair, she so astonishes her rude hostess by her magnificent beauty, that, doubting whether she were not a goddess, or, at the least, one of Diana's nymphs, she is almost ready to fall down and adore her; and, in truth, enthusiastically exclaims the poet,

To adore thing so divine as beauty were but right.

She awakens the same wonder and awe in the witch's son, a lazy good-for-nothing fellow, who lives with his mother, when she first flashes upon his sight on his return home at undertime (or the decline of the day); and, even for a considerable while that she remains with them, although he soon begins to look upon her with other thoughts, and she on her part by her meek and mild demeanour and her gentle speech encourages their familiarity, yet something divine about her still restrains him from uttering his feelings and wishes. "His caitiff thought durst not so high aspire." At length, however, finding both herself and her palfrey completely restored, she quietly withdraws herself from the "desert mansion" one morning before the dawn of day. The hag and her son, on awaking and finding their guest gone, both fall to moaning as if they had been undone; the son in particular is frantic with grief and rage. The witch now sets to work to endeavour either to bring her back again, or to work her destruction, by her devilish arts and incantations.

> Eftsoons out of her hidden cave she called
> An hideous beast of horrible aspect,
> That could the stoutest courage have appalled;
> Monstrous, mishaped, and all his back was spect
> With thousand spots of colours quaint elect;[f]
> Thereto so swift that it all beasts did pass:
> Like never yet did living eye detect;
> But likest it to an hyena was
> That feeds on women's flesh, as others feed on grass.

This beast she charges to pursue Florimel, and either

[f] Quaintly chosen.

capture or devour her. "The monster, swift as word that from her went," soon comes within sight of the flying damsel; and, spite first of the efforts of her nimble steed and then of her own fleet limbs, she would have become his prey, had she not, as she reached the seashore, leapt into a little boat that chanced to lie floating close to the spot, with the old fisherman asleep in it while his nets are drying on the sand, and instantly pushed it off with the oar. The monster is obliged to satisfy himself with wreaking his spite on the palfrey; but, while he is tearing the poor milk-white beast to pieces, suddenly there comes riding up to the place the good knight Sir Satyrane, whom the reader will remember as Una's protector in the Sixth Canto of the First Book, and who, we may here notice, is supposed to be intended to represent Sir John Perrot, generally believed to be a natural son of Henry VIII., who had been Lord Deputy of Ireland from 1583 to 1588; but, in 1590, when these first three Books of the Fairy Queen were published, was lying a prisoner in the Tower, where, after having been brought to trial and by an iniquitous verdict found guilty of high treason, he died in September, 1592. Satyrane, it seems, is a lover of Florimel, and, knowing her palfrey, he greatly fears that some evil has happened "to that fair maid, the flower of woman's pride." He finds, too, her golden girdle, which she had dropt in her flight, and that confirms his apprehensions. But this riband, "which that virgin wore about her slender waist," proves immediately of great service in binding the monster, whom Satyrane only subdues by the most Herculean exertions, and neither with strength nor sword can destroy—" his maker with her charms had framed him so well:" as soon as he felt the touch of the girdle, he roared aloud, we are told,

> For great despite of that unwonted band,
> Yet dared not his victor to withstand,
> But trembled like a lamb fled from the prey;
> And all the way him followed on the strand
> As he had long been learned to obey;
> Yet never learned he such service till that day.

But a new adventure is at hand for the stout Sir Satyrane. As he is thus leading the beast along he perceives at a distance a giantess flying on a dapple grey courser from a knight who pursues her with all his might, while before her, lying athwart her horse, she bears a doleful squire bound hand and foot. Satyrane lets go his captive beast, and, when he couches his spear and runs at the giantess, she also instantly addresses herself to fight and throws aside her load:

> Like as a goshawk, that in foot doth bear
> A trembling culver,ᵍ having spied on height
> An eagle that with plumy wings doth shear
> The subtile air, stooping with all his might,
> The quarry throws to ground with fell despite,
> And to the battle doth herself prepare:
> So ran the giantess unto the fight;
> Her fiery eyes with furious sparks did stare,
> And with blasphemous banns High God in pieces tear.

She proves more than a match for Satyrane, whom, after having stunned him with a blow of her huge iron mace, she plucks out of his saddle, and is carrying off with her, laid athwart her horse, much as she had had the squire, when the other knight comes up and attacks her, and she is again compelled to drop her prey. With this new assailant, however, she has no inclination to fight, but tries to escape from him by flight as before. Meanwhile Satyrane comes up to the squire, whom he finds to be a singularly handsome youth, and who, as soon as he has been set at liberty from his fetters, proceeds to explain what they have seen. The giantess, he tells Satyrane, is the terrible Argante, of the race of the Titans; she and her twin brother, the mighty Oliphant, were the children of Earth, by her own son Typhœus. She is a very monster and miracle of licentiousness; he himself, the squire states, is only one of innumerable youths whom she had carried off. "As for my name," says he, "it mistreth not (it signifies not) to tell:"

"Call me the Squire of Dames; that me beseemeth well."

ᵍ Pigeon.

The knight, he goes on to relate, whom Sir Satyrane
had seen pursuing the giantess, is no knight, but a "fair
virgin," called Palladine, famous for deeds of arms, above
all dames and even many knights: "Ne any," says he,

—————" may that monster match in fight,
But she, or such as she, that is so chaste a wight."

The Squire of Dames then relates his own story, which
is imitated from the Host's Tale in the Twenty-eighth
Canto of the Orlando Furioso. Fair Columbel, the
gentle lady whom he loves and serves, having charged
him to go forth and try how many other ladies he could
win, he had found such favour with the sex, that ere the
end of the year he had returned to her, bringing with
him the pledges of no fewer than three hundred con-
quests. His reward was that he should forthwith resume
his travels, and not again present himself before her till
he should have found as many other dames who should
"abide for ever chaste and sound," for all the suit he
could make to them. "Ah gentle squire," quoth
Satyrane,

——————————" tell at one word,
How many foundst thou such to put in thy record?"

"Indeed, Sir Knight," said he, "one word may tell
All that I ever found so wisely stayed,
For only three they were disposed so well;
And yet three years I now abroad have strayed
To find them out."

And of the three the only one who refused the love of
the comely squire on principle was a damsel of low de-
gree, the inmate of a country cottage; yet he admits that
this one was as fair as she was good.

"Perdy," said Satyrane, "thou Squire of Dames,
Great labour fondly hast thou hent[h] in hand,
To get small thanks, and therewith many blames;
That may amongst Alcides' labours stand."
Thence back returning to the former land,

---
[h] Taken.

Where late he left the beast he overcame,
He found him not; for he had broke his band,
And was returned again unto his dame,
To tell what tidings of fair Florimel became.

Canto VIII. (52 stanzas).—The sight of Florimel's girdle, which he takes as evidence of her death, drives the witch's son to distraction; upon which his mother boldly sets to work to fabricate by her art a lady of snow so like that it will be next to impossible to find out that she is not the one that has been lost. The snow, gathered by herself in a shady glade of the Riphæan hills, she tempers " with fine mercury, and virgin wax that never yet was sealed," and with the whole mingles an infusion of vermilion so as to produce a lively sanguine. Then,

> Instead of eyes two burning lamps she set
> In silver sockets, shining like the skies,
> And a quick moving spirit did arret[i]
> To stir and roll them like to women's eyes:
> Instead of yellow locks she did devise
> With golden wire to weave her curled head:
> Yet golden wire was not so yellow thrice
> As Florimel's fair hair: and, in the stead
> Of life, she put a sprite to rule the carcass dead.

The spirit is one that long ago had fallen from heaven with the Prince of Darkness, one that was fraught above all others with fawning guile,

And all the wiles of women's wit knew passing well.

The witch's son has no doubt that it is Florimel, and makes himself very happy, though the spirit continues to maintain a coy demeanour. At length one day, while they are walking in the woods together, they are seen by the vaunting Braggadoccio, who boldly seizing the lady sets her on Trompart's steed, and rides off with her But he is soon forced to resign her to "an armed knight upon a courser strong," whom they meet, and out of whose hands Braggadoccio is glad to escape by a cha-

[i] Appoint.

racteristic stratagem with his person safe, though with
the loss of his love. The knight supposes that it is
Florimel he has found; but that lady is far away, under-
going great distresses and fortunes strange. Her first
danger has been from the passion kindled in the old
fisherman, when, on awakening from his sleep, he beheld
that marvellous beauty of hers,

 Which with rare light his boat did beautify.

"O!" exclaims the poet,

 O! ye brave knights, that boast this lady's love,
 Where be ye now!
  . . . .

 —— If that thou, Sir Satyrane, didst weet,
 Or thou, Sir Peridure, her sorry state,
 How soon would ye assemble many a fleet,
 To fetch from sea that ye at land lost late!
 Towers, cities, kingdoms, ye would ruinate
 In your avengement and despiteous rage,
 Ne ought your burning fury mote abate
 But, if Sir Calidore could it presage,
 No living creature could his cruelty assuage.

But, in the absence of all these her old adorers, heaven
does not leave her without succour. It chances in her
extremity that Proteus, shepherd of the seas, passes near,

 Along the foamy waves driving his finny drove;

and he, at her cries, steering to the place his swift
chariot,—

 Which, with a team of scaly phocas bound,
 Was drawn upon the waves that foamed him around—

soon rescues her from the brutal fisherman. When she
first looked up and beheld her deliverer,

 For shame, but more for fear of his grim sight,
 Down in her lap she hid her face, and loudly shright :ᴶ

but Proteus did his best to recomfort her:

 ᴶ Shrieked.

Her up betwixt his rugged hands he reared,
And with his frory [k] lips full softly kist.
Whiles the cold icicles from his rough beard
Dropped adown upon her ivory breast:
Yet he himself so busily addrest,
That her out of astonishment he wrought;
And, out of that same fisher's filthy nest
Removing her, into his chariot brought,
And there with many gentle terms her fair besought.

The fisherman, after dragging him for some time behind his chariot through the waves, he at last casts ashore; but Florimel he takes with him to his bower, a cave hollowed out under a mighty rock at the bottom of the sea:

There was his won;[l] ne living wight was seen,
Save one old nymph, hight Panope, to keep it clean.

Florimel steadily resists all the sea-god's allurements, and is proof against all the various disguises he assumes to win her love:

Sometimes he boasted that a god he hight;
But she a mortal creature loved best:
Then he would make himself a mortal wight;
But then she said she loved none but a Fairy knight.

Then like a Fairy knight himself he drest;
For every shape on him he could endue:
Then like a king he was to her exprest.
And offered kingdoms unto her in view
To be his leman and his lady true:
But, when all this he nothing saw prevail,
With harder means he cast her to subdue,
And with sharp threats he often did assail;
So thinking for to make her stubborn courage quail.

To dreadful shapes he did himself transform:
Now like a giant; now like to a fiend:
Then like a centaur; then like to a storm
Raging within the waves: thereby he weened
Her will to win unto his wished eend:[m]
But when with fear, nor favour, nor with all
He else could do, he saw himself esteemed,

[k] Frozen.   [l] Dwelling.   [m] End.

Down in a dungeon deep he let her fall,
And threatened there to make her his eternal thrall.

And here for the present the poet leaves her, with this laudatory tribute:—

Most virtuous virgin! glory be thy meed,
And crown of heavenly praise with saints above,
Where most sweet hymns of this thy famous deed
Are still amongst them sung, that far my rhymes exceed.

Meanwhile Satyrane,—

—— having ended with that Squire of Dames
A long discourse of his adventures vain,
The which himself than ladies more defames,—

has returned with his new companion to the road in which he was proceeding when he encountered the giantess. They have not gone far when they perceive

———————— a knight fair pricking on the plain,
As if he were on some adventure bent,

whom,

Both by the burning heart which on his breast
He bare, and by the colours in his crest,

Satyrane soon discovers to be his friend Sir Paridel. When they have saluted, Paridel tells him that mirth has been turned to mourning at Fairy Court by the news of the destruction of Marinel and the departure of Florimel to find him; "and after her," he adds,

———————————————" are gone
All the brave knights, that doen in arms excel,
To saveguard her ywandered all alone:
Amongst the rest my lot (unworthy) is to be one."

"Ah! gentle knight," said then Sir Satyrane,
"Thy labour all is lost; I greatly dread,
That hast a thankless service on thee ta'en,
And offerest sacrifice unto the dead:
For dead, I surely doubt, thou mayest aread
Henceforth for ever Florimel to be:
That all the noble Knights of Maidenhead,

Which her adored, may sore repent with me,
And all fair ladies may for ever sorry be."

He then relates what he had seen, the monster devouring her palfrey, adding that he had besides found her golden girdle cast away. Paridel, however, though he admits, with deepest sorrow, that "the lady's safety is sore to be drad," like a true-hearted knight, will not give up his quest; and Satyrane then also declares that he will not be long behind him. For the present they both agree, on the proposal of the Squire of Dames, to seek shelter for the night in a castle which they see a little way off. But when they come up to the gate, very much to their surprise, and contrary to all the usages of chivalry, they are refused admission:

——————————————— Wondrous sore
Thereat displeased they were, till that young squire
Gan them inform the cause why that same door
Was shut to all which lodging did desire:
The which to let you weet will further time require.

Canto IX. (53 stanzas).—In this castle, it seems, there dwells "a cankered crabbed carle," or sour ill-conditioned old man, Malbecco, very wealthy, and with his whole heart set upon gathering and keeping, but who is nevertheless sorely put to it by his wife, a beautiful lady much younger than himself, named Helenore, of whom he both is and has good reason to be exceedingly jealous, and whom accordingly he does his best to seclude in close bower, or chamber, from all men's sight. Our two knights, however, are quite agreed that an attempt must be made to get, some way or other, into the churl's stronghold. But, although they get speech of Malbecco, they can make no impression upon him either by soft words or threats; and after a while, a storm having come on, they have nothing for it but to take refuge in a little shed beside the gate, which has been erected for the accommodation of swine. Soon after the tempest drives to the same shelter another knight, who at first demands admittance in so lordly a strain that Paridel, whose hot spirit cannot bear

> To hear him threaten so despitefully,
> As if he did a dog in kennel rate
> That durst not bark ;—and rather had he die
> Than, when he was defied, in coward corner lie,—

reluctant as he is to fight in the dark, betakes him to his steed, and they have a tilt at one another; the result, however, of which is that both he and his horse are thrown to the ground at the first shock, nor can the Knight get upon his legs again till the Squire of Dames has helped him up. He is, notwithstanding, eager to renew the fight with his sword, but Satyrane now steps forth, and by his persuasion they are induced to make peace. The three now agree to join in an attack upon the castle, which they begin by taking measures to set fire to the inhospitable gates. On this Malbecco consents to admit them, and they are brought into a comely bower, or room, where they throw off their armour and dry their wet clothes at the fire.

> And eke that stranger knight amongst the rest
> Was for like need enforced to disarray ;
> Though, whenas veiled was her lofty crest,
> Her golden locks, that were in trammels gay
> Upbounden, did themselves adown display
> And raught ⁿ unto her heels; like sunny beams,
> That in a cloud their light did long time stay,
> Their vapour vaded,º show their golden gleams,
> And through the persant air shoot forth their azure
>   streams.

Having also doffed her habergeon, and let fall " her wellplight frock," which she was wont " to tuck about her short when she did ride," she stands before them a woman at all points—

> The fairest woman-wight that ever eye did see.

It is no other, in fact, than Britomart herself, as the effect of the touch of her spear, sure and instantaneous as the lightning, may have prepared the reader to expect.

ⁿ Reached. º Being dispersed.

"Every one," we are told, "her liked, and every one her loved;"—

> And Paridel, though partly discontent
> With his late fall and foul indignity,
> Yet was soon won his malice to relent,
> Through gracious regard of her fair eye.
> And knightly worth which he too late did try,
> Yet tried did adore.

Paridel, we may now mention, is understood to be the brave but unfortunate Charles Nevil, sixth and last of the Nevils, Earls of Westmoreland, who, having joined what is called the Earl of Northumberland's rebellion in 1569, for the restoration of popery and the liberation of Mary Stuart, had on the failure of that attempt escaped to the Continent, where he was still living in obscurity and poverty when this first portion of the Fairy Queen was published. He was notorious for his devotion to the sex and his innumerable amours.

When they are about to sit down to supper, Malbecco, on their request to have a sight of his lady, tries to put them off with all sorts of excuses—

> Her crazed health, her late recourse to rest,
> And humid evening, ill for sick folk's case;

but they compel him to produce her:—

> She came in presence with right comely grace,
> And fairly them saluted, as became,
> And showed herself in all a gentle courteous dame.

At table Satyrane is seated over against her, and Paridel by her side; and the latter and she soon come to a good understanding, the luckless husband having his suspicious eye (he seems to have had but one) all the while chiefly directed upon the other much less dangerous knight. It is unnecessary to dwell upon the stratagems by which they are stated to have communicated their secret thoughts. After supper Helenore proposes that each knight should tell his kindred and his name.

Then Paridel, in whom a kindly pride
Of gracious speech, and skill his words to frame,
Abounded, being glad of so fit tide,
Him to commend to her, thus spake, of all well eyed:

" Troy, that art now nought but an idle name,
And in thine ashes buried low dost lie,
Though whilome far much greater than thy fame,
Before that angry gods and cruel sky
Upon thee heaped a direful destiny;
What boots it boast thy glorious descent,
And fetch from heaven thy great genealogy,
Sith all thy worthy praises being blent
Their offspring hath embased, and later glory shent!"

After this exordium he proceeds to deduce his own descent from Paris, whose son Parius, by Œnone, carried with him the remnant of the Trojans to the Isle of Paros, previously called Nausa, and there reigned many years, and left his kingdom to his son Paridas; "from whom," he concludes,—

——" I Paridel by kin descend:
But, for fair lady's love and glorious gain,
My native soil have left, my days to spend
In sueing[p] deeds of arms, my live's[q] and labour's end."

This rueful story, " of Trojan wars and Priam's city sacked," strongly excites the feelings of Britomart, herself of Trojan extraction;

For noble Britons sprung from Trojans bold,
And Troynovant was built of old Troy's ashes cold.

" O lamentable fall of famous town!" she sighing exclaims; and then she describes it as only an illustration of the general fate of all things human—an ensample of man's wretched state,

That flowers so fresh at morn, and fades at evening late.

At her request Paridel relates the fortunes of Æneas and of the other remnant of the Trojans who followed that chief to Latium, and there founded Alba Longa and

[p] Pursuing.   [q] Life's.

Rome. But a third kingdom, says Britomart when he has finished, is yet to arise out of the scattered offspring of the Trojans, and a third town that in its glory shall far surpass both the first and second Troy:

"It Troynovant is hight, that with the waves
Of wealthy Thames washed is along,
Upon whose stubborn neck (whereat he raves
With roaring rage, and sore himself does throng,
That all men fear to tempt his billows strong)
She fastened hath her foot; which stands so high,
That it a wonder of the world is song
In foreign lands; and all which passen by,
Beholding it from far, do think it threats the sky."

That city, she adds, was founded by the Trojan Brute, who "Highgate made the mean (or boundary) thereof by west, and Overt-gate by north." Paridel prays the lady to pardon his heedlessness in forgetting the story which he had heard from aged Mnemon, who said,

"That of the antique Trojan stock there grew
Another plant, that raught to wondrous height,
And far abroad his mighty branches threw
Into the utmost angle of the world he knew."

The Brute, or Brutus, of whom Britomart had spoken, he proceeds to say, was the son of Sylvius, son of Ascanius (or Iulus), and, having by mischance killed his father, left his native Italy with a band of youthful followers, who after long wandering came at last to the island of Britain, then inhabited by

—— an huge nation of the giants' brood,
That fed on living flesh, and drunk men's vital blood.

These Brutus subdued "through weary wars and labours long"—

A famous history to be enrolled
In everlasting monuments of brass,
That all the antique worthies' merits far did pass;—

and founded both great Troynovant (or London) and fair Lincoln—than which no cities are to be found fairer, except only Cleopolis. "So ended Paridel:

But all the while, that he these speeches spent,
Upon his lips hung fair Dame Helenore
With vigilant regard and due attent,
Fashioning worlds of fancies evermore
In her frail wit, that now her quite forlore:[r]
The whiles, unwares, away her wondering eye
And greedy ears her weak heart from her bore
Which he perceiving, ever privily,
In speaking, many false belgardes[s] at her let fly.

Much to Malbecco's relief, however, it is now time to retire to rest. "So all unto their bowers were brought."

Canto X. (60 stanzas).—The next morning Britomart and Satyrane proceed on their journey; but Paridel complains that the hurts he had received in his last encounter with Britomart will not yet let him ride, and remains in his quarters, in spite of his sore grudging host. Malbecco thinks to prevent all mischief by carefully watching his slippery concern of a wife;

Ne doth he suffer her, nor night nor day,
Out of his sight herself once to absent.

But Paridel kept better watch than he,
A fit occasion for his turn to find.
False Love! why do men say thou canst not see,
And in their foolish fancy feign thee blind,
That with thy charms the sharpest sight dost bind,
And to thy will abuse? Thou walkest free,
And seest every secret of the mind;
Thou seest all, yet none at all sees thee:
All that is by the working of thy deity.

So perfect in that art was Paridel,
That he Malbecco's halfen eye did wile;
His halfen eye he wiled wondrous well,
And Helenore's both eyes did eke beguile,
Both eyes and heart at once, during the while
That he there sojourned his wounds to heal;
That Cupid self, it seeing, close did smile

---

[r] Forsook.   [s] Kind glances.

To weet how he her love away did steal,
And bade that none their joyous treason should reveal.

" The learned lover," omits no opportunity, nor the least advantage, in his double task of both deceiving the husband and completing his conquest of the lady;—

Now singing sweetly to surprise her sprites,
Now making lays of love and lover's pain,
Bransles,[t] ballads, virelays, and verses vain;
Oft purposes, oft riddles, he devised,
And thousands like which flowed in his brain,
With which he fed her fancy, and enticed
To take to his new love, and leave her old despised.

And every where he might and every while
He did her service dutiful, and sued
At hand with humble pride and pleasing guile;
So closely yet, that none but she it viewed,
Who well perceived all, and all indued.[u]
Thus finely did he his false nets dispread,
With which he many weak hearts had subdued
Of yore, and many had alike misled:
What wonder then if she were likewise carried?

The end is, that " fair Dame Helenore," according to a device proposed by herself, is openly carried off one night by Paridel, after she has set fire to the closet in which her husband keeps his treasure, in the confusion and distraction into which the old miser is thrown between his desire to rescue his wife and his counter-desire to save his money.

The wretched man hearing her call for aid,
And ready seeing him with her to fly,
In his disquiet mind was much dismayed:
But when again he backward cast his eye,
And saw the wicked fire so furiously
Consume his heart, and scorch his idol's face,
He was therewith distressed diversely,
Ne wist he how to turn, nor to what place:
Was never wretched man in such a woeful case.

---

[t] Brawls, the dance so called, or the tune, as here.
[u] Digested, a term of falconry.

Aye, when to him she cried, to her he turned
And left the fire; love money overcame:
But, when he marked how his money burned,
He left his wife; money did love disclaim:
Both was he loth to lose his loved dame,
And loth to leave his liefest* pelf behind;
Yet, sith he no'te^w save both, he saved that same
Which was the dearest to his dunghill mind,
The god of his desire, the joy of misers blind.

He is frantic with rage, however, when, after the fire has been extinguished, he finds the lady to be fairly gone and out of his reach; and, when he somewhat regains self-command, all his thoughts are set to work to contrive how he may recover possession of her. At last, taking part of his treasure with him (his wife had helped herself with a liberal hand before she went off), and burying the rest in the ground, he sets out dressed like a poor pilgrim, and seeks her everywhere by sea and land; but all in vain. In course of time, however, he falls in with Braggadoccio, attended, as usual, by Trompart; and, after some parley, that mock knight agrees to accompany him in his search, and the three travel together for a long time " through many a wood, and many an uncouth way." Meanwhile, Paridel and Helenore have parted company after a very brief association; he has turned her off, and let her fly alone;

He n'ould be clogged; so had he served many one.
The gentle lady, loose at random left,
The green-wood long did walk, and wander wide
At wild adventure, like a forlorn weft;
Till on a day the satyrs her espied
Straying alone withouten groom or guide:
Her up they took, and with them home her led,
With them as housewife ever to abide,
To milk their goats, and make them cheese and bread.

Among her new friends she soon forgets both Malbecco,
"and eke Sir Paridel, all were he dear."
Now it so chances that, as Paridel is riding about the

^v Dearest, most loved.   ^w May not.

world in search of another adventure, he suddenly comes upon his old acquaintance Malbecco, journeying, as has just been told, with Braggadoccio and Trompart. As soon as the old man sees who it is he almost drops down dead with fear; but, recovering his senses though not his courage, he ventures with a lowly greeting to ask in a whisper after Helenore.

"I take no keep of her," said Paridel,
"She wonneth in the forest there before."

And so he rides off. The three now agree to proceed to the forest; Malbecco, before they enter it, retiring by himself and hiding his treasure for fear of being fallen upon by some of the many "wild woodmen" who, Trompart tells them, haunt the place, and are wont to rob and rend travellers.

Now when amid the thickest woods they were,
They heard a noise of many bagpipes shrill,
And shrieking hubbubs them approaching near,
Which all the forest did with horror fill:
That dreadful sound the boaster's heart did thrill
With such amazement, that in haste he fled,
Ne ever looked back for good or ill;
And after him eke fearful Trompart sped:
The old man could not fly, but fell to ground half dead;

Yet afterwards, close creeping as he might,
He in a bush did hide his fearful head.
The jolly satyrs full of fresh delight
Came dancing forth, and with them nimbly led
Fair Helenore with girlands all bespread,
Whom their May-lady they had newly made:
She, proud of that new honour which they read,
And of their lovely fellowship full glade,
Danced lively, and her face did with a laurel shade.

The silly man that in the thicket lay
Saw all this goodly sport, and grieved sore;
Yet durst he not against it do or say,
But did his heart with bitter thoughts engore,
To see the unkindness of his Helenore.
All day they danced with great lustihead,
And with their horned feet the green grass wore;

The whiles their goats upon the browses fed,
Till drooping Phœbus gan to hide his golden head.

Tho up they gan their merry pipes to truss,
And all their goodly herds did gather round;
But every satyr first did give a buss
To Helenore; so busses did abound.

Poor Malbecco's power of endurance is after this still more intolerably tormented; nor, although he obtains an opportunity of speaking to his wife, can he persuade her to return with him: she

—— by no means would to his will be won,
But chose amongst the jolly satyrs still to won.

He has found it necessary, in order to conceal himself, to assume the appearance of a goat—which, we are told, he managed to do

—— through the help of his fair horns on height,
And misty damp of misconceiving night.
And eke through likeness of his goatish beard;

but now when it is morning, and he has rejoined the rest of the herd, they all fall upon him, butting him on every side, and treading him down in the dirt. As soon as he can make his escape he runs off as fast as his feet will carry him; and first he makes for the place where he had buried his treasure; but the crafty Trompart has been there before him, and all is gone. On this,

With extreme fury he became quite mad,
And ran away; ran with himself away:
That who so strangely had him seen bestad,[x]
With upstart hair and staring eyes' dismay,
From Limbo lake him late escaped sure would say.

High over hills and over dales he fled,
As if the wind him on his wings had borne;
Ne bank nor bush could stay him, when he sped
His nimble feet, as treading still on thorn:
Grief, and Despite, and Jealousy, and Scorn,
Did all the way him follow hard behind;
And he himself himself loathed so forlorn,[y]

---

[x] Bested, distressed.   [y] Forsaken.

So shamefully forlorn of womankind:
That, as a snake, still lurked in his wounded mind.

He never stops till he comes to a rocky hill overhanging
the sea, over which he throws himself in desperation:

But, through long anguish and self murdering thought,
He was so wasted and forpined [z] quite,
That all his substance was consumed to nought,
And nothing left but like an airy sprite;
That on the rocks he fell so flit and light
That he thereby received no hurt at all,
But chanced on a craggy cliff to light;
Whence he with crooked claws so long did crawl,
That at the last he found a cave with entrance small.

Into the same he creeps, and thenceforth there
Resolved to build his baleful mansion
In dreary darkness and continual fear
Of that rock's fall, which ever and anon
Threats with huge ruin him to fall upon,
That he dare never sleep, but that one eye
Still ope he keeps for that occasion;
Ne ever rests he in tranquillity,
The roaring billows beat his bower so boisterously.

Ne ever is he wont on aught to feed
But toads and frogs, his pasture poisonous,
Which in his cold complexion do breed
A filthy blood, or humour rancorous,
Matter of doubt and dread suspicious,
That doth with cureless care consume the heart,
Corrupts the stomach with gall vicious,
Cross-cuts the liver with internal smart,
And doth transfix the soul with death's eternal dart.

Yet can he never die, but dying lives,
And doth himself with sorrow new sustain,
That death and life at once unto him gives,
And painful pleasure turns to pleasing pain.
There dwells he ever, miserable swain,
Hateful both to himself and every wight;
Where he, through privy grief and horror vain,

---

[z] Pined away.

Is woxen so deformed, that he has quite
Forgot he was a man, and Jealousy is hight.

Canto XI. (55 stanzas).—The poet now winds his way back to Sir Satyrane and Britomart, who, as will be remembered, had left the castle of Malbecco together, through a brief but passionate anathema of Jealousy, concluding—

And ye, fair ladies, that your kingdoms make
In the hearts of men, them govern wisely well,
And of fair Britomart ensample take,
That was as true in love as turtle to her make.

As the two ride along they see at a distance a young man flying from a huge giant, who proves to be Oliphant, the brother of the vile Argante, and as great a monster of the one sex as she is of the other. Britomart immediately dashes forward to attack him, and is quickly followed by Satyrane, on which, abandoning the chase of the youth, he takes to flight, and, being "long and swift as any roe," outruns them both.

It was not Satyrane, whom he did fear,
But Britomart, the flower of chastity;
For he the power of chaste hands might not bear,
But always did their dread encounter fly.

At last he takes refuge in a forest where the Knight and the lady part company in seeking for him. Proceeding along by herself, Britomart after some time comes to a fountain, beside which lies on the grass a knight,

——————— and by him near
His habergeon, his helmet, and his spear:
A little off, his shield was rudely thrown,
On which the winged boy in colours clear
Depainted was, full easy to be known,
And he thereby, wherever it in field was shown.

He lies with his face grovelling upon the ground, and, after many sobs and groans, is heard to break forth into a torrent of fervid words, in which he calls impatiently upon the justice of heaven, exclaiming,

> "If good find grace, and righteousness reward,
> Why then is Amoret in caitiff band,
> Sith that more bounteous creature never fared
> On foot upon the face of living land!
> Or, if that heavenly justice may withstand
> The wrongful outrage of unrighteous men,
> Why then is Busirane with wicked hand
> Suffered, these seven months' day, in secret den
> My lady and my love so cruelly to pen!"

This, in fact, is Sir Scudamore, of whom we have heard as the lover and the beloved of Amoret at the close of the Sixth Canto. She is kept, it appears, in durance and torment by Busirane, "all for she Scudamore will not denay." Britomart accosts him, and, after his grief has been somewhat composed by her words of sympathy, he explains further that the tyrant in whose hands Amoret is is a great enchanter, and that he keeps her guarded in her dungeon by many dreadful fiends. Desperate as the case looks, Britomart does not hesitate to devote herself to the enterprise of the lady's rescue :—

> "I will, with proof of last extremity,
> Deliver her fro thence, or with her for you die."
>
> "Ah! gentlest knight alive," said Scudamore,
> "What huge heroic magnanimity
> Dwells in thy bounteous breast? what couldst thou more,
> If she were thine, and thou as now am I?
> O spare thy happy days, and them apply
> To better boot; but let me die that ought:
> More is more loss; one is enough to die!"
> "Life is not lost," said she, "for which is bought
> Endless renown; that, more than death, is to be sought."

The castle of Busirane is within a bow-shot of where they are. Riding up to it they dismount from their horses, when they find neither a warder nor even a gate to bar their entry, but within the porch a blazing fire mixed with smoke and sulphur, which so overpowers their senses with horror that they are forced instantly to retire. Even Britomart is dismayed by this reception, and, turning back to Scudamore, exclaims,

"What monstrous enmity provoke we here?
Foolhardy as the earth's children, the which made
Battle against the gods, so we a god invade."

In reply to her, Scudamore can only repeat his old cry of despair; the fire, he assures her, can neither be removed nor extinguished; wherefore, says he,

" What is there else but cease these fruitless pains,
And leave me to my former languishing!
Fair Amoret must dwell in wicked chains,
And Scudamore here die with sorrowing!"

Britomart, however, will not so abandon the heroic adventure; throwing her shield before her face, and pointing her sword forward, she boldly marches up to and assails the flame,

———— the which eftsoons gave place,
And did itself divide with equal space,
That through she passed; as a thunder-bolt
Pierceth the yielding air, and doth displace
The soaring clouds into sad showers ymolt.[a]

When Scudamore, however, attempts to follow her, he finds that he cannot pass, and is driven back all scorched and miserably burnt; so that the brave championess remains within the castle alone. She has now entered

The utmost room, and passed the foremost door;
The utmost room abounding with all precious store·

For, round about the walls yclothed were
With goodly arras of great majesty,
Woven with gold and silk so close and near
That the rich metal lurked privily,
As feigning to be hid from envious eye;
Yet here, and there, and every where, unwares,
It showed itself and shone unwillingly;
Like to a discoloured snake, whose hidden snares
Through the green grass his long bright burnished back
  declares.

Great numbers of fair pictures still further adorn the tapestry, "all of love and all of lustihead;"

[a] Molten, melted

And eke all Cupid's wars they did repeat,
And cruel battles, which he whilome fought
Gainst all the gods to make his empire great·
Besides the huge massacres, which he wrought
On mighty kings and kesars into thraldom brought.

There are all the love adventures of thundering Jove, with Helle, with Europa, with Danae :

Then was he turned into a snowy swan,
To win fair Leda to his lovely trade :
O wondrous skill, and sweet wit of the man,
That her in daffodillies sleeping made
From scorching heat her dainty limbs to shade!
Whiles the proud bird, ruffing his feathers wide
And brushing his fair breast, did her invade,
She slept; yet twixt her eyelids closely spied
How towards her he rushed, and smiled at his pride.

Then he was shown with Semele and with Alcmena. And after that

Twice was he seen in soaring eagle's shape,
And with wide wings to beat the buxom air :
Once, when he with Asterie did scape
Again, whenas the Trojan boy so fair
He snatched from Ida hill, and with him bare :
Wondrous delight it was there to behold
How the rude shepherds after him did stare,
Trembling through fear lest down he fallen should
And often to him calling to take surer hold.

In satyr's shape Antiopa he snatched ;
And like a fire, when he Ægin' assayed :
A shepherd, when Mnemosyne he catched ;
And like a serpent to the Thracian maid.
Whiles thus on earth great Jove these pageants played,
The winged boy did thrust into his throne,
And, scoffing, thus unto his mother said ;
" Lo! now the heavens obey to me alone,
And take me for their Jove, whiles Jove to earth is
    gone."

Nor were the loves of the other gods forgotten :

And thou, fair Phœbus, in thy colours bright
Wast there enwoven,

with the stories of Daphne, of Hyacinthus, of Coronis,
of Clymene, and her son Phaethon—

> Who, bold to guide the chariot of the sun,
> Himself in thousand pieces fondly rent,
> And all the world with flashing fier brent;
> So like, that all the walls did seem to flame—

of Isse, the daughter of Admetus, and many more.

> Next unto him was Neptune pictured,
> In his divine resemblance woudrous like:
> His face was rugged, and his hoary head
> Dropped with brackish dew: his three-forked pike
> He sternly shook, and therewith fierce did strike
> The raging billows, that on every side
> They trembling stood, and made a long broad dyke,
> That his swift chariot might have passage wide,
> Which four great hippodames did draw in team-wise tied.
>
> His sea-horses did seem to snort amain,
> And from their nosthrils blow the briny stream,
> That made the sparkling waves to smoke again
> And flame with gold; but the white foamy cream
> Did shine with silver, and shoot forth his beam:
> The god himself did pensive seem and sad,
> And hung adown his head as he did dream;
> For privy love his breast impierced had,
> Ne ought but dear Bisaltis aye could make him glad.
>
> He loved eke Iphimedia dear,
> And Æolus' fair daughter, Arne hight,
> For whom he turned himself into a steer,
> And fed on fodder to beguile her sight.
> Also, to win Deucalion's daughter bright,
> He turned himself into a dolphin fair;
> And, like a winged horse, he took his flight
> To snaky-lock Medusa to repair,
> On whom he got fair Pegasus that flitteth in the air.

Who would ween that sullen Saturn ever thought of love? Yet love is sometimes sullen and Saturnlike, as this God himself proved when he transformed himself into a centaur for Erigone:

So proved it eke that gracious god of wine,
When, for to compass Philyra's hard love,
He turned himself into a fruitful vine,
And into her fair bosom made his grapes decline.

[The fact, however, is that it was Bacchus who loved Erigone, and Saturn Philyra; nor did the latter turn himself into a centaur, but into a horse.] It were long to tell the amours of Mars with Venus, and with many other nymphs; or how the little God of Love did not spare his own dear mother, nor sometimes even himself,

That he might taste the sweet consuming woe,
Which he had wrought to many others moe.

. . . . .

Kings, queens, lords, ladies, knights, and damsels gent,
Were heaped together with the vulgar sort,
And mingled with the rascal rabblement,
Without respect of person or of port,
To show Dan Cupid's power and great effort:
And round about a border was entrailed
Of broken bows and arrows shivered short;
And a long bloody river through them railed,
So lively, and so like, that living sense it failed.[b]

So much for the paintings on the tapestry. Then,

——— at the upper end of that fair room
There was an altar built of precious stone
Of passing value and of great renown,
On which there stood an image all alone
Of massy gold, which with his own light shone;
And wings it had with sundry colours dight,
More sundry colours than the proud pavone[c]
Bears in his boasted fan, or Iris bright
When her discoloured bow she spreads through heaven bright.[*]

Blindfold he was; and in his cruel fist
A mortal bow and arrows keen did hold,
With which he shot at random when him list,
Some headed with sad lead, some with pure gold;

---

[b] Deceived.   [c] Peacock.
[*] It probably should be "heaven's height."

(Ah! man, beware how thou those darts behold!)
A wounded dragon under him did lie,
Whose hideous tail his left foot did enfold,
And with a shaft was shot through either eye,
That no man forth might draw, ne no man remedy.

And underneath his feet was written thus,
"Unto the Victor of the gods this be:"
And all the people in that ample house
Did to that image bow their humble knee.

Transfixed with astonishment, Britomart gazes long upon the splendid scene around her; then, looking back, she perceives written over the door the words *Be Bold;* she cannot make out what the inscription may mean; but, "no whit thereby discouraged," she advances boldly into the next room.

Much fairer than the former was that room,
And richlier, by many parts, arrayed;
For not with arras made in painful loom,
But with pure gold it all was overlaid,
Wrought with wild anticks[d] which their follies played
In the rich metal, as they living were:
A thousand monstrous forms therein were made,
Such as false Love doth oft upon him wear;
For love in thousand monstrous forms doth oft appear.

And, all about, the glistring walls were hong
With warlike spoils and with victorious preys
Of mighty conquerors and captains strong,
Which were whilome captived in their days
To cruel love, and wrought their own decays:
Their swords and spears were broke, and hauberques rent,
And their proud girlands of triumphant bays
Trodden in dust with fury insolent,
To show the victor's might and merciless intent.

Britomart marvels greatly that all this while no living thing has appeared—that there should be nothing but emptiness and solemn silence over all the place. Then, as she looks around, she sees again the words *Be bold, Be bold,* written over every door; till at last, at the

[d] Images.

upper end of the room in which she is, she discovers one iron door on which is written *Be not too bold*. This perplexes her still more; but chance of penetrating the mystery for the present there seems none; night, too, now begins to wrap everything in darkness; so all she can do is to remain where she is, without either laying aside her armour or resigning herself to sleep.

Canto XII. (45 stanzas).—At last, when it is quite dark, a trumpet sounds, and then, after a storm of thunder and lightning and earthquake, and a stench of smoke and sulphur, lasting " from the fourth hour of the night until the sixth,"—

> All suddenly a stormy whirlwind blew
> Throughout the house, that clapped every door,
> With which that iron wicket open flew,
> As it with mighty levers had been tore;
> And forth issued, as on the ready floor
> Of some theatre, a grave personage
> That in his hand a branch of laurel bore,
> With comely haviour and countenance sage,
> Yclad in costly garments fit for tragic stage.
>
> Proceeding to the midst he still did stand,
> As if in mind he somewhat had to say;
> And to the vulgar beckoning with his hand,
> In sign of silence, as to hear a play,
> By lively actions he gan bewray
> Some argument of matter passioned;
> Which done, he back retired soft away,
> And passing by, his name discovered,
> Ease, on his robe in golden letters cyphered.
>
> The noble maid still standing all this viewed,
> And marvelled at his strange intendiment:
> With that a joyous fellowship issued
> Of minstrels making goodly merriment,
> With wanton bards, and rhymers impudent;
> All which together sung most cheerfully
> A lay of love's delight with sweet concent: [e]
> After whom marched a jolly company,
> In manner of a mask, enranged orderly.

---

[e] Harmony.

The whiles a most delicious harmony
In full strange notes was sweetly heard to sound,
That the rare sweetness of the melody
The feeble senses wholly did confound,
And the frail soul in deep delight nigh drowned :
And, when it ceased, shrill trumpets loud did bray,
That their report did far away rebound ;
And, when they ceased, it gan again to play,
The whiles the maskers marched forth in trim array.

The first was Fancy, like a lovely boy
Of rare aspect and beauty without peer,
Matchable either to that imp of Troy,
Whom Jove did love and chose his cup to bear ;
Or that same dainty lad, which was so dear
To great Alcides, that, whenas he died,
He wailed womanlike with many a tear,
And every wood and every valley wide
He filled with Hylas' name ; the nymphs eke Hylas cried.

His garment neither was of silk nor say
But painted plumes in goodly order dight,
Like as the sunburnt Indians do array
Their tawny bodies in their proudest plight :
As those same plumes, so seemed he vain and light,
That by his gait might easily appear ;
For still he fared as dancing in delight,
And in his hand a windy fan did bear,
That in the idle air he moved still here and there.

And him beside marched amorous Desire,
Who seemed of riper years than the other swain,
Yet was that other swain this elder's sire,
And gave him being, common to them twain :
His garment was disguised very vain,
And his embroidered bonnet sat awry :
Twixt both his hands few sparks he close did strain,
Which still he blew and kindled busily,
That soon they life conceived, and forth in flames did fly.

Next after him went Doubt, who was yclad
In a discoloured coat of strange disguise,
That at his back a broad capuccio had,
And sleeves dependent Albanese-wise ;

Hood.

He looked askew with his mistrustful eyes;
And nicely trod, as thorns lay in his way,
Or that the floor to shrink he did avise;
And on a broken reed he still did stay
His feeble steps, which shrunk when hard thereon he
  lay.

With him went Danger, clothed in ragged weed
Made of bear's skin, that him more dreadful made;
Yet his own face was dreadful, ne did need
Strange horror to deform his grisly shade:
A net in the one had, and a rusty blade
In the other was; this Mischief, that Mishap;
With the one his foes he threatened to invade,
With the other he his friends meant to enwrap:
For whom he could not kill he practised to entrap.

Next him was Fear, all armed from top to toe,
Yet thought himself not safe enough thereby,
But feared each shadow moving to or fro;
And, his own arms when glittering he did spy
Or clashing heard, he fast away did fly,
As ashes pale of hue, and winged heeled;
And evermore on Danger fixed his eye,
Gainst whom he always bent a brazen shield,
Which his right hand unarmed fearfully did wield.

With him went Hope in rank, a handsome maid,
Of cheerful look and lovely to behold;
In silken samite ᵍ she was light arrayed,
And her fair locks were woven up in gold:
She always smiled, and in her hand did hold
An holy-water-sprinkle, dipped in dew,
With which she sprinkled favours manifold
On whom she list, and did great liking shew,
Great liking unto many, but true love to few.

And after them Dissemblance and Suspect
Marched in one rank, yet an unequal pair;
For she was gentle and of mild aspect,
Courteous to all and seeming debonaire,
Goodly adorned and exceeding fair;
Yet was that all but painted and purloined,
And her bright brows were decked with borrowed hair;

ᵍ A stuff partly of silk.

Her deeds were forged, and her words false coined,
And always in her hand two clues of silk she twined:
But he was foul, ill-favoured, and grim,
Under his eyebrows looking still askance;
And ever, as Dissemblance laughed on him,
He lowered on her with dangerous eye-glance,
Shewing his nature in his countenance;
His rolling eyes did never rest in place,
But walked each where for fear of hid mischance,
Holding a lattice still before his face,
Through which he still did peep as forward he did pace.

Next him went Grief and Fury matched yfere;[h]
Grief all in sable sorrowfully clad,
Down hanging his dull head with heavy cheer,
Yet inly being more than seeming sad:
A pair of pincers in his hand he had,
With which he pinched people to the heart,
That from thenceforth a wretched life they lad,
In wilful languor and consuming smart,
Dying each day with inward wounds of dolour's dart.

But Fury was full ill apparelled
In rags, that naked nigh she did appear,
With ghastly looks and dreadful drearihead;
And from her back her garments she did tear,
And from her head oft rent her snarled[i] hair:
In her right hand a firebrand she did toss
About her head, still roaming here and there;
As a dismayed deer in chase embost,[j]
Forgetful of his safety, hath his right way lost.

After them went Displeasure and Pleasance,
He looking lumpish and full sullen sad,
And hanging down his heavy countenance;
She cheerful, fresh, and full of joyance glad,
As if no sorrow she ne felt ne drad;[k]
That evil matched pair they seemed to be:
An angry wasp the one in a vial had,
The other in her's an honey lady-bee.
Thus marched these six couples forth in fair degree.

After all these there marched a most fair dame,
Led of two grisly villains, the one Despite,

---

[h] Together.   [i] Entangled.   [j] Wearied out.   [k] Dreaded.

The other cleped¹ Cruelty by name:
She doleful lady, like a dreary sprite
Called by strong charms out of eternal night,
Had Death's own image figured in her face,
Full of sad signs, fearful to living sight;
Yet in that horror showed a seemly grace,
And with her feeble feet did move a comely pace.

Her breast all naked, as net ᵐ ivory,
Without adorn of gold or silver bright,
Wherewith the craftsman wonts it beautify,
Of her due honour was dispoiled quite;
And a wide wound therein (O rueful sight!)
Entrenched deep with knife accursed keen,
Yet freshly bleeding forth her fainting sprite,
(The work of cruel hand) was to be seen,
That dyed in sanguine red her skin all snowy clean:

At that wide orifice her trembling heart
Was drawn forth, and in silver basin laid,
Quite through transfixed with a deadly dart,
And in her blood yet steaming fresh embayed.ⁿ
And those two villains (which her steps upstayed,
When her weak feet could scarcely her sustain,
And fading vital powers gan to fade),
Her forward still with torture did constrain,
And evermore increased her consuming pain.

Next after her, the Winged God himself
Came riding on a lion ravenous,
Taught to obey the menage of that elf
That man and beast with power imperious
Subdueth to his kingdom tyrannous:
His blindfold eyes he bade awhile unbind,
That his proud spoil of that same dolorous
Fair dame he might behold in perfect kind;
Which seen, he much rejoiced in his cruel mind.

Of which full proud, himself uprearing high,
He looked round about with stern disdain,
And did survey his goodly company;
And, marshalling the evil-ordered train,
With that the darts which his right hand did strain

---

¹ Called.   ᵐ Pure.   ⁿ Bathed.

Full dreadfully he shook, that all did quake,
And clapped on high his coloured winges twain,
That all his many° it afraid did make:
Tho, blinding him again, his way he forth did take.

Behind him was Reproach, Repentance, Shame:
Reproach the first, Shame next, Repent behind:
Repentance feeble, sorrowful, and lame;
Reproach despiteful, careless, and unkind;
Shame most ill-favoured, bestial, and blind:
Shame lowered, Repentance sighed, Reproach did scold;
Reproach sharp stings, Repentance whips entwined,
Shame burning brand-irons in her hand did hold:
All three to each unlike, yet all made in one mould.

And after them a rude confused rout
Of persons flocked, whose names is hard to read:
Amongst them was stern Strife; and Anger stout;
Unquiet Care; and fond Unthriftihead;
Lewd Loss of Time; and Sorrow seeming dead;
Inconstand Change; and False Disloyalty;
Consuming Riotise; and guilty Dread
Of heavenly vengeance; faint Infirmity:
Vile Poverty: and, lastly, Death with infamy.

There were full many moe like maladies,
Whose names and natures I note readen well;
So many moe, as there be phantasies
In wavering women's wit, that none can tell,
Or pains in love, or punishments in hell:
All which disguised marched in masking-wise
About the chamber by the damosel:
And then returned, having marched thrice,
Into the inner room from whence they first did rise.

In the argument at the head of the Canto this splendid show, so wonderful for the profusion of allegoric invention displayed in it, is called the Masque of Cupid; and, as already noticed, it has been supposed to be perhaps an adaptation of the author's early composition, *The Court of Cupid*, mentioned by E. K. in his Epistle to Harvey prefixed to the Shepherd's Calendar.*

As soon as they have retired, the door is again fast

° Meiny, or retinue.   * See Vol. I., p. 27.

locked, driven to by a blast of wind even as it had been driven open. Britomart courageously advances to it, but tries in vain to open it, first by force then by art. She resolves to remain in the room where she is till the following morning. when she concludes the mask will probably again come forth. Accordingly, after another night, towards the close of the second watch, open flies the brazen door as before, and in walks bold Britomart:—

 So soon as she was entered, round about
 She cast her eyes to see what was become
 Of all those persons which she saw without.
 But lo! they straight were vanished all and some;
 Ne living wight she saw in all that room,
 Save that same woeful lady; both whose hands
 Were bounden fast, that did her ill become,
 And her small waist girt round with iron bands
 Unto a brazen pillar, by the which she stands.

The lady is Amoret; and before her sits the vile enchanter Busirane himself, writing strange magic characters with the living blood dropping from her dying breast, in which the dart still seems planted—" and all perforce to make her him to love." As soon as he sees Britomart, starting up, and overthrowing in his haste his wicked books, he draws a knife from his pocket, and runs fiercely up to Amoret to plunge it into her; but Britomart, " to him leaping light," prevents the blow and overpowers him. Turning, however, upon her, he wounds her slightly in the breast; on which, " exceeding wroth," the virgin draws her sword " to give him the reward for such vile outrage due;—"

 So mightily she smote him, that to ground
 He fell half dead; next stroke him should have slain,
 Had not the lady, which by him stood bound,
 Dernly ᵖ unto her called to abstain
 From doing him to die; for else her pain
 Should be remediless; sith none but he
 Which wrought it could the same recure again.

     Earnestly.

Therewith she stayed her hand, loth stayed to be ;
For life she him envied, and longed revenge to see :

And to him said, " Thou wicked man, whose meed
For so huge mischief and vile villainy
Is death, or if that ought do death exceed ;
Be sure that nought may save thee from to die
But if that thou this dame do presently
Restore unto her health and former state :
This do, and live ; else die undoubtedly."
He, glad of life, that looked for death but late,
Did yield himself right willing to prolong his date :

And rising up gan straight to overlook
Those cursed leaves, his charms back to reverse :
Full dreadful things out of that baleful book
He read, and measured many a sad verse,
That horror gan the virgin's heart to pierce,
And her fair locks up stared stiff on end,
Hearing him those same bloody lines rehearse ;
And, all the while he read, she did extend
Her sword high over him, if ought he did offend.

Anon she gan perceive the house to quake,
And all the doors to rattle round about ;
Yet all that did not her dismayed make,
Nor slack her threatful hand for dangers' doubt,
But still with steadfast eye and courage stout
Abode, to weet what end would come of all :
At last that mighty chain, which round about
Her tender waist was wound, adown gan fall,
And that great brazen pillar broke in pieces small.

The cruel steel, which thrilled her dying heart,
Fell softly forth, as of his own accord ;
And the wide wound, which lately did dispart
Her bleeding breast and riven bowels gored,
Was closed up as it had not been sored ;
And every part to safety full sound,
As she were never hurt, was soon restored :
Tho when she felt herself to be unbound
And perfect whole, prostrate she fell unto the ground ;

Before fair Britomart she fell prostrate,
Saying, " Ah ! noble knight, what worthy meed

Can wretched lady, quit from woeful state,
Yield you in lieu of this your gracious deed?
Your virtue self her own reward shall breed,
Even immortal praise and glory wide,
Which I your vassal, by your prowess freed,
Shall through the world make to be notified,
And goodly well advance that goodly well was tried."

Britomart, raising her from the ground, tells her to put away all sorrow—all "remembrance of late teen,"— adding,

"Instead thereof, know that your loving make
Hath no less grief endured for your gentle sake."

The championess then, laying her strong hand upon the enchanter, binds him with the same chain with which Amoret had been lately bound, and leads him away captive. Returning now by the way she had come, she finds all those goodly rooms, " which erst she saw so rich and royally arrayed," utterly vanished; and, when she descends to " that perilous porch," the dreadful fire likewise quenched and gone. But when she comes to where she had left Scudamore and her old squire, neither of them is to be seen. After having waited long for Britomart's re-appearance, they had concluded that she must have perished, and had set out to seek for further aid—" where," says the poet, bringing to a close the Canto and the Book—

— let them wend at will, whilst here I do respire.

As the poem, however, was originally written and published, in the place of the three last stanzas, which relate the coming forth of Britomart and Amoret, and state what had induced Scudamore and Glauce to take their departure, were other seven stanzas giving a different turn to the story. Scudamore was found where he had been left; the delighted lovers threw themselves into one another's arms—

No word they spake, nor earthly thing they felt,
But like two senseless stocks in long embracements
    dwelt;—

and this first portion of the work, all probably that was then composed, was finished off in the following lines:—

> Thus do those lovers with sweet countervail,[q]
> Each other of love's bitter fruit despoil.
> But now my team begins to faint and fail,
> All woxen weary of their journal[r] toil;
> Therefore I will their sweaty yokes assoil
> At this same furrow's end till a new day:
> And ye, fair swains, after your long turmoil,
> Now cease your work, and at your pleasure play;
> Now cease your work; to-morrow is an holiday.

In the alteration which he made when he reprinted the poem with its continuation, Spenser judiciously availed himself of the opportunity of keeping up the excitement of suspense with regard to Scudamore and Amoret, as well as with regard to Britomart and Arthegal, Florimel, and other personages that figure in this third Book. The second portion of the Fairy Queen, consisting of Books Fourth, Fifth, and Sixth, was published (along with a reprint of the three former Books) in 1596.

[q] Mutual requital.   [r] Diurnal.

Book Fourth.

The Fourth Book of the Fairy Queen is entitled *The Legend of Cambel and Triamond* (misprinted in the old editions *Telamond*), or *of Friendship*. It is preceded by five introductory stanzas, setting out as follows, with what is no doubt an allusion to Burleigh and the little favour, or rather avowed contempt, with which the former portion of the work had been regarded, both for its form and its subject, by the wise but not poetical Lord Treasurer:—

> The rugged forehead, that with grave foresight
> Welds[s] kingdoms' causes, and affairs of state,
> My looser rhymes, I wote, doth sharply wite,[t]
> For praising love as I have done of late,
> And magnifying lovers' dear debate,
> By which frail youth is oft to folly led
> Through false allurement of that pleasing bait,
> That better were in virtues discipled,[u]
> Than with vain poems' weeds to have their fancies fed.
>
> Such ones ill judge of love that cannot love,
> Ne in their frozen hearts feel kindly flame :
> Forthy[v] they ought not thing unknown reprove,
> Ne natural affection faultless blame
> For faults of few that have abused the same ;
> For it of honour and all virtue is
> The root, and brings forth glorious flowers of fame,
> That crown true lovers with immortal bliss,
> The meed of them that love, and do not live amiss.

All great works, he proceeds to affirm, of former

[s] Wields. [t] Blame.
[u] Disciplined.
[v] Therefore, on that account.

ages will be found to have either begun or ended in love; and even the father of philosophy, Socrates, was wont often to make this passion the subject of discourse with " his Critias" (that name being apparently used by mistake for Crito, from a forgetfulness similar to what we had occasion to notice in regard to the same name in the seventh Canto of the second Book). To such therefore as so wrongfully deem of love he does not sing at all, but " to that sacred saint" his sovereign queen, in whose chaste breast all treasures of true love are unlocked,

  Bove all her sex that ever yet was seen.

" To her," he exclaims,

  ———— I sing of love, that loveth best,
  And best is loved of all alive, I ween;
  To her this song most fitly is addressed,
  The Queen of Love and Prince of Peace from heaven blest.

  Canto I. (54 stanzas).—This Canto carries on the adventures of Amoret, the story of whose previous sufferings, and of the trials she has still to encounter, is declared to be so sad a one, " that I," says Spenser,

  ———— with tears full oft do pity it,
  And oftentimes do wish it never had been writ.

For never had she any enjoyment of life since the time when Scudamore won her from twenty knights, all of whom he had to fight and conquer before she became his; the vile enchanter Busirane having contrived on her wedding-day, in the midst of the bridal feast, to carry her off, as if in sport, by means of that Masque of Love of his, and having since detained her for seven long months in durance and torment, till she was delivered by Britomart, as related in the last Canto of the preceding Book. But her misfortunes are not yet at an end. Scudamore, as we have seen, is still lost to her and she is left alone with the Briton maid, whose sex of course she does not suspect. It would be a pleasant tale, says the poet, to tell " the diverse usage and demeanour daint" of the one to the other, as they rode along:

> For Amoret right fearful was and faint
> Lest she with blame her honour should attaint,
> That every word did tremble as she spake,
> And every look was coy and wondrous quaint,
> And every limb that touched her did quake;
> Yet could she not but courteous countenance to her make.

At last one evening they come to a castle, where many knights and ladies are assembled to witness and take part in deeds of arms:—

> Amongst all which was none more fair than she,
> That many of them moved to eye her sore.
> The custom of that place was such, that he
> Which had no love nor leman there in store
> Should either win him one, or lie without the door.

A jolly knight, who lays claim to Amoret, is easily and speedily disposed of by " the warlike virgin;" yet, although he had been overthrown by her in fight, as he seems to be a youth of valour, she, who is as courteous as stout, is loth that he should be either forced to pass the night in the open air, or that the custom of the place should be broken. Having first, therefore, obtained an assurance that in any circumstances Amoret should remain under her protection, she then surprises them all by claiming the admission of the knight into the castle as due to her, his conqueror, in her quality of a lady:

> With that, her glistering helmet she unlaced;
> Which doft, her golden locks, that were upbound
> Still in a knot, unto her heels down traced,*
> And like a silken veil in compass round
> About her back and all her body wound:
> Like as the shining sky in summer's night,
> What time the days with scorching heat abound,
> Is crested all with lines of fiery light,
> That it prodigious seems in common people's sight.

Some think that the transformation is the work of enchantment; some that she is Bellona, the Goddess of War, visibly revealed to them " with shield and armour fit." But to Amoret especially the discovery is a great

* Passed.

relief. The two spend the night in conversing of their
loves, and then on the morrow at sunrise resume their
journey. At length they spy two armed knights pacing
towards them, each with a lady, as seems, riding by his
side ; but ladies they are none, although fair enough in
face and outward show : the one is the false Duessa, in
yet another of her endless disguises—

    For she could don so many shapes in sight
    As ever could chamelion colours new ;
    So could she forge all colours, save the true :

the other was no whit better than she, but rather, if pos-
sible, much worse : " her name was Ate, mother of de-
bate and all dissension," raised by Duessa

    ———————————— from below
    Out of the dwellings of the damned sprites,
    Where she in darkness wastes her cursed days and nights.

Her dwelling is " in a darksome delve, far under ground,"
" hard by the gates of hell ;" environed with thorns and
brakes, yet with many ways to enter, although with none
whereby to issue forth :—

    And all within the riven walls were hung
    With ragged monuments of times forepast,
    All which the sad effects of discord sung :
    There were rent robes and broken sceptres placed ;
    Altars defiled, and holy things defaced ;
    Disshivered spears, and shields ytorn in twain ;
    Great cities ransacked, and strong castles rased :
    Nations captived, and huge armies slain :
    Of all which ruins there some relics did remain.

    There was the sign of antique Babylon ;
    Of fatal Thebes ; of Rome that reigned long ;
    Of sacred Salem ; and sad Ilion,
    For memory of which on high there hong
    The golden apple, cause of all their wrong,
    For which the three fair goddesses did strive :
    There also was the name of Nimrod strong ·
    Of Alexander, and his princes five ;
    Which shared to them the spoils that he had got alive :

And there the relies of the drunken fray
The which amongst the Lapithees befell:
And of the bloody feast, which sent away
So many centaurs' drunken souls to hell,
That under great Alcides' fury fell:
And of the dreadful discord, which did drive
The noble Argonauts to outrage fell,
That each of life sought others to deprive,
All mindless of the golden fleece, which made them
   strive.

And eke of private persons many moe,
That were too long a work to count them all:
Some, of sworn friends that did their faith forego:
Some, of born brethren proved unnatural:
Some, of dear lovers foes perpetual:
Witness their broken bands there to be seen,
Their girlands rent, their bowers despoiled all;
The moniments whereof there biding been,
As plain as at the first when they were fresh and green.

Such was her house within: but all without,
The barren ground was full of wicked weeds,
Which she herself had sowen all about,
Now growen great, at first of little seeds,
The seeds of evil words and factious deeds;
Which, when to ripeness due they growen are,
Bring forth an infinite increase, that breeds
Tumultuous trouble, and contentions jar,
The which most often end in bloodshed and in war.

And those same cursed seeds do also serve
To her for bread, and yield her living food:
For life it is to her, when others sterve
Through mischievous debate and deadly feud,
That she may suck their life and drink their blood,
With which she from her childhood had been fed:
For she at first was born of hellish brood,
And by infernal furies nourished;
That by her monstrous shape might easily be read.

Her face most foul and filthy was to see,
With squinted eyes contrary ways intended,
And loathly mouth, unmeet a mouth to be,
That nought but gall and venom comprehended,

And wicked words that God and man offended:
Her lying tongue was in two parts divided,
And both the parts did speak, and both contended;
And as her tongue so was her heart discided,[x]
That never thought one thing, but doubly still was
    guided.

Als. as she double spake, so heard she double,
With matchless ears deformed and distort,
Filled with false rumours and seditious trouble,
Bred in assemblies of the vulgar sort,
That still are led with every light report:
And, as her ears, so eke her feet were odd,
And much unlike; the one long, the other short,
And both misplaced; that, when the one forward yode,[y]
The other back retired and contrary trode.

Likewise unequal were her handes twain;
That one did reach, the other pushed away;
That one did make, the other marred again,
And sought to bring all things unto decay;
Whereby great riches, gathered many a day,
She in short space did often bring to nought,
And their possessors often did dismay:
For all her study was and all her thought
How she might overthrow the things that Concord
    wrought.

So much her malice did her might surpass,
That even the Almighty self she did malign,
Because to man so merciful he was,
And unto all his creatures so benign,
Sith she herself was of his grace indign:[z]
For all this world's fair workmanship she tried
Unto his last confusion to bring,
And that great golden chain quite to divide,
With which it blessed Concord hath together tied.

The two knights are our former acquaintance, Paridel, who accompanies Ate, and a new personage, Sir Blandamour, " a man of mickle might," and " that bore great sway in arms and chivalry," who has attached himself to Duessa;

---

[x] Cut in two.   [y] Went.   [z] Unworthy.

> For, though, like withered tree that wanteth juice,
> She old and crooked were, yet now of late
> As fresh and fragrant as the flower-de-luce
> She was become, by change of her estate,
> And made full goodly joyance to her new-found mate.

When they perceive Britomart and Amoret, Blandamour proposes to Paridel that he should attack the former, who must be supposed to have resumed her knightly attire; but Paridel remembers his late mischance, as related in the Ninth Canto of the last Book, and willingly leaves the enterprize to his friend, who thereupon makes his onset gallantly enough, but meets with the same sudden discomfiture as all those who encounter the warlike Britoness and her enchanted spear. However, when Britomart and Amoret have passed on, he is again set on his horse by his companions, and the four proceed on their way as before, till they meet two other knights, one of whom Blandamour immediately perceives to be Sir Scudamore,

> ———————— by that he bore
> The God of Love with wings displayed wide;
> Whom mortally he hated evermore,
> Both for his worth, that all men did adore,
> And eke because his love he won by right.

Unable, from his bruised condition, to "wreak his old despite," he applies to Paridel to do as he had just been done by:—

> "Ah! Sir," said Paridel, "do not dismay
> Yourself for this; myself will for you fight,
> As ye have done for me: The left hand rubs the right."

Paridel and Scudamore meet like too opposing "billows in the Irish Sounds;" but the former is soon overthrown. Blandamour upon this, though he can do no more, attacks the victor with words of reproach and insult. Duessa sarcastically beseeches him not to distress himself or be wroth that his love "list love another knight;"—

> "For love is free, and led with self-delight,
> Ne will enforced be with maisterdom or might:"—

but Ate, striking in, exclaims that she can but laugh both
at Scudamore and Blandamour for striving and storming
about one who cares for neither, but loves another,
with whom she both lovingly journeys and sleeps. When
Scudamore interrupts her with a passionate asseveration
that she lies, she repeats her statement with a more pre-
cise detail of circumstances:—

> Which whenas Scudamore did hear, his heart
> Was thrilled with inward grief: as, when in chase
> The Parthian strikes a stag with shivering dart,
> The beast astonished stands in middest of his smart;
>
> So stood Sir Scudamore when this he heard;
> Ne word he had to speak for great dismay,
> But looked on Glauce grim.

Glauce, it may be recollected, had accompanied Scud-
amore when he set out from the house of Busirane, as
related in the concluding stanza of the preceding Book.
Blandamour and Duessa now taunt and triumph over the
unhappy knight; he on the other hand is too much dis-
tressed to answer, and after they have left him and Glauce
by themselves he is hardly prevented by the sober and
soothing words with which the old woman endeavours to
assuage his fury from sacrificing her to his rage and thirst
of revenge as an abettor of the disloyalty which he im-
putes to Britomart. Glauce of course knows that there
is and can be no ground for what he believes; but we
are to suppose that the fear and perturbation in which
she is, or her fidelity to her mistress and reluctance to
betray her secret, withhold her from relieving Scudamore
and also averting all danger from herself by the requisite
easy and conclusive explanation. There are, however,
it may be remarked, several things in this Canto which
are somewhat perplexing, but about which the commen-
tators give themselves no trouble; especially the whole
of the part played by Ate—the contradiction between her
first introduction as having the appearance of a beautiful
lady and the subsequent description of her foul and filthy
face, and her position in relation to Paridel, who is at
first represented as having her riding by his side in the

same manner as Blandamour has Duessa, but is notwithstanding soon after expressly stated to be unprovided with any particular lady-love for the present. The figure seems to have taken successively two distinct shapes under the poet's forming fancy, or to have been originally designed for something different from what she eventually turns out.

Canto II. (54 stanzas).—" Firebrand of hell, first tined (or kindled) in Phlegethon by a thousand furies," exclaims the poet in commencing this stanza, " is wicked Discord "—

—————— whose small sparks once blown
None but a god or godlike man can slake :
Such as was Orpheus, that, when strife was grown
Amongst those famous imps of Greece, did take
His silver harp in hand and shortly friends them make.

When the story is resumed we find ourselves in company of Blandamour and Paridel, and their two female fellow-travellers—" the one a fiend, the other an incarnate devil." It may be remembered that in the Eighth Canto of the last Book the snowy lady formed after the likeness of Florimel, after falling into the hands of Braggadoccio, was carried off from that vaunting dastard by a knight who is there left unnamed. This knight, who, we are now informed, is called the bold Sir Ferraugh, is the next person whom the four encounter, riding along in high delight with his fair-seeming prize. He is attacked and overthrown by Blandamour, and the false Florimel passes to a new proprietor. She is more expert than Blandamour himself in every subtile sleight, and, although he

—————— by his false allurements' wily draft[a]
Had thousand women of their love beraft,[b]

yet he is now completely deceived and taken in, and every day becomes more enamoured and enslaved. Ate, however, after a time stirs up Paridel to demand his share of the lady, according to a covenant which he says

[a] Strategem.   [b] Bereft.

they had made to divide between them whatever spoil or prey should be taken by either. A long and desperate fight ensues, which the poet supposes might have gone on till this day, if there had not come up by chance another notable personage of the last Book, the Squire of Dames, who, well knowing them both of old, prevails upon the two combatants, though not without difficulty, to suspend their animosity. The Squire is greatly delighted to see the snowy lady—" for none alive but joyed in Florimel," and he, as well as all others, had thought her dead or lost. He tells them that Satyrane having found her girdle, which he had ever since worn for her sake, had on that account excited the envy and displeasure of many other knights; to put an end to which he had lately proclaimed a solemn feast and tournay, " to which," he adds, " all knights with them their ladies are to bring :"

" And of them all she that is fairest found
Shall have that golden girdle for reward;
And of those knights who is most stout on ground
Shall to that fairest lady be prefard.^c
Since therefore she herself is now your ward,
To you that ornament of her's pertains,
Against all those that challenge it, to guard,
And save her honour with your venturous pains;
That shall you win more glory than ye here find gains."

This prospect reunites the two, for the present at least, so that they ride along in outward harmony as before, though their friendship, as indeed it always had been, is but hollow and precarious. Thus proceeding, they overtake two knights riding close beside each other as if in intimate converse, with their two ladies similarly associated not far behind them; and the Squire being sent forward to ascertain who they are, comes back with the intelligence that they are " two of the prowest knights in Fairy Land," Cambel and Triamond, and that the ladies are Canace and Cambin " their two lovers dear." The poet now prepares himself for what he is about to

^c Preferred.

relate by invocation of his greatest English predecessor :—

> Whilome, as antique stories tellen us,
> Those two were foes the fellonest [d] on ground,
> And battle made the dreadest dangerous
> That ever shrilling trumpet did resound;
> Though now their acts be nowhere to be found,
> As that renowmed poet them compiled
> With warlike numbers and heroic sound,
> Dan Chaucer, well of English undefiled,
> On fame's eternal beadroll worthy to be filyd.
>
> But wicked Time, that all good thoughts doth waste,
> And works of noblest wits to nought outwear,
> That famous moniment hath quite defaced,
> And robbed the world of threasure endless dear,
> The which mote have enriched all us here.
> O cursed eld, the canker-worm of writs!
> How may these rhymes, so rude as doth appear,
> Hope to endure, sith works of heavenly wits
> Are quite devoured, and brought to nought by little bits!
>
> Then pardon, O most sacred happy spirit,
> That I thy labours lost may thus revive,
> And steal from thee the meed of thy due merit,
> That none durst ever whilst thou wast alive,
> And, being dead, in vain yet many strive:
> Ne dare I like; but, through infusion sweet
> Of thine own spirit which doth in me survive,
> I follow here the footing of thy feet,
> That with thy meaning so I may the rather meet.

The allusion is to the unfinished Tale of the Squire in the Canterbury Tales, the last lines of which are,

> " And after wol I speak of Cambalo,
> That fought in listes with the brethren two
> For Canace, ere that he might her win,
> And there I left I wol again begin."

Cambalo, Camballo, Camballus, Cambello, or Cambel,— for all these transformations the name is made to undergo

[d] Fiercest.

according to the exigences of the measure and the
rhyme—was the brother of Canace; and she

——————— was the learnedst lady in her days,
Well seen in every science that mote be,
And every secret work of nature's ways;
In witty riddles; and in wise soothsays;
In power of herbs; and tunes of beasts and birds;
And, that augmented all her other praise,
She modest was in all her deeds and words.
And wondrous chaste of life, yet loved of knights and
   lords.

Many lords and knights loved her, and the more she
refused to return the affection of any one of them, "so
much the more she loved was and sought." At last,
their contention having produced many bloody fights,
one day, having assembled all the troop of warlike
wooers, Cambel, who was both stout and wise, proposed
to them that they should each in succession fight for her
with himself, and that whoever should conquer him
should carry off his sister. "Bold was the challenge, as
himself was bold;" but what chiefly gave him confidence
was not so much his own strength and hardihood as a
ring provided for him by his sister, one of many virtues
of which was that it "had power to staunch all wounds
that mortally did bleed." Now,

Amongst those knights there were three brethren bold,
Three bolder brethren never were yborn,
Born of one mother in one happy mould,
Born at one burden in one happy morn;
Thrice happy mother, and thrice happy morn,
That bore three such, three such not to be fond:[e]
Her name was Agape, whose children wern[f]
All three as one; the first hight Priamond,
The second Diamond, the youngest Triamond.

Stout Priamond, but not so strong to strike;
Strong Diamond, but not so stout a knight;
But Triamond was stout and strong alike:
On horseback used Triamond to fight,

---

[e] Found.   [f] Were.

And Priamond on foot had more delight;
But horse and foot knew Diamond to wield ;
With curtaxe used Diamond to smite,
And Triamond to handle spear and shield,
But spear and curtaxe both used Priamond in field.

These three did love each other dearly well,
And with so firm affection were allied
As if but one soul in them all did dwell,
Which did her power into three parts divide ;
Like three fair branches budding far and wide,
That from one root derived their vital sap :
And like that root, that doth her life divide,
Their mother was ; and had full blessed hap
These three so noble babes to bring forth at one clap.

Their mother was a fairy, their father a young and noble knight, into whose hands she had one day fallen in a forest,

As she sate careless by a crystal flood,
Combing her golden locks.

As they grew up their love of arms and adventures so alarmed their mother that to relieve her anxiety she had betaken her, in order to learn their destiny, to the house of the Three Fatal Sisters :—

Down in the bottom of the deep abyss,
Where Demogorgon, in dull darkness pent,
Far from the view of gods and heaven's bliss
The hideous Chaos keeps, their dreadful dwelling is.

There she them found all sitting round about
The direful distaff standing in the mid,
And with unwearied fingers drawing out
The lines of life, from living knowledge hid.
Sad Clotho held the rock, the whiles the thread
By grisly Lachesis was spun with pain,
That cruel Atropos eftsoons undid,
With cursed knife cutting the twist in twain ;
Most wretched men, whose days depend on threads so
   vain !

After having saluted them she sate by them for a while in

silence, "beholding how the threads of life they span;" then, trembling and pale, she told them her object:—

> To whom fierce Atropos; "Bold fay, that durst
> Come see the secret of the life of man,
> Well worthy thou to be of Jove accurst
> And eke thy children's threads to be asunder burst!"

Clotho, however, consented to show her her children's threads, and much distressed she was to see them as thin as those spun by spiders, and also so short that they seemed already almost at an end. She besought them "to draw them longer out, and better twine;" but the inexorable Lachesis answered that that was impossible—

> ———— "Fond dame! that deem'st of things divine
> As of humane, that they may altered be,
> And changed at pleasure for those imps of thine:
> Not so; for what the Fates do once decree,
> Not all the gods can change, nor Jove himself can free!"

She then made a last request:

> "Grant this; that when ye shred with fatal knife
> His line which is the eldest of the three,
> Which is of them the shortest, as I see,
> Eftsoons his life may pass into the next;
> And, when the next shall likewise ended be,
> That both their lives may likewise be annext
> Unto the third, that his may be so trebly wext."

This they granted; upon which she departed in content. When she came home she concealed from her sons what she had learned;

> But evermore, when she fit time could find,
> She warned them to tend their safeties well,
> And love each other dear, whatever them befell.

This counsel they duly followed, no discord ever dividing them; and now, to add to their mutual affection, they were all three united in love of Canace. Out of this state of things arose the great battle to be related in the next Canto.

Canto III. (52 stanzas).—" O why," asks the poet, in commencing the continuation of the story of the three sons of Agape,

> O! why do wretched men so much desire
> To draw their days unto the utmost date,
> And do not rather wish them soon expire;
> Knowing the misery of their estate,
> And thousand perils which them still await,
> Tossing them like a boat amid the main,
> That every hour they knock at Deathes gate!
> And he that happy seems and least in pain,
> Yet is as nigh his end as he that most doth plain.

He holds this fairy mother, therefore, but fond and vain,
> The which, in seeking for her children three
> Long life, thereby did more prolong their pain.

Yet while they lived, he adds, more happy creatures than they seemed to be none ever saw, nor any of nobler courtesy, nor more dearly loved, nor more renowned. All the other suitors, not unreasonably, declined the encounter with Cambel and his miraculous ring; the three brothers alone accepted his challenge to fight with him for Canace. And now the appointed morning was come; " the field with lists was all about inclosed;"— on the one side sate six judges to watch and declare the issue of the fight—on the other

> ———————— in fresh array
> Fair Canace upon a stately stage
> Was set, to see the fortune of that fray,
> And to be seen.

First Cambel entered the lists; soon after, the three brothers,
> With scutcheons gilt and banners broad displayed;
> And, marching thrice in warlike ordinance,
> Thrice lowted lowly to the noble Maid;
> The whiles shrill trumpets and loud clarions sweetly
>   played.

The first that comes forth to answer the challenger's call is Priamond, the eldest; after a fierce combat, in which Cambel, although, protected by the ring, he loses no blood, yet receives some severe bruises and wounds, he is slain by his weasand-pipe being cleft through his gorget, and in a gush of purple blood his weary ghost is let forth :

> His weary ghost, assoiled from fleshly band,
> Did not, as others wont, directly fly
> Unto her rest in Pluto's grisly land ;
> Ne into air did vanish presently ;
> Ne changed was into a star in sky ;
> But through traduction was eftsoons derived,
> Like as his mother prayed the Destiny,
> Into his other brethren that survived,
> In whom he lived anew, of former life deprived.

Instantly the next brother, Diamond, sad and sorry enough, yet giving no time to grief, started forward to offer himself to the like chance : " his foe was soon addressed ; the trumpets freshly blew."

> With that they both together fiercely met,
> As if that each meant other to devour;
> And with their axes both so sorely bet,
> That neither plate nor mail, whereas their power
> They felt, could once sustain the hideous stour,
> But rived were, like rotten wood, asunder ;
> Whilst through their rifts the ruddy blood did shower,
> And fire did flash, like lightning after thunder,
> That filled the lookers on at once with ruth and wonder.

> As when two tigers pricked with hunger's rage
> Have by good fortune found some beast's fresh spoil,
> On which they ween their famine to assuage,
> And gain a feastful guerdon of their toil ;
> Both falling out do stir up strifeful broil,
> And cruel battle twixt themselves do make,
> Whiles neither lets the other touch the soil,[g]
> But either sdains[h] with other to partake :
> So cruelly those knights strove for that lady's sake.

The fight is long, but ends like the former ; Diamond's head is severed from his shoulders by Cambel's axe. Yet the decapitated man continues on the perpendicular :—

---

[g] The prey (properly, the mire in which an animal of chase wallows).

[h] Disdains.

The headless trunk, as heedless of that stour,
Stood still awhile, and his fast footing kept;
Till, feeling life to fail, it fell, and deadly slept.[i]

They which that piteous spectacle beheld
Were much amazed the headless trunk to see
Stand up so long and weapon vain to weld,[j]
Unweeting of the Fates' divine decree
For life's succession in those brethren three.
For notwithstanding that one soul was reft,
Yet, had the body not dismembered be,
It would have lived, and revived eft;[k]
But, finding no fit seat, the lifeless corse it left.

It left; but that same soul which therein dwelt,
Straight entering into Triamond him filled
With double life and grief.

Lightly leaping forward, the third and last brother loses not a moment in confronting the victor—who on his part meets his new foe with equal alacrity.

Well mote ye wonder how that noble knight,
After he had so often wounded been,
Could stand on foot now to renew the fight:
But, had ye then him forth advancing seen,
Some newborn wight ye would him surely ween;
So fresh he seemed and so fierce in sight;
Like as a snake, whom weary winter's teen[l]
Hath worn to nought, now feeling summer's might
Casts off his ragged skin and freshly doth him dight.

All was through virtue of the ring he wore;
The which not only did not from him let
One drop of blood to fall, but did restore
His weakened powers, and dulled spirits whet,
Through working of the stone therein yset.
Else how could one of equal might with most,
Against so many no less mighty met,
Once think to match three such on equal cost,
Three such as able were to match a puissant host?

---

[i] Slept in death.
[j] And Cambel's weapon wielded in vain?
[k] Again.   [l] Injury.

Yet nought thereof was Triamond adread,
Ne desperate [n] of glorious victory;
But sharply him assailed, and sore bested
With heaps of strokes, which he at him let fly
As thick as hail forth poured from the sky:
He strook, he souced,[o] he foined,[p] he hewed, he lashed,
And did his iron brand so fast apply,
That from the same the fiery sparkles flashed,
As fast as water-sprinkles gainst a rock are dashed.

Cambel is forced for a time to give ground; but in his turn he forces Triamond to retreat:—

Like as the tide, that comes fro the ocean main,
Flows up the Shenan [q] with contrary force,
And, over-ruling him in his own reign,
Drives back the current of his kindly [r] course,
And makes it seem to have some other source;
But, when the flood is spent, then, back again
His borrowed waters forced to re-disburse,
He sends the sea his own with double gain,
And tribute eke withall, as to his sovereign.

In this way the battle for a long time continues varying to and fro, Triamond, however, gradually growing fainter from loss of blood:

But Cambel still more strong and greater grew,
Ne felt his blood to waste, ne powers emperished,
Through that ring's virtue, that with vigour new,
Still, whenas he enfeebled was, him cherished.
And all his wounds and all his bruises guerished:[s]
Like as a withered tree, through husband's [t] toil,
Is often seen full freshly to have flourisht,
And fruitful apples to have borne awhile,
As fresh as when it first was planted in the soil.

Through which advantage, in his strength he rose
And smote the other with so wondrous might,
That through the seam which did his hauberk close
Into his throat and life it pierced quite,

---

[m] Terrified.   [n] Hopeless.   [o] Came plunging down.
   [p] Pushed.   [q] The Shannon.
[r] ...tural.   [s] Cured.   [t] Husbandman's.

> That down he fell as dead in all men's sight:
> Yet dead he was not; yet he sure did die,
> As all men do that lose the living sprite:
> So did one soul out of his body fly
> Unto her native home from mortal misery.
>
> But natheless whilst all the lookers-on
> Him dead behight,[u] as he to all appeared,
> All unawares he started up anon,
> As one that had out of a dream been reared,
> And fresh assailed his foe: who half afeard
> Of the uncouth sight, as he some ghost had seen,
> Stood still amazed, holding his idle sweard;[v]
> Till, having often by him stricken been,
> He forced was to strike and save himself from teen.

Cambel, however, after this fights less furiously, "as one in fear the Stygian gods to offend." At last, each receiving a tremendous stroke from the other at the same moment, they both at once fall to all appearance dead upon the field. But lo, when the judges have risen, the marshals broken up the lists, and Canace given herself up to weeping and wailing, up start again both combatants, the one out of his swoon, the other breathing a new life, and instantly fall to fighting afresh. They strike and hew away at one another for a further length of time; and the case still hangs in doubt, when

> All suddenly they heard a troublous noise,
> That seemed some perilous tumult to design,
> Confused with women's cries and shouts of boys,
> Such as the troubled theatres ofttimes annoys.
>
> Thereat the champions both stood still a space,
> To weeten what that sudden clamour meant:
> Lo! where they spied with speedy whirling pace
> One in a chariot of strange furniment[w]
> Towards them driving like a storm out sent.
> The chariot decked was in wondrous wise
> With gold and many a gorgeous ornament,
> After the Persian monarchs' antique guise,
> Such as the maker self could best by art devise.

---

[u] Affirmed.   [v] Sword.   [w] Furniture.

The chariot is drawn by two lions, and in it sits a most beautiful lady, seeming "born of angels' brood," and with a look of bounty, or goodness, equal to her beauty. This is Cambina, a daughter of the Fairy Agape, who, having been trained in magic by her mother, and having by her mighty art learned the evil plight in which her brother Triamond now is, has come to aid him, and to put an end to the deadly strife between him and Cambel.

> And, as she passed through the unruly preace [x]
> Of people thronging thick her to behold,
> Her angry team, breaking their bonds of peace,
> Great heaps of them, like sheep in narrow fold,
> For haste did over-run in dust enrolled;
> That, thorough rude confusion of the rout.
> Some fearing shrieked, some being harmed howled,
> Some laughed for sport, some did for wonder shout,
> And some, that would seem wise, their wonder turned to doubt.
>
> In her right hand a rod of peace she bore,
> About the which two serpents weren wound,
> Entrailed [y] mutually in lovely lore,
> And by the tails together firmly bound,
> And both were with one olive girland crowned;
> (Like to the rod which Maia's son doth wield,
> Wherewith the hellish fiends he doth confound;)
> And in her other hand a cup she hild, [z]
> The which was with Nepenthe to the brim upfilled.
>
> Nepenthe is a drink of sovereign grace,
> Devised by the gods for to assuage
> Heart's grief, and bitter gall away to chase
> Which stirs up anguish and contentious rage:
> Instead thereof sweet peace and quietage
> It doth establish in the troubled mind.
> Few men, but such as sober are and sage,
> Are by the gods to drink thereof assigned;
> But such as drink, eternal happiness do find.
>
> Such famous men, such worthies of the earth,
> As Jove will have advanced to the sky,
> And there made gods, though born of mortal birth,

---

[x] Press.   [y] Interwoven.   [z] Held

For their high merits and great dignity,
Are wont, before they may to heaven fly,
To drink hereof; whereby all cares forepast
Are washed away quite from their memory:
So did those old heroes hereof taste,
Before that they in bliss amongst the gods were placed.

Much more of price and of more gracious power
Is this, than that same water of Ardenne,
The which Rinaldo drunk in happy hour,
Described by that famous Tuscan pen:
For that had might to change the hearts of men
Fro love to hate, a change of evil choice:
But this doth hatred make in love to bren,[a]
And heavy heart with comfort doth rejoice.
Who would not to this virtue rather yield his voice?

[The fountain here alluded to was made by Merlin to cure Sir Tristram (who, however, never drank of it) of his love for Isotta, or Isolde, and is mentioned by Boyardo in the First Book of the Orlando Innamorato.]

When she has reached the lists, Cambina softly smites the rail with her rod, and forthwith it flies open and gives her passage. Then descending from her coach she salutes first her brother and next Cambel, for whom, it is intimated, she entertains a secret love. As they continue to fight she throws herself down on the bloody ground, and, mixing prayers with her tears, and reasons with her prayers, entreats them to desist.

But, whenas all might nought with them prevail,
She smote them lightly with her powerful wand:
Then suddenly, as if their hearts did fail,
Their wrathful blades down fell out of their hand,
And they, like men astonished, still did stand.
Thus, whilst their minds were doubtfully distraught,
And mighty spirits bound with mightier band,
Her golden cup to them for drink she raught,[b]
Whereof, full glad for thirst, each drunk an hearty draught:

Of which so soon as they once tasted had,
Wonder it is that sudden change to see:

---

[a] Burn.   [b] Reached.

> Instead of strokes, each other kissed glad,
> And lovely halst,ᶜ from fear of treason free,
> And plighted hands, for ever friends to be.
> When all men saw this sudden change of things,
> So mortal foes so friendly to agree,
> For passing joy, which so great marvel brings,
> They all gan shout aloud, that all the heaven rings.

Canace now comes down from her seat to know what it is that has happened; she and Cambina become friends on the spot; the trumpets sound, and all the people arising depart in glee and gladness;

> And wise Cambina, taking by her side
> Fair Canace as fresh as morning rose,
> Unto her coach remounting, home did ride,
> Admired of all the people and much glorified.
>
> Where making joyous feast their days they spent
> In perfect love, devoid of hateful strife,
> Allied with bands of mutual complement;
> For Triamond had Canace to wife,
> With whom he led a long and happy life;
> And Cambel took Cambina to his fere,ᵈ
> The which as life were each to other lief.ᵉ
> So all alike did love, and loved were,
> That since their days such lovers were not found elsewhere.

Canto IV. (48 stanzas).—The main story of the poem is now resumed from the point where Cambel, Triamond, Cambina, and Canace are overtaken by Blandamour, Paridel, the Squire of Dames, Duessa, Ate, and the false Florimel, in the second Canto. Blandamour, vainglorious and insolent, notwithstanding the entreaty of the courteous squire that he would let them and their ladies pass on in quiet, assails the two stranger knights, as was his wont, with his foul tongue—so that, stung by his unprovoked abuse—" for evil deeds may better than bad words be borne "—they begin to adjust their shields and to lay hold on their spears, when Cambina interposes, and by her mild persuasions prevents the quarrel from

---

ᶜ Embraced.   ᵈ Companion, wife.   ᵉ Dear.

going farther. They all now ride on together, discoursing of the tourney, till after a while they perceive advancing towards them " one in bright arms, with ready spear in rest," who, however, upon observing Paridel ready to take him in hand, quickly assumes a gay and good-humoured demeanour, and joins their company. But, as soon as he looks about him and sees the snowy Florimel, he lays claim to her as his own lost property. It is, in fact, Braggadoccio, from whom, it may be remembered, the false lady had been carried off by Ferraugh. Blandamour hears his demand with infinite scorn, and proposes that they shall immediately decide the controversy in the usual way by a passage of arms, and that, while the victor shall have the bright Florimel for his prize, the other shall be obliged to console himself with the old hag Ate—" and with her always ride till he another get."

  That offer pleased all the company:
  So Florimel with Ate forth was brought,
  At which they all gan laugh full merrily:
  But Braggadoccio said, he never thought
  For such an hag, that seemed worse than nought,
  His person to emperil so in fight:
  But if to match that lady they had sought
  Another like, that were like fair and bright.
  His life he then would spend to justify his right.

  At which his vain excuse they all gan smile,
  As scorning his unmanly cowardice:
  And Florimel him foully gan revile,
  That for her sake refused to enterprize
  The battle, offered in so knightly wise;
  And Ate eke provoked him privily
  With love of her,[d] and shame of much misprize.[e]
  But nought he cared for friend or enemy;
  For in base mind nor friendship dwells nor enmity.

  But Cambel thus did shut up all in jest;
  " Brave knights and ladies, certes ye do wrong

---

  [d] That is, of Florimel.
 [e] Contempt, to which he exposed himself.

> To stir up strife, when most us needeth rest,
> That we may us reserve both fresh and strong
> Against the tournament which is not long,[f]
> When whoso list to fight may fight his fill:
> Till then your challenges ye may prolong;
> And then it shall be tried, if ye will,
> Whether shall have the hag, or hold the lady still."

So they all ride on in merry mood, "that masked mock-knight" affording them good sport all the while; till on the appointed day they come to the place of tournament, where they find already assembled "many a brave knight, and many a dainty dame." All take their places, knights and ladies marching in couples linked together:—

> Then first of all forth came Sir Satyrane,
> Bearing that precious relic in an ark
> Of gold, that bad eyes might it not profane;
> Which drawing softly forth out of the dark,
> He open shewed, that all men it mote mark;
> A gorgeous girdle, curiously embost
> With pearl and precious stone, worth many a mark;
> Yet did the workmanship far pass the cost:
> It was the same which lately Florimel had lost.
>
> The same aloft he hung in open view,
> To be the prize of beauty and of might;
> The which, eftsoons discovered, to it drew
> The eyes of all, allured with close delight,
> And hearts quite robbed with so glorious sight,
> That all men threw out vows and wishes vain.
> Thrice happy lady, and thrice happy knight,
> Them seemed that could so goodly riches gain,
> So worthy of the peril, worthy of the pain.

But how the girdle has come into the hands of Satyrane is not explained. It was indeed found by him when he came up to the spot where Florimel had dropped it in her flight from the beast sent in pursuit of her by the witch (B. iii. C. 7, s. 31); but he afterwards employed it to bind that monster (s. 36), which, we are expressly told (C. 8, s. 2), returned so bound to the

---

[f] Not far off.

witch, who immediately (s. 3) took the girdle and ran with it to show to her son as an evidence that Florimel was destroyed.

Satyrane then takes his spear and " maiden-headed shield," and presents himself ready for the fight. The first who comes forth against him is a paynim knight, called Bruncheval the Bold. They are thrown to the ground together at the first encounter. On this another knight, the noble Ferramont, rides up to the aid of Satyrane, and against him Blandamour advances. Blandamour and his horse are both thrown down, and then Paridel rides forth to the rescue of his friend; but he meets the same fate. It is Braggadoccio's turn to strike in next, but of course he does not stir; and so Triamond sternly steps forth, and at last bears down the hitherto invincible Ferramont. Neither can Sir Devon, nor Sir Douglas, nor Sir Palimord, who all come up in succession, better stand his fury and force. Satyrane, however, now recovers out of his swoon,—

> And looking round about, like one dismayed,
> Whenas he saw the merciless affray
> Which doughty Triamond had wrought that day
> Unto the noble knights of Maidenhead,
> His mighty heart did almost rend in tway
> For very gall, that rather wholly dead
> Himself he wished have been than in so bad a stead.

Mounting his steed he dashes fiercely forward,

> Like spark of fire that from the anvil glode, ᵍ

and, aiming " his beam-like spear " with all his strength, wounds Triamond so severely in the side, that the utmost the latter can do is to manage to withdraw himself without being observed.

> Then gan the part of challengers anew
> To range the field, and victor-like to reign,
> That none against them battle durst maintain.
> By that the gloomy evening on them fell,
> That forced them from fighting to refrain,

ᵍ Glided.

> And trumpets' sound to cease did them compel:
> So Satyrane that day was judged to bear the bell.

The next morning Triamond is still unable to appear; but Cambel, without informing him, arrays himself in his friend's shield and arms, and so presents himself before the triumphing Satyrane. Having encountered, they are at the first onset thrown to the ground together, but, quickly springing up and betaking themselves to their swords, they continue the fight, till, Satyrane's horse stumbling, Cambel by a blow on his helmet unseats him, and throws him down among the animal's feet. He himself instantly dismounts and is about to disarm his prostrate adversary, when a hundred knights rush up to the rescue of Satyrane, and all fall to pounding him with their swords at once. Stoutly as he resists they succeed in taking him captive. When news of this is brought to Triamond, he soon forgets his wound, and, starting up, seeks for his arms; which when he cannot find, he hastily takes those of Cambel, and issuing forth rushes into the thick of the knights who hold his friend a prisoner, and soon compels them to let him go. The two knights, joining together, carry everything before them—till at last the trumpets sound, and the prize is unanimously declared to be theirs. Neither, however, will accept it from the other; so that the doom, or final adjudication, is deferred to a third day. On that Satyrane again finds none who can withstand him, and victory seems to rest with him and his party:—

> Ne was there knight that ever thought of arms,
> But that his utmost prowess there made knowen:
> That, by their many wounds and careless harms,
> By shivered spears and swords all under strown,
> By scattered shields, was easy to be shown.
> There might ye see loose steeds at random run,
> Whose luckless riders late were overthrown;
> And squires make haste to help their lords fordone:
> But still the knights of Maidenhead the better won.

At last, however, there enters from the opposite side a stranger knight, whose quaint disguise perplexes every body:—

> For all his armour was like salvage weed
> With woody moss bedight, and all his steed
> With oaken leaves attrapt, that seemed fit
> For salvage wight, and thereto well agreed
> His word, which on his ragged shield was writ,
> *Salvagesse sans finesse,* shewing secret wit.

He instantly charges the first knight that catches his eye, who happens to be the stout Sir Sanglier; and, after jerking him out of his saddle at the first encounter, treats a second, Sir Brianor, in the same fashion:—

> Then, ere his hand he reared, he overthrew
> Seven knights one after other as they came:
> And, when his spear was brust,[h] his sword he drew,
> The instrument of wrath, and with the same
> Fared like a lion in his bloody game,
> Hewing and slashing shields and helmets bright,
> And beating down whatever nigh him came,
> That every one gan shun his dreadful sight,
> No less than death itself, in dangerous affright.

The wondering crowd name him the Salvage Knight; but his true name, though few know it, is Arthegal—

> The doughtiest knight that lived that day, and most of might.

By evening, however, another stranger knight appears, and eclipses the glory of this victorious champion: first attacking him, and sending him over his horse's tail, and then disposing of Cambel, Triamond, Blandamour, and many others, who successively encounter her, in the same summary way. For this is no other that Britomart, with her enchanted spear, whose force no man can bide. And the Canto concludes thus:—

> Like as in summer's day when raging heat
> Doth burn the earth and boiled rivers dry,
> That all brute beasts, forced to refrain fro meat,
> Do hunt for shade where shrouded they may lie,
> And, missing it, fain[i] from themselves to fly;
> All travellers tormented are with pain:
> A watery cloud doth overcast the sky,

---

[h] Burst.   [i] Desire, long.

And poureth forth a sudden shower of rain,
That all the wretched world recomforteth again:
So did the warlike Britomart restore
The prize to knights of Maidenhead that day,
Which else was like to have been lost, and bore
The praise of prowess from them all away.
Then shrilling trumpets loudly gan to bray,
And bade them leave their labours and long toil
To joyous feast and other gentle play,
Where beauty's prize should win that precious spoil :
Where I with sound of trump will also rest awhile.

Canto V. (46 stanzas).—The contest of the ladies for Florimel's girdle, which forms the main incident in the first part of this Canto, is founded on the same favourite fiction with the story of King Arthur's drinking horn in the *Lai du Corn*, and the *Morte d'Arthur*, or that of the drinking horn in the romances of Tristan and of Percival, the fabliau called *Le Court Mantel* (translated by Way under the title of the Mantle Made Amiss), the ballad of *The Boy and the Mantle* in 'Percy's Reliques,' the tale of the enchanted cup in the second Canto of the Orlando Furioso, and Fontaine's *La Coupe Enchantée*. The Canto opens with these lines ;—

It hath been through all ages ever seen,
That with the praise of arms and chivalry
The prize of beauty still hath joined been ;
And that for reason's special privity ;
For either doth on other much rely :
For he me seems most fit the fair to serve,
That can her best defend from villainy ;
And she most fit his service doth deserve,
That fairest is, and from her faith will never swerve.

The girdle of fair Florimel, the poet proceeds to state, which many of the ladies were eager to win not so much for virtuous use, as for glory vain—

———— gave the virtue of chaste love
And wivehood true to all that it did bear;
But whosoever contrary doth prove,
Might not the same about her middle wear
But it would loose or else asunder tear.

It is said to have been formerly the girdle of Venus, and to have been greatly valued by her as long as " she used to live in wively sort :"—

>Her husband Vulcan whilome for her sake,
>When first he loved her with heart entire,
>This precious ornament, they say, did make,
>And wrought in Lemnos with unquenched fire:
>And afterwards did for her love's first hire
>Give it to her.
>
>. . . . . .
>
>The same one day, when she herself disposed
>To visit her beloved paramour,
>The God of War, she from her middle loosed,
>And left behind her in her secret bower
>On Acidalian mount, where many an hour
>She with the pleasant Graces wont to play.
>There Florimel in her first age's flower
>Was fostered by those Graces as they say,
>And brought with her from thence that goodly belt away.

By Florimel this belt, the name of which is the Cestus, was held dear as her life; no wonder, then, that many ladies are now anxious to win it;

>For peerless she was thought that did it bear.

As soon as the feast is ended the selected judges descend " into the Martian field" (meaning, apparently, the Campus Martius). And, first, it is declared, that Satyrane, Triamond, and the Knight of the Ebon Spear, as Britomart is called, have been the victors in the three days' fighting ; and Britomart, as the last, the chief:—

>———————— to her, therefore,
>The fairest lady was adjudged for paramour.

It is now, then, to be determined which best deserves to be accounted that paragon of beauty. First, Cambel brings forward his Cambina ; next, Triamond, his Canace ; after her, Paridel, his false Duessa (Blandamour must have made over Duessa to Paridel, we suppose, upon coming into possession of the snowy lady) ; then

Sir Ferramont, his Lucida; and after these a hundred other ladies appear; "all which," says the poet,

> ―――― whoso dare think for to enchase,[j]
> Him needeth sure a golden pen I ween
> To tell the feature of each goodly face.
> For, since the day that they created been,
> So many heavenly faces were not seen
> Assembled in one place : ne he that thought
> For Chian folk to portrait Beauty's Queen,
> By view of all the fairest to him brought,
> So many fair did see, as here he might have sought.

At last Britomart exhibits her Amoret, and all think that she shall "surely bear the bell away," till Blandamour who imagines he has "the true and very Florimel," produces his snowy lady,

> The sight of whom once seen did all the rest dismay.
> For all afore that seemed fair and bright
> Now base and contemptible did appear,
> Compared to her, that shone as Phœbus' light
> Amongst the lesser stars in evening clear.
> All that her saw with wonder ravished were,
> And weened no mortal creature she should be,
> But some celestial shape that flesh did bear :
> Yet all were glad there Florimel to see ;
> Yet thought that Florimel was not so fair as she.

> As guileful goldsmith that by secret skill
> With golden foil doth finely overspread
> Some baser metal, which commend he will
> Unto the vulgar for good gold instead,
> He much more goodly gloss thereon doth shed
> To hide his falsehood, that if it were true :
> So hard this idol was to be aread,[k]
> That Florimel herself in all men's view
> She seemed to pass : So forged things do fairest shew.

But, when by universal assent it is agreed that she shall have the girdle, and it is brought to be put about her waist, by no management can it be made to fit her : as soon as it is fastened it loosens itself and drops off, "as feeling secret blame." Of the very much astonished

---

[j] Set out.   [k] Understood, seen through.

spectators each has his own thoughts on the subject; she herself thinks it is done in spite:—

> Then many other ladies likewise tried
> About their tender loins to knit the same;
> But it would not on none of them abide,
> But, when they thought it fast, eftsoons it was untied.
> Which when that scornful Squire of Dames did view,
> He loudly gan to laugh, and thus to jest;
> "Alas for pity that so fair a crew,
> As like cannot be seen from east to west,
> Cannot find one this girdle to invest!
> Fie on the man that did it first invent,
> To shame us all with this *ungirt unblest!*
> Let never lady to his love assent,
> That hath this day so many so unmanly shent."[1]

At this "all knights gan laugh, and ladies lour;" till at last the gentle Amoret comes forward to prove the power of the girdle, and having put it round her finds it fit "withouten breach or let." Florimel, however, still urges her claim, and, although on a further trial the belt proves in her hands as unmanageable as before, it is nevertheless adjudged to her, and she herself is assigned to the Knight of the Ebon Spear. But Britomart will not so lightly forego her Amoret for this strange dame. Upon this it is decided by the judges that the Salvage Knight (or Arthegal), as having been the second best of the combatants, shall have her; but he is found to have already gone away " in great displeasure that he could not get her." She is then offered to Triamond; but he loves Canace, "and other none." So at last she is adjudged to Satyrane. But Blandamour, Paridel, and a crowd of other knights, stirred up by Ate, will by no means submit to this arrangement; among the rest Braggadoccio puts in his claim, calling upon the lady herself to testify to his right; and she on being questioned confesses that all he affirms is true.

> Thereat exceeding wroth was Satyrane;
> And wroth with Satyrane was Blandamour;

---
[1] Disgraced.

And wroth with Blandamour was Erivane;
And at them both Sir Paridel did lour.

Satyrane, considerably perplexed, and feeling that "sweet is alone the love that comes with willingness," proposes that the fair lady shall be set in the midst of them, and allowed to choose for herself. They all accordingly encircle her, gazing, wishing, vowing, praying, and calling upon the Queen of Beauty, or Venus, for her aid; when, after looking long at each, as if she wished she could please them all, she at last walks up to Braggadoccio. Frantic with mortification and rage, the others are some of them for taking her from him by main force, some for making him maintain his right in fair fight to the fair lady. He little minds their angry words, but yet deems it prudent to make off with his prize during the night. The rest then set out after him—and in that pursuit the story for the present leaves them.

Britomart, however, taking with her the lovely Amoret, proceeds upon her own proper adventure, the quest of her Arthegal—

> Unlucky maid, to seek her enemy!
> Unlucky maid, to seek him far and wide,
> Whom, when he was unto herself most nigh,
> She through his late disguisement could him not descry!

Meanwhile Amoret's lover, Scudamore, has been travelling on, enduring all the pangs of jealousy and unsatisfied thirst of revenge—feelings which will not be allayed by all that his companion, old Glauce, can say or do. It is now nightfall, and the aspect of the heavens portends the coming on of a fearful storm, when not far off they spy a little cottage, " like some poor man's nest."

> Under a steep hill's side it placed was,
> There where the mouldered earth had caved[m] the bank;
> And fast beside a little brook did pass
> Of muddy water, that like puddle stank,
> By which few crooked sallows grew in rank:

---

[m] Hollowed out.

Whereto approaching nigh, they heard the sound
Of many iron hammers beating rank,ⁿ
And answering their weary turns around,
That seemed some blacksmith dwelt in that desert ground.°

There entering in, they found the goodman self
Full busily unto his work ybent;
Who was to weetᵖ a wretched wearishᑫ elf,
With hollow eyes and rawbone cheeks forspent,ʳ
As if he had in prison long been pent:
Full black and grisly did his face appear,
Besmeared with smoke that nigh his eye-sight blent;ˢ
With rugged beard, and hoary shagged hair,
The which he never wont to comb or comely shear.

Rude was his garment, and to rags all rent;
Ne better had he, ne for better cared:
With blistered hands amongst the cinders brent,
And fingers filthy with long nails unpaired,
Right fit to rend the food on which he fared.
His name was Care; a blacksmith by his trade,
That neither day nor night from working spared,
But to small purpose iron wedges made;
Those be unquiet thoughts that careful minds invade.

In which his work he had six servants prest,ᵗ
About the anvil standing evermore
With huge great hammers, that did never rest
From heaping strokes which thereon sousedᵘ sore:
All six strong grooms, but one than other more;
For by degrees they all were disagreed;
So likewise did the hammers which they bore
Like bells in greatness orderly succeed,
That he, which was the last, the first did far exceed.

He like a monstrous giant seemed in sight,
Far passing Bronteus or Pyracmon great,

ⁿ Fiercely.
° "Seem-ed" in two syllables; and "blacksmith," with the accent on the last.
ᵖ Was visibly—manifestly (to wit).   ᑫ Worn out.
ʳ Completely spent.   ˢ Confounded.
ᵗ Ready at hand.   ᵘ Fell down with force.

> The which in Lipari do day and night
> Frame thunderbolts for Jove's avengeful threat.
> So dreadfully he did the anvil beat,
> That seemed to dust he shortly would it drive:
> So huge his hammer, and so fierce his heat,
> That seemed a rock of diamond it could rive
> And rend asunder quite, if he thereto list strive.
>
> Sir Scudamore there entering much admired
> The manner of their work and weary pain:
> And, having long beheld, at last inquired
> The cause and end thereof; but all in vain;
> For they for nought would from their work refrain,
> Ne let his speeches come unto their ear.
> And eke the breathful bellows blew amain,
> Like to the northern wind, that none could hear:
> Those Pensiveness did move; and Sighs the bellows were.

Seeing all this, the warrior attempts no more speech, but lays him down to rest in his armour on the floor; and so does "that old aged dame, his faithful squire." Gentle sleep, however, will not come to close his heavy eyes; he tosses from side to side, and often, in his mental fever, rises and lies down again;

> And evermore, when he to sleep did think,
> The hammers' sound his senses did molest;
> And evermore, when he began to wink,
> The bellows' noise disturbed his quiet rest,
> Ne suffered sleep to settle in his breast.
> And all the night the dogs did bark and howl
> About the house, at scent of stranger guest:
> And now the crowing cock, and now the owl
> Loud shrieking, him afflicted to the very soul.

And, if he at any time chances to drop asleep for a moment, presently one of the villains raps him upon his headpiece with his iron mall. At last, however, completely worn out he sinks into a repose, from which even all this commotion and torment cannot awaken him. But then the one master-thought that fills his heart—the thought of the disloyalty of Amoret and Britomart—assails his idle brain in the form of a dream.

With that the wicked carle, the maister smith,
A pair of red-hot iron tongs did take
Out of the burning cinders, and therewith
Under his side him nipt; that, forced to wake,
He felt his heart for very pain to quake,
And started up avenged for to be
On him the which his quiet slumber brake:
Yet, looking round about him, none could see;
Yet did the smart remain, though he himself did flee.

In this disquiet and wretchedness he passes all the night —"that too long night"—till morning comes, when he rises "like heavy lump of lead," and, climbing his lofty steed, pursues his journey, accompanied by Glauce, as before.

Canto VI. (47 stanzas).—The story is thus resumed:

What equal torment to the grief of mind
And pining anguish hid in gentle heart,
That inly feeds itself with thoughts unkind,
And nourisheth her own consuming smart!
What medicine can any leech's art
Yield such a sore, that doth her grievance hide,
And will to none her malady impart!
Such was the wound that Scudamore did gride:[v]
For which Dan Phœbus self cannot a salve provide.

Riding on with Glauce in great dejection of mind, Sir Scudamore suddenly perceives close by a forest an armed knight "sitting in shade beside his grazing steed," who at their approach eagerly advances towards them with a threatening demeanour, to which Scudamore is not slow to respond; but, as soon as the stranger observes the arms of his opponent, he lowers his spear, much to the surprise of the other addresses him by name, and entreats his pardon, which Scudamore readily accords, at the same time requesting to know the name of a stranger who has shown himself so well acquainted with his. This information his new acquaintance begs to be excused from giving him for the present, but desires that he may be called, as he is by others, the Salvage Knight. It is, in fact, Sir Arthegal, or Artegal, as, for some unapparent reason,

[v] Pierce.

the name is henceforward spelled. Sir Scudamore then asks him if he dwells in the forest; to which the other replies that he is waiting to take vengeance, whenever he shall pass that way, on a stranger knight from whom he has suffered shame and dishonour:—

> "Shame be his meed," quoth he, " that meaneth shame!
> But what is he by whom ye shamed were?"
> "A stranger knight," said he, "unknown by name,
> But known by fame, and by an ebon spear
> With which he all that met him down did bear.
> He, in an open tournay lately held,
> Fro me the honour of that game did rear;
> And, having me, all weary erst, down felled,
> The fairest lady reft, and ever since withheld."

When Scudamore hears of the ebon spear, he knows right well who it is, and his anger and jealousy are immediately roused by the recollection of the supposed wrongs that he has received at the hands of Britomart, whose apparently treacherous conduct he recounts to the Salvage Knight, and offers to join him in chastising their common enemy when an opportunity shall offer.

So both to wreak their wraths on Britomart agree.

While they are thus talking, the subject of their discourse appears, " soft riding towards them,"

> Attired in foreign arms and strange array.

Scudamore entreats that he may be the first to take his revenge, as his injury is of earlier date than that of his companion. His request is granted, and he proceeds with great fierceness to attack " the noble maid," who on her part readily addresses herself to welcome him;

> But entertained him in so rude a wise,
> That to the ground she smote both horse and man;
> Whence neither greatly hasted to arise,
> But on their common harms together did devise.

At this mischance of Scudamore, Artegal, with his former rage still farther inflamed, " eft aventuring," that is, quickly advancing, his steel-headed lance, rides against the victor, but, to his no small amazement, is also himself unhorsed in an instant. Lightly starting up, however, he attacks his adversary with his sword so furiously that, mounted as she is, she is compelled to give ground; and presently, as she is wheeling round to avoid his blows, one of them, after glancing down her back, falls on her horse, and quite chining, or dividing, the unfortunate beast behind the saddle, compels her to alight:—

> Like as the lightning brond from riven sky,
> Thrown out by angry Jove in his vengeance,
> With dreadful force falls on some steeple high:
> Which battering down, it on the church doth glance,
> And tears it all with terrible mischance.
> Yet, she no whit dismayed, her steed forsook;
> And, casting from her that enchanted lance,
> Unto her sword and shield her soon betook:
> And therewithal at him right furiously she strook.

The vehemence of her first attack is irresistible, and Artegal is forced to fall back, while his blood flows forth through his rent and riven armour; but, as soon as he perceives her heat to be a little abated, he rises in his strength and assails her afresh;

> Heaping huge strokes as thick as shower of hail,
> And lashing dreadfully at every part,
> As if he thought her soul to disentrail.*
> Ah! cruel hand, and thrice more cruel heart,
> That work'st such wreck on her to whom thou dearest art!

As they continue the fight, Artegal recovers the strength he has lost from his wounds, while that of Britomart rather decreases:—

> At last his luckless hand he heaved on high,
> Having his forces all in one accrewed,ˣ
> And therewith strook at her so hideously,
> That seemed nought but death mote be her destiny.

> The wicked stroke upon her helmet chanced,
> And with the force which in itself it bore

---

* Draw or drive out.   ˣ United.

Her ventail ʸ shared away, and thenceforth glanced
Adown in vain, ne harmed her any more.
With that her angel's face, unseen afore,
Like to the ruddy morn appeared in sight,
Dewed with silver drops through sweating sore;
But somewhat redder than beseemed aright,
Through toilsome heat and labour of her weary fight:

And round about the same her yellow hair,
Having through stirring loosed their wonted band,
Like to a golden border did appear,
Framed in goldsmith's forge with cunning hand:
Yet goldsmith's cunning could not understand
To frame such subtile wire, so shiny clear;
For it did glister like the golden sand
The which Pactolus with his waters sheer ᶻ
Throws forth upon the rivage ᵃ round about him near.

The hand of Artegal is again upraised, but down falls the sword to ground " out of his fingers slack,"—

———— as if the steel had sense,
And felt some ruth, or sense his hand did lack,—

at the view of that overpowering beauty;

And he himself, long gazing thereupon,
At last fell humbly down upon his knee,
And of his wonder made religion,
Weening some heavenly goddess he did see,
Or else unweeting what it else might be.

All subdued he beseeches her pardon for the outrage he had done her; but the bold Britoness, not in the least softened by his adoration, the remembrance of that last stroke rankling in her mind, still stands over him, and, sternly looking down on him, bids him rise and resume the fight or receive instant death at her hand. She speaks in vain; he continues on his knee, and entreats her to pardon him or punish him as she pleases. By this time Scudamore has recovered his senses; and he too, looking on " that peerless pattern of Dame Nature's pride," is at first struck with terror, and then, his fear

ʸ Fore part of the helmet.   ᶻ Clear.   ᵃ Shore.

converted to faint devotion, thinks it is a divinity that he sees. Glauce now, seeing how matters stand, entreats her mistress to grant the two warriors " truce awhile:" Britomart consents; and then the knights raise their beavers, and she for the first time sees their countenances. As soon as she beholds " the lovely face of Artegal, tempered with sterness and stout majesty," she is startled and appalled by perceiving it to be the same that she had seen long since in the enchanted glass. Her uplifted hand drops down, and, ever as she attempts to raise it anew, all strength to hold the sword leaves it as soon as her eye again meets that manly visage ; nor will even her tongue obey her as she strives still to appear enraged, but brings forth speeches mild instead of angry words. Meanwile Scudamore, inwardly rejoicing at having found how false and groundless was all his jealous fear, addresses the submissive knight :—

——— " Certes, Sir Artegal,
I joy to see you lout[b] so low on ground,
And now become to live a lady's thrall,
That whilome in your mind wont to despise them all."

Poor Britomart does not hear that name, giving her full assurance that she has found him she has so long sought, without various violent and conflicting emotions, though she still continues to feign her former angry mood,—

Thinking to hide the depth by troubling of the flood.

Glauce now addresses the three. First, she reminds both Artegal and Scudamore, that they may now lay aside all the fears that had troubled them so much, lest Britomart should " woo away" their loves. Then she exhorts Artegal not henceforth to make it matter of regret or self-reproach that he has a second time been conquered by a woman's hand ;—" for," says she,

—" whilome they have conquered sea and land,
And heaven itself, that nought may them withstand:"

" Ne," she adds,

---

[b] Stoop, bow.

—— "henceforth be rebellious unto love,
That is the crown of knighthood, and the band
Of noble minds derived from above,
Which, being knit with virtue, never will remove."

Britomart she recommends to repress somewhat of her wrathful spirit, the fire of which, she tells her, "were better turned to other flame," and to lend a favourable ear to her lover, only, however, on condition that he fulfil the penance she shall lay upon him—

" For lovers' heaven must pass by sorrow's hell."

" Thereat," we are told,

——— full inly blushed Britomart;
But Artegal, close-smiling, joyed in secret heart.

During all this while Scudamore is longing to hear news of his Amoret; and he now begs Britomart (whom, however, somewhat oddly, he still addresses by the title Sir) to give him the desired information. It would appear that, after releasing her from the hands of the enchanter, Britomart had taken every care of her, preserving her "from peril and from fear" with all possible tenderness and affection; till one day as they were travelling through a desert, being both weary, they alighted and sate down to rest, when Britomart, having fallen asleep, found on awaking her companion gone; nor were all her subsequent efforts to obtain tidings of her of any avail. Scudamore is overwhelmed with grief and deadly fear at this account; but after a while is somewhat re-assured by Britomart kindly vowing " by heaven's light" never to leave him till they shall have found his lady love, and avenged themselves on her reaver. Every thing being thus arranged, they take their steeds, and set forward to a resting place to which Artegal undertakes to conduct them;

Where goodly solace was unto them made,
And daily feasting both in bower and hall,
Until that they their wounds well healed had,
And weary limbs recured after late usage bad.

In all this time Sir Artegal, too, we are told, was making way "unto the love of noble Britomart;" and that, notwithstanding the pains she took "with womanish art" to conceal the impression he had made on her heart,

> So well he wooed her, and so well he wrought her,
> With fair entreaty and sweet blandishment,
> That at the length unto a bay[c] he brought her,
> So as she to his speeches was content
> To lend an ear, and softly to relent.
> At last, through many vows which forth he poured
> And many oaths, she yielded her consent
> To be his love, and take him for her lord,
> Till they with marriage meet might finish that accord.

But at last, after they have rested here for a long while, Artegal, to the great grief of Britomart, finds it necessary to depart in order to proceed upon an adventure in which he had been engaged when they met. It is with much difficulty that he obtains her permission to go; but on his pledging his faith to her by a "thousand vows from bottom of his heart," and promising to return to her as soon as he shall have achieved his object, for which he only demands three months, she yields her consent.

> So, early on the morrow next, he went
> Forth on his way to which he was ybent;
> Ne wight him to attend, or way to guide,
> As whilome was the custom ancient
> Mongst knights when on adventures they did ride;
> Save that she algates[d] him a while accompanied.

> And by the way she sundry purpose found
> Of this or that, the time for to delay,
> And of the perils whereto he was bound,
> The fear whereof seemed much her to affray:
> But all she did was but to wear out day.
> Full oftentimes she leave of him did take;
> And eft again devised somewhat to say,
> Which she forgot, whereby excuse to make:
> So loth she was his company for to forsake.

---

[c] Stand.   [d] Nevertheless.

However, at last, when all her speeches are spent, she leaves him to himself; and, returning to Scudamore, sets out with him in quest of Amoret—" her second care, though in another kind." They go back to the forest where she had disappeared, and seek her there and every where, without success. But, concludes the Canto,

 ————— by what hapless fate
Or hard misfortune she was thence conveyed,
And stolen away from her beloved mate,
Were long to tell: therefore I here will stay
Until another tide, that I it finish may.

Canto VII. (47 stanzas).—" Great God of Love," exclaims the poet in now proceeding with the story of Amoret,

 Great God of Love, that with thy cruel darts
Dost conquer greatest conquerors on ground,
And set'st thy kingdom in the captive hearts
Of kings and kesars to thy service bound;
What glory or what guerdon hast thou found
In feeble ladies tyranning so sore,
And adding anguish to the bitter wound
With which their lives thou lanched'st[e] long afore,
By heaping storms of trouble on them daily more?

It seems that, when Britomart fell asleep, Amoret had amused herself by taking a walk through the wood, and in the course of her ramble had been suddenly fallen upon and snatched up by a personage who is thus engagingly painted:—

 It was to weet a wild and salvage man;
Yet was no man, but only like in shape,
And eke in stature higher by a span;
All overgrown with hair, that could awhape[f]
An hardy heart; and his wide mouth did gape
With huge great teeth, like to a tusked boar:
For he lived all on ravin and on rape
Of men and beasts; and fed on fleshly gore,
The sign whereof yet stained his bloody lips afore.

---

  [e] Pierced'st.   [f] Terrify.

His nether lip was not like man nor beast,
But like a wide deep poke down hanging low,
In which he wont the relics of his feast
And cruel spoil, which he had spared, to stow:
And over it his huge great nose did grow,
Full dreadfully empurpled all with blood;
And down both sides two wide long ears did glow,
And raught[g] down to his waste when up he stood,
More great than the ears of elephants by Indus' flood.

His waist was with a wreath of ivy green
Engirt about, ne other garment wore;
For all his hair was like a garment seen;
And in his hand a tall young oak he bore,
Whose knotty snags were sharpened all afore,
And beathed[h] in fire for steel to be in stead.
But whence he was, or of what womb ybore,
Of beasts, or of the earth, I have not read;
But certes was with milk of wolves and tigers fed.

The hideous monster rushed away with her through the briars and bushes to his cave, and there throwing her in left her more dead than alive. When she came to herself she heard in the darkness some one sighing and sobbing near her; this was one of her own sex, another of the wretch's victims, who had been already twenty days in the cavern, and in that time had seen "seven women by him slain and eaten clean," that being his regular mode of finishing his atrocities as soon as his amorous fit was over. Only she and an old woman, besides Amoret, remained; "and of us three," said she, "to-morrow he will sure eat one." She then told her own story. The daughter of a great lord, she had loved a squire of low degree—who yet was fit, if her eyes did not deceive her, " by any lady's side for leman to have lain." Having resolved for his sake to abandon sire, and friends, and all for ever, she one day left her home to meet him at a place they had agreed upon between them, and was caught by this " shame of men and plague of woman-kind," who, said she,

---

[g] Reached.   [h] Heated.

> —— "trussing me, as eagle doth his prey,
> Me hither brought with him as swift as wind;
> Where yet untouched till this present day,
> I rest his wretched thrall, the sad Æmilia."

While they are discoursing the villain himself returns to the cave. Horrified at his proceedings, Amoret soon breaks away in desperation, and (taking advantage, apparently, of his having neglected to replace the stone which closed the entrance) rushes forth screaming, while he runs after her.

> Full fast she flies, and far afore him goes
> Ne feels the thorns and thickets prick her tender toes.
>
> Nor hedge, nor ditch, nor hill, nor dale she stays,[1]
> But over-leaps them all, like roebuck light,
> And through the thickest makes her nighest ways;
> And evermore, when with regardful sight
> She looking back espies the grisly wight
> Approaching nigh, she gins to mend her pace,
> And makes her fear a spur to haste her flight;
> More swift than Myrrh' or Daphne in her race,
> Or any of the Thracian Nymphs in salvage chase.

It must be supposed that this is the same forest in which Florimel was seen flying from the foster in the First Canto of the preceding Book, and in which Timias, the prince's gentle squire, was found in the Fifth Canto of that Book by Belphoebe and conveyed by her to her pavilion. It chances that that lady is at this very time, as is her wont, hunting here the leopards and the bears with her sister wood-nymphs and "that lovely boy;" and it is the fortune of Timias to come up just as the cursed caitiff has again caught Amoret, and, grinning in self-gratulation, is bearing her off under his arm. For some time he wards off the squire's blows by using the captive lady as a buckler;

> And if it chanced (as needs it must in fight),
> Whilst he on him was greedy to be wroke,[2]

---

[1] Stops for.
[2] While Timias was eager to be avenged on him.

That any little blow on her did light.
Then would he laugh aloud, and gather great delight.

At last, however, Timias succeeds in thrusting his spear through the villain's hand ; on which

A stream of coal-black blood thence gushed amain,
That all her silken garments did with blood bestain ;

and, throwing his burthen on the earth, he falls upon the squire with such a storm of blows that the latter is compelled to give ground. Luckily the noise attracts Belphoebe,

Whom when that thief approaching nigh espied
With bow in hand and arrows ready bent,
He by his former combat would not bide,
But fled away with ghastly dreariment,
Well knowing her to be his death's sole instrument.

She, however, pursues, "with winged feet, as nimble as the wind," and with such success that, just as he is entering his hellish den,

She sent an arrow forth with mighty draught,
That in the very door him overcaught,
And, in his nape arriving, through it thrilled :
His greedy throat therewith in two distraught,
That all his vital spirits thereby spilled,
And all his hairy breast with gory blood was filled.

Whom when on ground she grovelling saw to roll,
She ran in haste his life to have bereft ;
But, ere she could him reach, the sinful soul,
Having his carrion corse quite senseless left,
Was fled to hell, surcharged with spoil and theft :
Yet over him she there long gazing stood,
And eft admired his monstrous shape, and eft
His mighty limbs, whilst all with filthy blood
The place there over-flown seemed like a sudden flood.

Thenceforth she passed into his dreadful den,
Where nought but darksome dreariness she found,
Ne creature saw, but harkened now and then
Some little whispering, and soft-groaning sound.
With that she asked, what ghosts there under ground

Lay hid in horror of eternal night;
And bade them, if so be they were not bound,
To come and show themselves before the light,
Now freed from fear and danger of that dismal wight.

On this Æmilia comes forth, all trembling, and after her the hag, her fellow prisoner, a foul and loathsome wretch —" leman fit for such a lover dear." They all three then return together to the place where she had left Timias with Amoret:—

There she him found by that new lovely mate,
Who lay the whiles in swoon, full sadly set,
From her fair eyes wiping the dewy wet
Which softly stilled, and kissing them atween,
And handling soft the hurts which she did get:
For of that carle she sorely bruised had been;
Als[k] of his own rash hand one wound was to be seen.

Which when she saw with sudden glancing eye,
Her noble heart, with sight thereof, was filled
With deep disdain and great indignity,
That in her wrath she thought them both have thrilled
With that self arrow which the carle had killed:
Yet held her wrathful hand from vengeance sore:
But drawing nigh, ere he her well beheld,
" Is this the faith?" she said—and said no more,
But turned her face, and fled away for evermore.

He, seeing her depart, arose up light,
Right sore aggrieved at her sharp reproof,
And followed fast: but, when he came in sight,
He durst not nigh approach, but kept aloof,
For dread of her displeasure's utmost proof:
And evermore, when he did grace entreat,
And framed speeches fit for his behoof,
Her mortal arrows she at him did threat,
And forced him back with foul dishonour to retreat.

At last, when long he followed had in vain,
Yet found no ease of grief nor hope of grace,
Unto those woods he turned back again,
Full of sad anguish and in heavy case:

---

[k] Also.

And, finding there fit solitary place
For woful wight, chose out a gloomy glade,
Where hardly eye mote see bright heaven's face
For mossy trees, which covered all with shade
And sad melancholy; there he his cabin made.

His wonted warlike weapons all he broke
And threw away, with vow to use no more,
Ne thenceforth ever strike in battle stroke,
Ne ever word to speak to woman more;
But in that wilderness, of men forlore¹
And of the wicked world forgotten quite,
His hard mishap in dolour to deplore,
And waste his wretched days in woful plight:
So on himself to wreak his folly's own despite.

And eke his garment, to be thereto meet,
He wilfully did cut and shape anew;
And his fair locks, that wont with ointment sweet
To be embalmed, and sweat out dainty dew,
He let to grow and grisly to concrew,ᵐ
Uncombed, uncurled, and carelessly unshed;
That in short time his face they overgrew,
And over all his shoulders did dispread,
That who he whilome was uneathⁿ was to be read.

There he continued in his careful plight,
Wretchedly wearing out his youthly years,
Through wilful penury consumed quite,
That like a pined ghost he soon appears:
For other food than that wild forest bears,
Ne other drink there did he ever taste
Than running water tempered with his tears,
The more his weakened body so to waste:
That out of all men's knowledge he was worn at last

In this very remarkable passage there can be no doubt that the real incident alluded to is Raleigh's amour with Elizabeth Throgmorton, one of Elizabeth's maids of honour, by which he is understood to have drawn down upon himself for a time the passionate displeasure of his royal mistress. The circumstance appears to have happened in the year 1592, and Raleigh afterwards made all

---

ˡ Forsaken.   ᵐ Grow together.   ⁿ Scarcely

the reparation in his power by marrying the lady. The reader will admire not only the ingenuity of the allegory, but the singular combination which it presents of boldness in the conception and the highest delicacy in the execution.

The story goes on to relate, that one day Prince Arthur, seeking adventures, chanced to come to the cabin in which Timias thus abode, "spending his days in dolour and despair," and never suspected who he was. When the prince addressed him, and expressed pity for his miserable state,

    — to his speech he answered no whit,
    But stood still mute, as if he had been dumb,
    Ne sign of sense did show, ne common wit,
    As one with grief and anguish overcome;
    And unto everything did answer mum:
    And ever, when the prince unto him spake,
    He louted lowly, as did him become,
    And humble homage did unto him make;
    Midst sorrow showing joyous semblance for his sake.

Greatly wondering, the prince yet was led to think he had in former days been conversant with arms and knightliness, both by secret signs of a gentler nature which were discernible even through all that rudeness of demeanour, and by observing him handle his naked sword and try its edge;

    And eke by that he saw on every tree
    How he the name of one engraven had
    Which likely was his liefest love to be,
    From whom he now so sorely was bestad;[o]
    Which was by him Belphoebe rightly rad:[p]
    Yet who was that Belphoebe he ne wist;
    Yet saw he often how he wexed glad
    When he it heard, and how the ground he kist
    Wherein it written was, and how himself he blist.

Nothing that Arthur can do, however, is of any avail to soothe his dejection and wretchedness; and he at last leaves him, for time, which alone can, to work his restoration.

    [o] Distressingly removed?   [p] Read.

Canto VIII. (64 stanzas).—It is well said by the wise man that the displeasure of the mighty is more dread and desperate than death itself;

> Like as it fell to this unhappy boy,
> Whose tender heart the fair Belphoebe had
> With one stern look so daunted, that no joy
> In all his life, which afterwards he lad,[q]
> He ever tasted; but with penance sad
> And pensive sorrow pined and wore away,
> Ne ever laughed, ne once showed countenance glad,
> But always wept and wailed night and day,
> As blasted bloosm through heat doth languish and decay.

The first thing that awakens him from his settled melancholy is the song of a turtle dove, who, having herself lately lost her love, takes pity on him, and tunes her notes to a lamentable lay,

> So sensibly[r] compiled that in the same
> Him seemed oft he heard his own right name.

The gentle bird daily repairs without fear to his dwelling, to comfort him with her sympathizing melody;

> And every day, for guerdon of her song,
> He part of his small feast to her would share;
> That, at the last, of all his woe and wrong
> Companion she became, and so continued long.

One day as she is sitting by his side he brings forth some memorials, or relics, he still retains of Belphoebe's former kindness—among the rest a ruby shaped like a bleeding heart, with a gold chain attached to it; and this he takes, and with a riband, in which are his lady's colours, hangs it about the turtle's neck; when lo!

> All unawares the bird, when she did find
> Herself so decked, her nimble wings displayed,
> And flew away as lightly as the wind.

Timias grieves that he should so lightly have lost both his jewel and "the dear companion of his care:" but "that sweet bird" has only gone off to carry the token

[q] Led.   [r] Feelingly.

to where wons his fair Belphoebe. She finds the lady resting herself after the fatigues of the chase in a shady arbour, and, alighting on the ground before her, begins to sing her customary mournful song. At length Belphoebe perceives the well-known jewel, and instantly puts forward her hand to seize it;—

> But the swift bird obeyed not her behest,
> But swerved aside, and there again did stay;
> She followed her, and thought again it to essay.
>
> And ever, when she nigh approached, the dove
> Would flit a little forward, and then stay
> Till she drew near, and then again remove:
> So tempting her still to pursue the prey,
> And still from her escaping soft away:
> Till that at length into that forest wide
> She drew her far, and led with slow delay:
> In the end she her unto that place did guide
> Whereas that woful man in languor did abide.

The dove flies to the hand of Timias; Belphoebe does not recognize him; but he, as soon as he beholds her, falls down at her feet and kisses the ground on which she treads, and washes it with his gushing tears. Wondering at his behaviour, she addresses him, exhorting him to rouse himself from the grief and lethargy that seem to oppress him. Then for the first time he breaks his long silence, and tells her that it is she herself that has reduced him to the state in which he is, and that she alone can restore him to the light. His words of sorrow move her mighty heart to pity and mild regard; and the end is that he is restored to his former favour, and long leads a happy life as before, fearless of chance or change, and mindless even of his own dear lord the noble prince, who hears nothing of what has become of him, but wanders through the endless world seeking him evermore in vain. At last one day, riding through that wood, the prince there finds Æmilia and Amoret, who are represented as being still both "in full sad and sorrowful estate," the one from the effects of her ill-treatment in the cave, the other from the wound she had received at the hand of Timias while effecting her rescue. Arthur, however, soon restores the latter by a few drops of the precious medicinal liquor he always carries about with him; and Æmilia also recovers her health. They then tell him their story; upon hearing which a strong desire seizes him to discover the warlike virgin by whom they had been delivered. He can, however, learn nothing more of her from the ladies; and therefore he lifts them from the ground ("no service loathsome to a gentle kind"), and, placing them both together on his horse, sets out with them, walking himself on foot by their side. It will be observed that nothing has been said of how Æmilia and Amoret have disposed of themselves since Belphoebe and Timias left them, which must have been a goodly while since, seeing how much had happened to Timias in the interval; and the expression used here—"he them from ground did rear"—might almost seem to imply that they had remained ever since sitting on the ground. This must be admitted to be carrying the shadowy and mysterious, or the complexity and perplexity which with Spenser seems to be part and parcel of his poetical system, sufficiently far. The matter, however, does not give any trouble to his dozing editors. The prince and the two ladies, after getting out of the forest, come at nightfall to a little cottage; entering which, they find only an old woman, raggedly attired, sitting upon the ground; her hair is all in disorder, and she gnaws her nails "for fellness and for ire," sucking venom thence for her heart and mind:—

> A foul and loathly creature sure in sight,
> And in conditions to be loathed no less:
> For she was stuffed with rancour and despite
> Up to the throat, that oft with bitterness
> It forth would break and gush in great excess,
> Pouring out streams of poison and of gall
> Gainst all that truth or virtue do profess;
> Whom she with leasings* lewdly did miscall
> And wickedly backbite; her name men Slander call.

---
* Lies.

> Her nature is, all goodness to abuse,
> And causeless crimes continually to frame,
> With which she guiltless persons may accuse,
> And steal away the crown of their good name:
> Ne ever knight so bold, ne ever dame
> So chaste and loyal lived, but she would strive
> With forged cause them falsely to defame;
> Ne ever thing so well was done alive,
> But she with blame would blot, and of due praise deprive.
>
> Her words were not, as common words are, meant
> To express the meaning of the inward mind,
> But noisome breath, and poisonous spirit sent
> From inward parts, with cankered malice lined,
> And breathed forth with blast of bitter wind;
> Which, passing through the ears, would pierce the heart,
> And wound the soul itself with grief unkind:
> For, like the sting of asps that kill with smart,
> Her spiteful words did prick and wound the inner part.

Little meet to host such guests is a hag like this—albeit one " whom," says the poet, as if with a bitterness inspired by some personal injury, " greatest princes' courts would welcome him;"—but necessity leaves no choice; and, besides, that age despised vain luxury, and was enured to hardness and to homely fare. They therefore do not complain of having to spend the evening in cold and hunger, but only that the hag scolds and rails at them for so taking up their lodging without her consent. Nor do the two ladies take any harm or run any danger in thus spending the hours with this noble knight; that antique age, yet in the infancy of time, lived in simplicity and in blameless innocence;

> The lion there did with the lamb consort,
> And eke the dove sate by the falcon's side;
> Ne each of other feared fraud or tort,[t]
> But did in safe security abide:

but when the world grew old, it grew worse—whence, says our poet (adopting or proposing a very whimsical etymology), it has its name, *quasi* war-old (or worse-old). Then fair grew foul, and foul grew fair; then

[t] Wrong.

beauty, originally designed to represent a bright resemblance of the great Creator, became only the bait or provocative of passion :—

> And that, which wont to vanquish God and man,
> Was made the vassal of the victor's might ;
> Then did her glorious flower wex dead and wan,
> Despised and trodden down of all that overran :
>
> And now it is so utterly decayed,
> That any bud thereof doth scarce remain,
> But if few plants, preserved through heavenly aid,
> In prince's court do hap to sprout again,
> Dewed with her drops of bounty sovereign,
> Which from that goodly glorious flower proceed,
> Sprung of the ancient stock of prince's strain,
> Now the only remnant of that royal breed,
> Whose noble kind at first was sure of heavenly seed.

As soon as it is day the "gentle crew"—that is the prince and the two ladies—set out again as before, he on foot, they mounted together on his horse ; but when they leave the hag follows them, reviling them with the worst names and imputations, so that his noble heart is stung with vexation, and the two ladies are covered with shame. Even when they are out of sight, and when there are none to hear her hateful words, she continues to send her barkings and backbitings after them :—

> Like as a cur doth felly bite and tear
> The stone, which passed stranger at him threw ;
> So she, them seeing past the reach of ear,
> Against the stones and trees did rail anew,
> Till she had dulled the sting which in her tongue's end grew.

They meanwhile pass on, though rather slowly, till they perceive galloping towards them a squire bearing before him on his steed a dwarf, who all the way cries aloud for help,

> That seemed his shrieks would rend the brazen sky ;

while after them rides in hot pursuit on a dromedary, venting a torrent of threats and curses, a man of huge stature, and of the most astounding aspect; for from his eyes proceed two fiery beams, sharper than points of needles, that, like the glance of the basilisk, are deadly poison to all who incautiously look upon him, and slay his enemies before they are aware. At the loud call of the squire, the prince, lifting the ladies down, quickly mounts his steed; but their foe is upon them, and has struck both squire and dwarf to the earth, by a blow aimed at Arthur, which he wards off with his shield, almost before " the royal child " has had time to draw his sword. A dreadful battle ensues: the Pagan, swearing by Mahound that he will have his adversary's life, smites at him with his murderous mace so as " that seemed nought the souse thereof could bear;" but, with his usual activity and dexterity in such cases, the prince so manages that, notwithstanding,

>———————————— ere he wist, he found
> His head before him tumbling on the ground;
> The whiles his babbling tongue did yet blaspheme
> And curse his god that did him so confound;
> The whiles his life ran forth in bloody stream,
> His soul descended down into the Stygian ream.[a]

At this issue, however, although the squire rejoices, the dwarf manifests only sorrow and distress, howling aloud at seeing his lord lie slain, and rending his hair and scratching his face in his misery.

> Then gan the prince at leisure to inquire
> Of all the accident there happened plain,
> And what he was whose eyes did flame with fire:
> All which was thus to him declared by that squire.

He informs him that the mighty man he has slain was the son of a giantess, and had conquered many great kingdoms and nations, not, however, in war, or by " hosts of men with banners broad displayed;"

> But by the power of his infectious sight,
> With which he killed all that came within his might.

---

[a] Realm.

Never had he found man so strong but he had thus borne him down, nor woman so fair that he did not bring her to bay; for his chief desire was to make spoil of strength and beauty, and waste them away to nought, by casting secretly into their hearts and inward parts flakes of the fire of licentious passion from those false eyes. "Therefore," continues the squire,

>———————— Corflambo was he called aright,
> Though nameless there his body now doth lie;
> Yet hath he left one daughter that is hight
> The fair Pœana: who seems outwardly
> So fair as ever yet saw living eye;
> And, were her virtue like her beauty bright,
> She were as fair as any under sky:
> But ah! she given is to vain delight,
> And eke too loose of life, and eke of love too light.

He then proceeds to relate that he had a friend, a gentle squire of inferior degree, named Amias, who loved and was beloved by a lady of high parentage, the fair Æmilia. They had agreed to meet (as we have already heard from Æmilia herself) at a certain spot; but on his way (as she had fallen into the hands of the brutal savage of the cavern) the squire was caught by Corflambo, and carried away to his dungeon, where he still remains " of all unsuccoured and unsought." There, however, he was one day seen by Pœana, and no sooner seen than loved. In the hope of thereby regaining his liberty, notwithstanding his engagement and firm attachment to Æmilia, he granted a cold profession of affection to the giant's daughter; yet she still detains him. She allows him, however, so much liberty as to walk about her gardens of delight with a keeper, who is the dwarf now present, " her darling base," and the trusted minister to whom she has consigned the whole custody and control of all her captives. Meanwhile tidings of the captivity of Amias came to the ears of his friend, whose name is Placidas; upon which the latter contrived to find his way to him, and for some time concealed himself in the gardens, till he was one day seen by the dwarf, who, however, mistook him for Amias, to whom he bore the closest resemblance, and thereupon informed his mistress that her captive was in the habit of stealing secretly out of his prison. The consequence was that Placidas, who, being brought before Pæana, was by her too taken for Amias, was committed to the same dungeon in which his friend lay. But Amias professed to be only made more miserable by the circumstance of his friend having lost his liberty as well as himself; "for," says Placidas,

—"all his joy, he said, in that distress
Was mine and his Æmilia's liberty.
Æmilia well he loved, as I mote guess;
Yet greater love to me than her he did profess."

At length, however, he agreed to allow Placidas to follow out his scheme. So the following day, when Amias was sent for by Pæana, Placidas went to her in his stead, and was very well received. Excusing his former rudeness, and promising a different behaviour in future, he soon induced her to let him have more liberty, and to command the dwarf to allow him a larger range in the gardens. "So," said he,

—"on a day, as by the flowery marge
Of a fresh stream I with that elf did play,
Finding no means how I might us enlarge,
But if that dwarf I could with me convey,
I lightly snatched him up and with me bore away."

And thus Placidas finishes his narrative, merely adding that the shrieks of the dwarf brought out Corflambo; but he was not for that to be disseised of his "gotten prey."

The ladies now come up, and Æmilia immediately recognizes her lover's friend. Having first ascertained from him that Amias lives, she afterwards listens with deep emotion to a repetition of all that he has just told Prince Arthur:—

Then, after many tears and sorrows spent,
She dear besought the prince of remedy:
Who thereto did with ready will consent,
And well performed; as shall appear by his event.*

---

* The fortune or issue he met with.

Canto IX. (41 stanzas).—In this Canto we are to see proved by example how much stronger is friendship than either love or natural affection, although at the same time it will appear that of those two last the former has most power over the heart:—

> For, though Pœana were as fair as morn,
> Yet did this trusty squire with proud disdain
> For his friend's sake her offered favours scorn,
> And she herself her sire of whom she was yborn.

The stratagem that Prince Arthur adopts for getting into the castle of the slain tyrant, where Amias is detained, is to take Corflambo's dead body, and, having again imprest, or fastened, the head to it, to set it on his dromedary, with Placidas laid before it, as if he had been taken captive; and then to force the dwarf to lead the beast along. When they come to the gate it is immediately opened without any suspicion by the warder, and Arthur enters. Here he finds the fair Pœana in her delicious bower, playing on a rote (by which Spenser must here be supposed to mean a kind of harp, whatever ground there may be for Ritson's assertion that the instrument, taking its name from the Latin word for a wheel, was really nothing else than what we now call a hurdy-gurdy). She is

> Complaining of her cruel paramour,
> And singing all her sorrow to the note;

and that so sweetly, that

> The prince half wrapped began on her to dote;
> Till, better him bethinking of the right,
> He her unawares attached, and captive held by might.

At first she calls to her father for aid, but she soon perceives the state to which he is reduced:—

> Then gan she loudly cry, and weep, and wail,
> And that same squire of treason to upbraid:
> But all in vain; her plaints might not prevail;
> Ne none there was to rescue her, ne none to bail.

The prince then compels the dwarf to open the door of

the prison, and above a score of knights and squires are released from bondage. Among the rest Amias is brought forth; he is weak and wan, and not like himself; but, as soon as they see him, Æmilia and Placidas both run up, and, clasping him in their arms, kiss him again and again, so that Pœana not only envies them, but falls " bitterly to ban," in her jealousy and rage. It would appear from this that Æmilia, and of course Amoret also, had either been sent for by the prince after he had gotten possession of the castle, or had entered along with him, although the poet has forgotten to say so. After regarding the two squires, however, a little longer, as they stand embracing one another, Pœana begins to doubt which of them is the one she so dearly loves—

> For they so like in person did appear,
> That she uneath [w] discerned whether whether were.

The Prince, too, and all the other knights and squires are equally amazed at their perfect resemblance.

A vast store of hoarded treasure is found in the castle :—

> Upon all which the Briton prince made seizure;
> And afterwards continued there awhile
> To rest himself, and solace in soft pleasure
> Those weaker ladies after weary toil;
> To whom he did divide part of his purchased spoil.

For more joy, he even grants her liberty to " that captive lady fair, the fair Pœana," and sets her " in sumptuous chair, to feast and frolic " with the rest; but she nevertheless will show no gladsome countenance, grieving for the loss both of her sire and of her " land and fee," but most of all for loss of her love, the handsome squire (though whether she has yet made up her mind which of the two young men it is that she has been attached to, and would like to retain, we are not informed). The Prince, however, takes great pains to mollify her both by " good thewes," or courtesy of manner, and kind speeches :—

[w] Scarcely.

> And, for to shut up all in friendly love,
> Sith love was first the ground of all her grief,
> That trusty squire he wisely well did move
> Not to despise that dame which loved him lief,[x]
> Till he had made of her some better prief;[y]
> But to accept her to his wedded wife:
> Thereto he offered for to make him chief
> Of all her land and lordship during life:
> He yielded, and her took; so stinted all their strife.

From that day, it is added, they lived together long in peace and joy; and the fair Pæana, whose beauty, unsurpassed by that of any other lady of her time, had formerly been stained by such irregularities,

> ———————— thenceforth reformed her ways,
> That all men much admired her change, and spake her praise.

It may be presumed that, Placidas being thus provided for, Amias and Æmilia were also united; but all that is said is, that the Prince " perfectly compiled (that is, brought together) these pairs of friends in peace and settled rest;" and then, turning to his proper quest,[*] set out again, taking only Amoret with him. Poor Amoret, who has gone through so many dangers, does not find herself left alone and helpless " in the victor's power, like vassal bond," without some natural feelings of shame and fear; but she has no ground for any apprehension with so honourable a protector as Arthur:—

> —— all the while he by his side her bore,
> She was as safe as in a sanctuary;

and so they ride together for many miles, she hoping to find her love, he his, and not showing " their heart's privity " to one another. At length they come upon six knights, all, as appears, in a state of great excitement, and fighting with one another, but four of them engaged with especial activity and fury. These are four of the knights

---

[x] Dearly.   [y] Proof.
[*] This must be the word, although it is printed " guest " in all the editions.

from whose competition, as related in the Fifth Canto, the false Florimel had been won and carried off by Braggadoccio—namely, our old acquaintances Blandamour and Paridel, and two others, the stern Druon and the lewd Claribel. The other two are Britomart and Scudamore, whom, it may be remembered, we left setting out together in quest of Amoret at the end of the Sixth Canto; they have only just come up, and are standing aside, wondering at the confused contention of the rest, who, spurred on by Ate and Duessa, were waging this wild and doubtful strife " for love of that same snowy maid." And

>—— sometimes Paridel and Blandamour
> The better had, and bet^z the others back;
> Eftsoons^a the others did the field recoure,^b
> And on their foes did work full cruel wrack:
> Yet neither would their fiend-like fury slack,
> But evermore their malice did augment;
> Till that uneath^c they forced were, for lack
> Of breath, their raging rigour to relent,
> And rest themselves for to recover spirits spent.
>
> Then* gan they change their sides, and new parts take,
> For Paridel did take to Druon's side,
> For old despite which now forth newly brake
> Gainst Blandamour whom always he envied:
> And Blandamour to Claribel relied:^d
> So all afresh gan former fight renew.
> As when two barks, this carried with the tide,
> That with the wind, contrary courses sue,^e
> If wind and tide do change, their courses change anew.
>
> Thenceforth they much more furiously gan fare,
> As if but then the battle had begun;
> Ne helmets bright, ne hauberks strong did spare,
> That through the clefts the vermeil blood outspun,

---

^z Beat.
^b Recover.
^d Joined himself.
^a Presently.
^c With difficulty.
^e Pursue.

* In the original edition "their," which the modern editors have altered into "there."

And all adown their riven sides did run.
Such mortal malice wonder was to see
In friends professed, and so great outrage done:
But sooth is said, and tried in each degree,
Faint friends when they fall out most cruel foemen be.

But soon, perceiving Scudamore and Britomart, and remembering how they had been discomfited by the latter at the recent tournay, they all turn upon these two:—

Who wondering much at that so sudden fit,
Yet nought dismayed, them stoutly well withstood;
Ne yielded foot, ne once aback did flit,
But, being doubly smitten, likewise doubly smit.

The warlike dame was on her part assaid [f]
Of Claribel and Blandamour atone; [g]
And Paridel and Druon fiercely laid
At Scudamore, both his professed fone: [h]
Four charged two, and two surcharged one;
Yet did those two themselves so bravely bear,
That the other little gained by the loan,
But with their own repayed duly were,
And usury withall: such gain was gotten dear.

It is in vain that Britomart again and again tries to bring them to parley; they will no more stop for a moment to listen to her than will an eager mastiff be called off by words from the gored beast whose blood he has once tasted. Arthur, however, indignant to see the unequal match, now strikes in; he, too, after he has compelled them somewhat to give way, endeavours to pacify them with mild speeches; but, when this kind attempt produces no effect, he is not long in compelling them by force to crave respite and mercy. They then accuse Britomart of having both despoiled them of their public praise and beguiled them of their private loves; she easily shows the absurdity of these charges; and the Prince declares his judgment that they are much in the wrong. Then Britomart speaks again:—

[f] Attacked (essayed, or perhaps assailed).
[g] At once. [h] Foes.

"And yet," quoth she, " a greater wrong remains:
For I thereby my former love have lost;
Whom seeking ever since with endless pains
Hath me much sorrow and much travel cost;
Aye me, to see that gentle maid so tossed!"
But Scudamore then sighing deep thus said;
" Certes her loss ought me to sorrow most,
Whose right she is, wherever she be strayed,
Through many perils won, and many fortunes weighed:"

and so forth. This is not quite intelligible. For Britomart had not, as she here states, lost Amoret through anything that the four knights had done: she had lost her, as we have seen, after the tournament was over and she and they had parted and left the place in different directions. It is strange, too, that Amoret should remain all this while unnoticed by either Britomart or Scudamore, and that she herself should not ere now have recognized both the one and the other. If she had retired to a distance, or been left behind by Arthur (which it is not said that she did or was) when he threw himself into the fray, it would seem to be natural that she should now be brought forward when the fighting is all over. And what makes the case the more puzzling is, that, as we shall find, she is spoken of in the beginning of the next Canto as if she never had been absent. We think with Upton that something is clearly wanting, and that probably the poet intended to introduce here, after the speech of Scudamore, with some few necessary alterations, the stanzas which originally stood at the end of the Third Book describing the happy meeting between him and Amoret. As it is, no mention is made of Amoret in this place; but, a general harmony having now been established, and the whole party having agreed to pursue their journey together, Scudamore is besought by Sir Claribel (now characterized by the epithet " good ") to favour them, as they ride along, with a recital of the adventure he had undertaken for his fair lady's love: and all the rest joining in the request, Britomart especially urging it with earnest importunity, Scudamore consents to comply, as he does in the next Canto.

On the whole, this short Canto has the air of having been hastily composed merely to carry forward the narrative and connect what precedes with what follows, and neither to have been worked up with the poet's customary elaboration, nor even to have received his last corrections. The carelessness with which it would seem to have been thrown off and dismissed appears even in the usual metrical summary with which it is headed, where we are told that

> The Squire of Low Degree, released,
> Pæana takes to wife;—

whereas it is, indeed, the Squire of Low Degree, Amias, who is released, but his friend Placidas, the Trusty Squire, who marries Pæana. The inferiority of this Canto may have been artfully intended as a foil, the more to set off the splendid writing upon which we are now about to enter.

Canto X. (58 stanzas).—Sir Scudamore commences his narrative as follows:—

> "True he it said, whatever man it said,
> That love with gall and honey doth abound;
> But, if the one be with the other weighed,
> For every dram of honey therein found
> A pound of gall doth over it redound:[i]
> That I too true by trial have approved;
> For, since the day that first with deadly wound
> My heart was launched,[j] and learned to have loved,
> I never joyed hour, but still with care was moved.
>
> "And yet such grace is given them from above,
> That all the cares and evil which they meet
> May nought at all their settled minds remove,
> But seem, gainst common sense, to them most sweet,
> As boasting in their martyrdom unmeet:
> So all that ever yet I have endured
> I count as nought, and tread down under feet,
> Since of my love at length I rest assured
> That to disloyalty she will not be allured."

It will be a long story, he goes on to observe, to tell the

[i] Compensate. [j] Pierced.

long toil by which he had won the Shield of Love which he carries (and from which he has his name—*Scutum Amoris*, or *Scudo d'Amore*): but, since the company desire it, it shall be done. "Then, hark," he adds,

>———"ye gentle knights and ladies free,
>My hard mishaps that ye may learn to shun;
>For, though sweet love to conquer glorious be,
>Yet is the pain thereof much greater than the fee."

This address, it will be perceived, must include Amoret, for she is the only lady present, besides Britomart. His knowledge of her presence is still clearer from what follows, where he states that from the time when the report of this famous prize, namely the Shield, first flew abroad, he had been possessed with the thought that he was the man destined to carry it off, adding—

>"And that both shield and she whom I behold
>Might be my lucky lot, sith all by lot we hold."

So forth he proceeded on the adventure, and soon made his way to "the place of peril," an ancient, beautiful, and renowned temple of Venus—much more famous than either that in Paphos or that in Cyprus (Spenser seems to have forgotten that Paphos was merely the town in the isle of Cyprus where the principal temple of Venus stood), both built long subsequently,—

>"Though all the pillars of the one were gilt,
>And all the other's pavement were with ivory spilt." [k]

This temple of the goddess to which Scudamore repaired stood in an island so strongly fortified by nature, that there was only one passage by which access was possible.

>"It was a bridge ybuilt in goodly wise
>With curious corbs [l] and pendants graven fair,
>And, arched all with porches, did arise
>On stately pillars framed after the Doric guise."

At the farther end was built a strong and fair castle,

---

[k] Inlaid.   [l] Corbels.

in which were placed twenty valiant and experienced
knights. And, continues Sir Scudamore,

> " Before that castle was an open plain,
> And in the midst thereof a pillar placed;
> On which this shield, of many sought in vain,
> THE SHIELD OF LOVE, whose guerdon me hath graced,
> Was hanged on high with golden ribands laced;
> And in the marble stone was written this,
> With golden letters goodly well enchased;
> *Blessed the man that well can use this bliss:*
> *Whose ever be the shield, fair Amoret be his.*
>
> " Which when I read, my heart did inly earn,[m]
> And pant with hope of that adventure's hap:
> Ne stayed further news thereof to learn,
> But with my spear upon the shield did rap,
> That all the castle ringed with the clap.
> Straight forth issued a knight all armed to proof,
> And bravely mounted to his most mishap:
> Who, staying nought to question from aloof,
> Ran fierce at me, that fire glanced from his horse's hoof."

He boldly encountered this fiery champion, and soon
unseated him; then two others, who sprung out upon
him together, met with the same fate; in short, all the
twenty were left groaning on the plain; and the victor,
advancing to the pillar, and reading aloud the inscription,
took down the shield, and bore it away with him. All
this is modestly told by Scudamore in a single stanza.
He then proceeds:—

> " So forth without impediment I passed,
> Till to the bridge's utter gate I came;
> The which I found sure locked and chained fast.
> I knocked, but no man answered me by name;
> I called, but no man answered to my claim:
> Yet I persevered still to knock and call;
> Till at the last I spied within the same
> Where one stood peeping through a crevice small,
> To whom I called aloud, half angry therewithall.

---

[m] Yearn.

"That was to weet the porter of the place,
Unto whose trust the charge thereof was lent:
His name was Doubt, that had a double face.
The one forward looking, the other backward bent,
Therein resembling Janus ancient
Which hath in charge the ingate[n] of the year
And evermore his eyes about him went,
As if some proved peril he did fear,
Or did misdoubt some ill whose cause did not appear.

"On the one side he, on the other sat Delay,
Behind the gate, that none her might espy;
Whose manner was, all passengers to stay
And entertain with her occasions sly;
Through which some lost great hope unheedily,
Which never they recover might again;
And others, quite excluded forth, did lie
Long languishing there in unpitied pain,
And seeking often entrance afterwards in vain."

As soon as Doubt, looking through the chink, perceived the shield, he immediately knew it, opened the gate wide, and, the knight having passed in, closed it again. Delay now caught hold of him, trying to stay him with much prating and many foolish pretences, and to steal from him time, that precious treasure, whose smallest minute lost no riches may restore. "But," continues Scudamore,

"——— by no means my way I would forslow[o]
For aught that ever she could do or say;
But from my lofty steed dismounting low
Passed forth on foot, beholding all the way
The goodly works, and stones of rich assay,
Cast into sundry shapes by wondrous skill,
That like on earth no where I reckon may;
And, underneath, the river rolling still
With murmur soft, that seemed to serve the workman's
will.

"Thence forth I passed to the second gate,
The Gate of Good Desert, whose goodly pride

---

[n] Entrance, beginning.　　　[o] Delay.

And costly frame were long here to relate:
The same to all stood always open wide;
But in the porch did evermore abide
An hideous giant, dreadful to behold,
That stopped the entrance with his spacious stride,
And with the terror of his countenance bold
Full many did affray, that else fain enter wold:

His name was Danger, dreaded over all;
Who day and night did watch and duly ward
From fearful cowards entrance to forestall,
And faint-heart-fools, whom show of peril hard
Could terrify from fortune's fair adward:
For oftentimes faint hearts, at first espial
Of his grim face, were from approaching scard:
Unworthy they of grace, whom one denial
Excludes from fairest hope withouten further trial.

Yet many doughty warriors, often tried
In greater perils to be stout and bold,
Durst not the sternness of his look abide;
But, soon as they his countenance did behold,
Began to faint, and feel their courage cold.
Again, some other, that in hard assays
Were cowards known, and little count did hold,
Either through gifts, or guile, or such like ways,
Crept in by stooping low, or stealing of the kays."[p]

Scudamore disdained either to stoop to him, or to creep between his legs; but, advancing his enchanted shield, began to lay about him with all his might; on which Danger immediately lowered his sword, and allowed him to pass freely on. Looking back, he now perceived that worse lay concealed behind the Giant than what appeared in front of him; for there lay lurking in ambush Hatred, Murder, Treason, Despite, and many more such foes, ready to entrap whosoever did not protect himself against them with vigilant circumspection. He was now fairly within the island; "the which," he says,

—— "did seem, unto my simple doom,[q]
The only pleasant and delightful place

---

[p] Pronounced *kays* (or as Spenser spells it, *kaies*), as indeed it commonly was down to a much later date.
[q] Judgment.

That ever trodden was of footing's trace:
For all that nature by her mother-wit
Could frame in earth, and form of substance base,
Was there; and all that nature did omit,
Art, playing second nature's part, supplied it.

No tree, that is of count, in greenwood grows,
From lowest juniper to cedar tall;
No flower in field, that dainty odour throws,
And decks his branch with blossoms over all,
But there was planted, or grew natural:
Nor sense of man so coy and curious nice,
But there mote find to please itself withall;
Nor heart could wish for any quaint device,
But there it present was, and did frail sense entice.

In such luxurious plenty of all pleasure,
It seemed a second paradise, I guess,
So lavishly enriched with nature's treasure,
That, if the happy souls, which do possess
The Elysian fields and live in lasting bliss,
Should happen this with living eye to see,
They soon would loath their lesser happiness,
And wish to life returned again to be,
That in this joyous place they mote have joyance free.

Fresh shadows, fit to shroud from sunny ray;
Fair lawns, to take the sun in season due;
Sweet springs, in which a thousand nymphs did play;
Soft-rumbling brooks, that gentle slumber drew;
High-reared mounts, the lands about to view;
Low-looking dales, disloined^r from common gaze;
Delightful bowers, to solace lovers true;
False labyrinths, fond runners' eyes to daze;
All which by nature made did nature self amaze.

And all without were walks and alleys dight
With divers trees enranged in even ranks;
And here and there were pleasant arbours pight,
And shady seats, and sundry flowering banks
To sit and rest the walker's weary shanks:
And therein thousand pairs of lovers walked,
Praising their god, and yielding him great thanks,

---

^r Removed.

> Ne ever aught but of their true loves talked,
> Ne ever for rebuke or blame of any balked."

Apart, and at a distance, from these were lovers of another sort, those namely whose desires were set only on virtue—whose spirits ever aspired after noble thoughts and valiant deeds. " Such," Scudamore proceeds,

> ——— " were great Hercules, and Hylas dear :
> True Jonathan, and David trusty tried ;
> Stout Theseus, and Pirithous his fere ;*
> Pylades, and Orestes by his side ;
> Mild Titus, and Gesippus without pride ;
> Damon and Pythias, whom death could not sever :
> All these, and all that ever had been tied
> In bands of friendship, there did live for ever ;
> Whose lives although decayed, yet loves decayed never
>
> Which whenas I, that never tasted bliss
> Nor happy hour, beheld with gazeful eye,
> I thought there was none other heaven than this ;
> And gan their endless happiness envy,
> That being free from fear and jealousy
> Might frankly there their loves' desire possess ;
> Whilst I through pains and perilous jeopardy
> Was forced to seek my life's dear patroness :
> Much dearer be the things which come through hard distress.
>
> Yet all those sights, and all that else I saw,
> Might not my steps withhold but that forthright
> Unto that purposed place I did me draw,
> Whereas my love was lodged day and night,
> The temple of great Venus, that is hight
> The Queen of Beauty, and of Love the mother,
> There worshipped of every living wight ;
> Whose goodly workmanship far passed all other
> That ever were on earth, all were they set together.
>
> Not that same famous temple of Diane,
> Whose height all Ephesus did oversee,
> And which all Asia sought with vows profane,
> One of the world's seven wonders said to be,

---

* Companion.

Might match with this by many a degree;
Nor that, which that wise king of Jewry framed
With endless cost to be the Almighty's see;
Nor all, that else through all the world is named
To all the heathen gods, might like to this be claimed.

I, much admiring that so goodly frame,
Unto the porch approached, which open stood;
But therein sat an amiable dame,
That seemed to be of very sober mood,
And in her semblant[t] showed great womanhood:
Strange was her tire; for on her head a crown
She wore, much like unto a Danisk[u] hood,
Powdered with pearl and stone; and all her gown
Enwoven was with gold, that raught[v] full low adown.

On either side of her two young men stood,
Both strongly armed, as fearing one another;
Yet were they brethren both of half the blood,
Begotten by two fathers of one mother,
Though of contrary natures each to other:
The one of them hight Love, the other Hate;
Hate was the elder, Love the younger brother;
Yet was the younger stronger in his state
Than the elder, and him maistered still in all debate.

Nathless that dame so well them tempered both,
That she them forced hand to join in hand,
All be that Hatred was thereto full loth,
And turned his face away, as he did stand,
Unwilling to behold that lovely band:
Yet she was of such grace and virtuous might,
That her commandment he could not withstand,
But bit his lip for felonous despite,
And gnashed his iron tusks at that displeasing sight.

Concord she cleeped[w] was in common reed,
Mother of blessed Peace and Friendship true;
They both her twins, both born of heavenly seed,
And she herself likewise divinely grew;
The which right well her works divine did shew:
For strength and wealth and happiness she lends,
And strife and war and anger does subdue;

---

[t] Appearance, air. [u] Danish. [v] Reached.
[w] Called.

Of little much, of foes she maketh friends,
And to afflicted minds sweet rest and quiet sends.

By her the heaven is in his course contained,
And all the world in state unmoved stands,
As their Almighty Maker first ordained,
And bound them with inviolable bands;
Else would the waters overflow the lands,
And fire devour the air, and hell them quite;
But that she holds them with her blessed hands.
She is the nurse of pleasure and delight,
And unto Venus' grace the gate doth open right.

By her I entering half dismayed was;
But she in gentle wise me entertained,
And twixt herself and Love did let me pass;
But Hatred would my entrance have restrained,
And with his club me threatened to have brained,
Had not the lady with her powerful speech
Him from his wicked will uneath refrained[x]:
And the other eke his malice did impeach,[y]
Till I was throughly past the peril of his reach.

Into the inmost temple thus I came,
Which fuming all with frankincense I found
And odours rising from the altar's flame.
Upon an hundred marble pillars round
The roof up high was reared from the ground,
All decked with crowns, and chains, and girlands gay,
And thousand precious gifts worth many a pound,
The which sad lovers for their vows did pay;
And all the ground was strewed with flowers as fresh as May.

An hundred altars round about were set,
All flaming with their sacrifices' fire,
That with the steam thereof the temple sweat,
Which rolled in clouds to heaven did aspire,
And in them bore true lovers' vows entire:
And eke an hundred brazen caldrons bright
To bathe in joy and amorous desire,
Every of which was to a damsel hight;
For all the priests were damsels in soft linen dight

---

[x] With some difficulty kept back.   [y] Hinder.

Right in the midst the goddess self did stand
Upon an altar of some costly mass,
Whose substance was uneath[z] to understand:
For neither precious stone, nor dureful brass,
Nor shinning gold, nor mouldering clay it was;
But much more rare and precious to esteem,
Pure in aspect, and like to crystal glass;
Yet glass was not, if one did rightly deem;
But, being fair and brickle,[a] likest glass did seem.

But it in shape and beauty did excel
All other idols which the heath'n adore,
Far passing that, which by surpassing skill
Phidias did make in Paphos' isle of yore,
With which that wretched Greek, that life forlore,[b]
Did fall in love: yet this much fairer shined,
But covered with a slender veil afore:
And both her feet and legs together twined
Were with a snake, whose head and tail were fast combined.

The cause why she was covered with a veil
Was hard to know, for that her priests the same
From people's knowledge laboured to conceal:
But sooth it was not sure for womanish shame,
Nor any blemish, which the work mote blame;
But for (they say) she hath both kinds in one,
Both male and female, both under one name:
She sire and mother is herself alone,
Begets and eke conceives, ne needeth other none.

And all about her neck and shoulders flew
A flock of little loves, and sports, and joys,
With nimble wings of gold and purple hue;
Whose shapes seemed not like to terrestrial boys,
But like to angels playing heavenly toys;
The whilst their eldest brother was away,
Cupid their eldest brother: he enjoys
The wide kingdom of love with lordly sway,
And to his law compels all creatures to obey.

And all about her altar scattered lay
Great sorts[c] of lovers piteously complaining,

---

[z] Difficult.   [a] Brittle.   [b] Forsook.
[c] Flocks.

Some of their loss, some of their love's delay,
Some of their pride, some paragons' disdaining,
Some fearing fraud, some fraudulently feigning,
As every one had cause of good or ill.
Amongst the rest some one, through love's constraining
Tormented sore, could not contain it still,
But thus brake forth, that all the temple it did fill."

The hymn or prayer to Venus that follows is a free translation of the exquisitely beautiful invocation with which Lucretius opens his great poem:—

"'Great Venus! Queen of Beauty and of Grace,
The joy of gods and men, that under sky
Dost fairest shine, and most adorn thy place;
That with thy smiling look dost pacify
The raging seas, and mak'st the storms to fly;
Thee, goddess, thee the winds, the clouds do fear;
And, when thou spread'st thy mantle forth on high,
The waters play, and pleasant lands appear,
And heavens laugh, and all the world shows joyous cheer.

Then doth the dædal[d] earth throw forth to thee
Out of her fruitful lap abundant flowers;
And then all living wights, soon as they see
The spring break forth out of his lusty bowers,
They all do learn to play the paramours:
First do the merry birds, thy pretty pages,
Privily pricked with thy lustful powers,
Chirp loud to thee out of their leafy cages,
And thee, their mother, call to cool their kindly rages.

Then do the salvage beasts begin to play
Their pleasant frisks, and loath their wonted food:
The lions roar; the tigers loudly bray;
The raging bulls rebellow through the wood,
And breaking forth dare tempt the deepest flood
To come where thou dost draw them with desire.

. . . . . .

So all the world by thee at first was made,
And daily yet thou dost the same repair:

---

[d] Productive. It is the original Latin word.

"Ne ought on earth that merry is and glad,
Ne ought on earth that lovely is and fair,
But thou the same for pleasure didst prepare:
Thou art the root of all that joyous is:
Great god of men and women, queen of the air,
Mother of laughter, and well-spring of bliss,
O grant that of my love at last I may not miss!' "

Sir Scudamore goes on, in lines too bright and musical for one of them to be spared:—

" So did he say: but I with murmur soft,
That none might hear the sorrow of my heart,
Yet inly groaning deep and sighing oft,
Besought her to grant ease unto my smart,
And to my wound her gracious help impart.
Whilst thus I spake, behold! with happy eye
I spied where at the idol's feet apart
A bevy of fair damsels close did lie,
Waiting whenas the anthem should be sung on high.

The first of them did seem of riper years
And graver countenance than all the rest:
Yet all the rest were eke her equal peers,
Yet unto her obeyed as the best:
Her name was Womanhood: that she expressed
By her sad semblant and demeanour wise;
For steadfast still her eyes did fixed rest,
Ne roved at random, after gazers' guise,
Whose luring baits oftimes do heedless hearts entise.

And next to her sate goodly Shamefacedness,
Ne ever durst her eyes from ground uprear,
Ne ever once did look up from her dess,^e
As if some blame of evil she did fear,
That in her cheeks made roses oft appear:
And her against sweet Cheerfulness was placed,
Whose eyes, like twinkling stars in evening clear,
Were decked with smiles that all sad humours chased,
And darted forth delights the which her goodly graced.

And next to her sate sober Modesty,
Holding her hand upon her gentle heart;

---

^e Seat.

And her against sate comely Courtesy,
That unto every person knew her part;
And her before was seated overthwart
Soft Silence, and submiss Obedience,
Both linked together never to dispart;
Both gifts of God not gotten but from thence;
Both girlands of his saints against their foes' offence.

Thus sate they all around in seemly rate[f]:
And in the midst of them a goodly Maid
(Even in the lap of Womanhood) there sate,
The which was all in lily-white arrayed,
With silver streams amongst the linen strayed;
Like to the Morn, when first her shining face
Hath to the gloomy world itself bewrayed:
That same was fairest Amoret in place.
Shining with beauty's light and heavenly virtue's grace.

Whom soon as I beheld, my heart gan throb
And weighed in doubt what best were to be done:
For sacrilege me seemed the church to rob:
And folly seemed to leave the thing undone,
Which with so strong attempt I had begun.
Tho, shaking off all doubt and shamefaced fear,
Which lady's love I heard had never won
Mongst men of worth, I to her stepped near,
And by the lily hand her laboured up to rear."

Upon this, Womanhood sharply rebuked him for being overbold in presuming to lay hands upon a virgin dedicated to the service of Venus. Scudamore replied in a few honest words, and at the same time disclosed his shield, which he had kept hidden ever since he entered the temple; at the sight on which, of Cupid emblazoned with his bow and shafts, the matron, awed, said no more. Meantime the knight all the while had kept hold of the fair virgin's hand, resolved for no entreaty to "forego so glorious spoil;" having his eye also evermore fixed upon the face of the goddess, "whom," he says,

——— " when I saw with amiable grace
To laugh on me, and favour my pretence,
I was emboldened with more confidence;

---

[f] Manner, arrangement.

And, nought for niceness nor for envy sparing,
In presence of them all forth led her thence,
All looking on, and like astonished staring,
Yet to lay hand on her not one of all them daring.

She often prayed, and often me besought,
Sometime with tender tears, to let her go,
Sometime with witching smiles: but yet, for nought
That ever she to me could say or do,
Could she her wished freedom fro me woo;
But forth I led her through the temple gate,
By which I hardly passed with much ado:
But that same lady[g] which me friended late
In entrance, did me also friend in my retrate.

No less did Danger threaten me with dread,
Whenas he saw me, maugre all his power,
That glorious spoil of Beauty with me lead,
Than Cerberus, when Orpheus did recoure[h]
His leman from the Stygian prince's bower.
But evermore my shield did me defend
Against the storm of every dreadful stour:
Thus safely with my love I thence did wend."

"And so," says the poet, "ended he his tale, where I this Canto end."

Canto XI. (53 stanzas).—We must also give nearly the whole of this Canto, one of the most conspicuous in the poem. It sets out thus:—

But ah! for pity that I have thus long
Left a fair lady languishing in pain!
Now well away! that I have done such wrong,
To let fair Florimel in bands remain,
In bands of love, and in sad thraldom's chain;
From which unless some heavenly power her free
By miracle, not yet appearing plain,
She lenger yet is like captived to be;
That even to think thereof it inly pities me.

Florimel, it may be remembered, was left, in the Eighth Canto of the preceding Book, in the hands of the sea-god Proteus, who, we were there told, after all his

[g] Concord.   [h] Recover.

attempts to win her favour had failed, at last threw her into a dungeon and threatened to keep her there in eternal durance.

> Deep in the bottom of an huge great rock
> The dungeon was, in which her bound he left,
> That neither iron bars, nor brazen lock,
> Did need to guard from force or secret theft
> Of all her lovers which would her have reft:
> For walled it was with waves, which raged and roared
> As they the cliff in pieces would have cleft;
> Besides, ten thousand monsters foul abhorred
> Did wait about it, gaping grisly, all begored.[i]
>
> And in the midst thereof did Horror dwell,
> And Darkness dread that never viewed day,
> Like to the baleful house of lowest hell,
> In which old Styx her aged bones alway
> (Old Styx the grandame of the gods) doth lay.
> There did this luckless maid seven months abide,
> Ne ever evening saw, ne morning's ray,
> Ne ever from the day the night descried,
> But thought it all one night, that did no hours divide.

And all this was for the love of Marinel—of Marinel, by whom she and all other women were despised. Meanwhile, however, he still lay languishing of the wound inflicted by a woman's hand, as related in the Fourth Canto of the last Book: and nothing that the nymph his mother can do to cure him is of any avail, till at last she hies for help to Tryphon, the sea-gods' surgeon, to whom she carries a whistle, curiously wrought of a fish's shell, for fee. If, therefore, we would have the poet to be perfectly consistent throughout the whole extent of his long performance, we must suppose that the message which we were before told she sent in haste for Tryphon to come to her, as soon as her son was brought home, had not been attended to by that "sovereign leech." But we shall take a truer view if we are contented to allow that he may be chargeable with a lapse of memory in regard to so minute a matter. Now, at any rate,

---

[i] Besmeared with gore.

Tryphon, hearkening to the nymph's request, applied his skill with such assiduity and success that Marinel was soon restored to health. His mother's maternal fears, nevertheless, long retained him in her ocean bower, very much against his will. At length it happened that all the deities of the sea and their offspring were assembled at a solemn feast held in the house of Proteus in honour of the marriage of the Thames and the Medway, that is, of the god of the former river with the goddess or nymph of the latter, whom, after long wooing, he had at last prevailed upon to consent to share his bed. The famous episode thus introduced, the commentators assume to be the same poem which Spenser speaks of in the year 1580 as already written by him on this subject. But that poem, entitled *Epithalamion Thamesis*, was, as we have seen, a specimen of what was called "English versifying," or a composition in some of the metres then attempted to be constructed on the principles of the ancient Greek and Latin prosody;* and it must therefore have been, at least in its form, entirely different from what we have here. Nor, considering the long interval that had elapsed, does it seem very probable that there would be much resemblance between the present and the former composition in any respect. The episode, as we have it, is altogether in Spenser's most matured style; and it may be assumed not to have been written even when the first three Books of the Fairy Queen were published, else it would probably have been introduced in that portion of the poem.

To the house of Proteus, then, all the water deities, the poet tell us, repaired on this occasion, both the greater and the least—

> As well which in the mighty ocean trade,
> As that in rivers swim, or brooks do wade—

adding, in Homeric fashion, that, if he had an hundred tongues, as many mouths, a voice of brass, and a memory

---

* See Vol. I. pp. 28, 29.

endless, or boundless, he could not recount them all in order. And then he proceeds:—

> Help therefore, O thou sacred imp of Jove,
> The nursling of dame Memory his dear,
> To whom those rolls, laid up in heaven above,
> And records of antiquity appear,
> To which no wit of man may comen near;
> Help me to tell the names of all those floods
> And all those nymphs, which then assembled were
> To that great banquet of the watery gods,
> And all their sundry kinds, and all their hid abodes.
>
> First came great Neptune, with his three-forked mace,
> That rules the seas and makes them rise or fall;
> His dewy locks did drop with brine apace
> Under his diadem imperial:
> And by his side his queen with coronal,
> Fair Amphitrite, most divinely fair,
> Whose ivory shoulders weren covered all,
> As with a robe, with her own silver hair,
> And decked with pearls which the Indian seas for her prepare.
>
> These marched far afore the other crew:
> And all the way before them, as they went,
> Triton his trumpet shrill before them blew,
> For goodly triumph and great jolliment,
> That made the rocks to roar as they were rent.
> And after them the royal issue came,
> Which of them sprung by lineal descent:
> First the sea-gods, which to themselves do claim
> The power to rule the billows, and the waves to tame.
>
> Phorcys, the father of that fatal brood,
> By whom those old heroes won such fame;
> And Glaucus, that wise soothsays understood;
> And tragic Ino's son, the which became
> A god of seas through his mad mother's blame,
> Now hight Palemon, and is sailors' friend;
> Great Brontes; and Astræus, that did shame
> Himself with incest of his kin unkenned;
> And huge Orion, that doth tempests still portend;
>
> The rich Cteatus; and Eurytus long;
> Neleus and Pelias, lovely brethren both;

Mighty Chrysaor; and Caïcus strong;
Eurypulus, that calms the waters wroth:
And fair Euphœmus, that upon them go'th,
As on the ground, without dismay or dread;
Fierce Eryx; and Alebius, that know'th
The waters' depth, and doth their bottom tread;
And sad Asopus, comely with his hoary head.

There also some most famous founders were
Of puissant nations, which the world possessed,
Yet sons of Neptune, now assembled here:
Ancient Ogȳges, even the ancientest;
And Inachus renowmed above the rest;
Phœnix; and Aon; and Pelasgus old;
Great Belus; Phœax; and Agenor best;
And mighty Albion, father of the bold
And warlike people which the Britain Islands hold:

For Albion was the son of Neptune, and passed dry-footed out of his own Britain, called Albion after him, into Gaul, now called France, to fight with Hercules, by whom what was mortal of him was slain; but the immortal spirit still lives, and comes with the rest of the progeny of Neptune to this great feast. Of the remainder of the Canto there is not a stanza that can be abridged or thrown out.

Next came the aged Ocean and his dame
Old Tethys, the oldest two of all the rest;
For all the rest of those two parents came,
Which afterward both sea and land possessed;
Of all which Nereus, the eldest and the best,
Did first proceed; than which none more upright,
Ne more sincere in word and deed professed;
Most void of guile, most free from foul despite,
Doing himself and teaching others to do right:

Thereto he was expert in prophecies,
And could the ledden[j] of the gods unfold;
Through which, when Paris brought his famous prize,
The fair Tyndarid lass, he him foretold
That her all Greece with many a champion bold

---

[j] Language.

Should fetch again, and finally destroy
Proud Priam's town: so wise is Nereus old,
And so well skilled; nathless he takes great joy
Oft-times amongst the wanton nymphs to sport and toy.

And after him the famous rivers came,
Which do the earth enrich and beautify:
The fertile Nile, which creatures new doth frame;
Long Rhodanus, whose source springs from the sky;
Fair Ister, flowing from the mountains high;
Divine Scamander, purpled yet with blood
Of Greeks and Trojans, which therein did die;
Pactolus glistering with his golden flood;
And Tigris fierce, whose streams of none may be with-
 stood;

Great Ganges; and immortal Euphrates;
Deep Indus; and Mæander intricate;
Slow Peneus; and tempestuous Phasides;
Swift Rhene; and Alpheus still immaculate;
Oraxes, feared for great Cyrus' fate;
Tybris, renowned for the Romans' fame;
Rich Oranochy,[k] though but knowen late;
And that huge river, which doth bear his name
Of warlike Amazons which do possess the same.

Joy on those warlike women, which so long
Can from all men so rich a kingdom hold!
And shame on you, O men, which boast your strong
And valiant hearts, in thoughts less hard and bold,
Yet quail in conquest of that land of gold!
But this to you, O Britons, most pertains,
To whom the right hereof itself hath sold;
The which, for sparing little cost or pains,
Lose so immortal glory, and so endless gains.

Then was there heard a most celestial sound
Of dainty music, which did next ensue
Before the spouse: that was Arion crowned;
Who, playing on his harp, unto him drew
The ears and hearts of all that goodly crew;
That even yet the dolphin, which him bore
Through the Ægean seas from pirates' view,

---

[k] The Orinoco.

Stood still by him astonished at his lore,
And all the raging seas for joy forgot to roar.

So went he playing on the watery plain :
Soon after whom the lovely bridegroom came,
The noble Thames, with all his goodly train.
But him before there went, as best became,
His ancient parents, namely the ancient Thame;
But much more aged was his wife than he,
The Ouse, whom men do Isis rightly name ;
Full weak and crooked creature seemed she,
And almost blind through eld, that scarce her way could see.

Therefore on either side she was sustained
Of two small grooms, which by their names were hight
The Churn and Charwell, two small streams, which pained
Themselves her footing to direct aright,
Which failed oft through faint and feeble plight:
But Thame was stronger, and of better stay ;
Yet seemed full aged by his outward sight,
With head all hoary, and his beard all gray,
Dewed with silver drops that trickled down alway :

And eke he somewhat seemed to stoop afore
With bowed back, by reason of the load
And ancient heavy burden which he bore
Of that fair city, wherein make abode
So many learned imps, that shoot abroad,
And with their branches spread all Britany,
No less than do her elder sister's [1] brood.
Joy to you both, ye double nursery
Of arts! but, Oxford, thine doth Thame most glorify.

But he their son,[m] full fresh and jolly was,
All decked in a robe of watchet[n] hue,
On which the waves, glittering like crystal glass,
So cunningly enwoven were, that few
Could weenen whether they were false or true :
And on his head like to a coronet
He wore, that seemed strange to common view,

Cambridge.   [m] Thames.   [n] Blue.

In which were many towers and castles set,
That it encompassed round as with a golden frʻ ɩ.
Like as the mother of the gods, they say,
In her great iron chariot wonts to ride,
When to Jove's palace she doth take her way,
Old Cybele, arrayed with pompous pride,
Wearing a diadem embattled wide
With hundred turrets, like a turribant: ᵒ
With such an one was Thamis beautified;
That was to weet the famous Troynovant,
In which her kingdom's throne is chiefly resiant.ᵖ

And round about him many a pretty page
Attended duly, ready to obey;
All little rivers which owe vassalage
To him, as to their lord, and tribute pay:
The chalky Kennet; and the Thetis grey;
The morish Cole; and the soft-sliding Brean;
The wanton Lee, that oft doth lose his way;
And the still Darent, in whose waters clean
Ten thousand fishes play and deck his pleasant stream.

Then came his neighbour floods which nigh him dwell,
And water all the English soil throughout;
They all on him this day attended well,
And with meet service waited him about;
Ne none disdained low to him to lout:
No, not the stately Severn grudged at all,
Ne storming Humber, though he looked stout;
But both him honoured as their principal,
And let their swelling waters low before him fall.

There was the speedy Tamar, which divides
The Cornish and the Devonish confines;
Through both whose borders swiftly down it glides,
And, meeting Plym, to Plymouth thence declines:
And Dart, nigh choked with sands of tinny mines:
But Avon marched in more stately path,
Proud of his adamants with which he shines
And glisters wide, as als of wondrous Bath,
And Bristow fair, which on his waves he builded hath.

And there came Stour with terrible aspect,
Bearing his six deformed heads on high,

ᵒ Turban. ᵖ Resident.

That doth his course through Blandford plains direct,
And washeth Winborne meeds in season dry.
Next him went Wilyburn with passage sly,
That of his wiliness his name doth take,
And of himself doth name the shire thereby:
And Mole, that like a mousling mole doth make
His way still under ground till Thames he overtake.

Then came the Rother, decked all with woods
Like a wood-god, and flowing fast to Rye;
And Sture, that parteth with his pleasant floods
The eastern Saxons from the southern nigh,
And Clare and Harwich both doth beautify.
Him followed Yar, soft washing Norwich wall,
And with him brought a present joyfully
Of his own fish unto their festival,
Whose like none else could shew, the which they ruffins
   call.

Next these the plenteous Ouse came far from land,
By many a city and by many a town,
And many rivers taking underhand
Into his waters, as he passeth down,
(The Clee, the Were, the Grant,^q the Sture, the Rowne.)
Thence doth by Huntingdon and Cambridge flit,
My mother Cambridge, whom as with a crown
He doth adorn, and is adorned of it
With many a gentle muse and many a learned wit.

And after him the fatal Welland went,
That if old saws prove true (which God forbid!)
Shall drown all Holland with his excrement.
And shall see Stamford, though now homely hid,
Then shine in learning more than ever did
Cambridge or Oxford, England's goodly beams.
And next to him the Nene down softly slid;
And bounteous Trent, that in himself enseams
Both thirty sorts of fish and thirty sundry streams.

Next these came Tyne, along whose stony bank
That Roman monarch built a brazen wall,
Which mote the feebled Britons strongly flank
Against the Picts that swarmed over all,

---

       q Misprinted Guant.

Which yet thereof Gualsever they do call:
And Tweed, the limit betwixt Logris land
And Albany: and Eden, though but small,
Yet often stained with blood of many a band
Of Scots and English both, that tined[r] on his strand

Then came those six sad brethren, like forlorn,
That whilome were, as antique fathers tell,
Six valiant knights of one fair nymph yborn,
Which did in noble deeds of arms excel,
And wonned there where now York people dwell;
Still Ure, swift Werf, and Oze the most of might,
High Swale, unquiet Nide, and troublous Skell;
All whom a Scythian king, that Humber hight,
Slew cruelly, and in the river drowned quite:

But passed not long, ere Brutus' warlike son
Locrinus them avenged, and the same date,
Which the proud Humber unto them had done,
By equal doom repaid on his own pate:
For in the self same river, where he late
Had drenched them, he drowned him again;
And named the river of his wretched fate;
Whose bad condition yet it doth retain,
Oft tossed with his storms which therein still remain.

These after came the stony shallow Lone,
That to old Loncaster his name doth lend;
And following Dee, which Britons long ygone
Did call divine, that doth by Chester tend;
And Conway, which out of his stream doth send
Plenty of pearls to deck his dames withal;
And Lindus, that his pikes doth most commend,
Of which the ancient Lincoln men do call:
All these together marched toward Proteus' hall.

Ne thence the Irish rivers absent were:
Sith no less famous than the rest they be,
And, joined in neighbourhood of kingdom near,
Why should they not likewise in love agree,
And joy likewise this solemn day to see?
They saw it all, and present were in place:
Though I them all, according their degree,

---

[r] Were killed.

Cannot recount, nor tell their hidden race,
Nor read the salvage countries thorough which they pace.

There was the Liffy rolling down the lea;
The Sandy Slane; the stony Aubrion;
The spacious Shenan spreading like a sea;
The pleasant Boyne; the fishy fruitful Ban;
Swift Awniduff, which of the English man
Is called Blackwater; and the Liffar deep;
Sad Trowis, that once his people overran;
Strong Allo tumbling from Slewlogher steep;
And Mulla mine, whose waves I whilome taught to weep.

And there the three renowmed brethren were,
Which that great giant Blomius begot
Of the fair nymph Rheüsa wandering there:
One day, as she to shun the season hot
Under Slewboome in shady grove was got,
This giant found her and by force deflowered;
Whereof conceiving, she in time forth brought
These three fair sons, which being thenceforth poured
In three great rivers ran, and many countries scoured.

The first the gentle Shure that, making way
By sweet Clonmell, adorns rich Waterford;
The next, the stubborn Newre whose waters grey
By fair Kilkenny and Rossponte board;
The third, the goodly Barrow which doth hoard
Great heaps of salmon in his deep bosom:
All which, long sundered, do at last accord
To join in one, ere to the sea they come;
So, flowing all from one, all one at last become.

There also was the wide embayed Mayre;
The pleasant Bandon crowned with many a wood;
The spreading Lee that, like an island fair,
Encloseth Cork with his divided flood;
And baleful Oure late stained with English blood:
With many more whose names no tongue can tell.
All which that day in order seemly good
Did on the Thames attend, and waited well
To do their dueful service, as to them befell.

Then came the bride, the lovely Medua came,
Clad in a vesture of unknowen gear

And uncouth fashion, yet her well became,
That seemed like silver sprinkled here and there
With glittering spangs that did like stars appear,
And waved upon, like water chamelot,*
To hide the metal, which yet everywhere
Bewrayed itself, to let men plainly wot
It was no mortal work, that seemed and yet was not.

Her goodly locks adown her back did flow
Unto her waist, with flowers bescattered,
The which ambrosial odours forth did throw
To all about, and all her shoulders spread
As a new spring; and likewise on her head
A chapelet of sundry flowers she wore,
From under which the dewy humour shed
Did trickle down her hair, like to the hoar
Congealed little drops which do the morn adore.

On her two pretty handmaids did attend,
One called the Theise, the other called the Crane:
Which on her waited things amiss to mend,
And both behind upheld her spreading train;
Under the which her feet appeared plain,
Her silver feet, fair washed against this day;
And her before there paced pages twain,
Both clad in colours like and like array,
The Donne and eke the Frith, both which prepared her way.

And after these the sea-nymphs marched all,
All goodly damsels, decked with long green hair,
Whom of their sire Nereïdes men call,
All which the Ocean's daughter to him bare,
The grey-eyed Doris; all which fifty are;
All which she there on her attending had:
Swift Proto; mild Eucrate; Thetis fair;
Soft Spio; sweet Eudore; Sao sad;
Light Doto; wanton Glauce; and Galene glad;

White-hand Eunica; proud Dynamene;
Joyous Thalia; goodly Amphitrite;
Lovely Pasithee; kind Eulimene;
Light-foot Cymothoë; and sweet Melite;

---

* Camlet.

Fairest Pherusa; Phao lily white;
Wondered Agave; Poris; and Nesæa;
With Erato that doth in love delight;
And Panopæ; and wise Protomedæa;
And snowy-necked Doris; and Milk-white Galathæa;

Speedy Hippothoë; and chaste Actea;
Large Lisianassa; and Pronæa sage;
Euagore; and light Pontoporea;
And, she that with the least word can assuage
The surging seas when they do sorest rage,
Cymodoce; and stout Autonoë;
And Neso; and Eione well in age;
And seeming still to smile Glauconome;
And, she that hight of many hestes, Polynome;

Fresh Alimeda decked with girland green;
Hyponeo with salt-bedewed wrests;[t]
Laomedia like the crystal sheen;
Liagore much praised for wise behests;
And Psamathe for her broad snowy breasts;
Cymo; Eupompe; and Themiste just;
And, she that virtue loves and vice detests,
Euarna; and Menippe true in trust;
And Nemertea learned well to rule her lust.[u]

All these the daughters of old Nereus were,
Which have the sea in charge to them assigned,
To rule his tides, and surges to uprear,
To bring forth storms, or fast them to upbind,
And sailors save from wrecks of wrathful wind.
And yet besides, three thousand more there were
Of the Ocean's seed, but[v] Jove's and Phœbus' kind;
The which in floods and fountains do appear,
And all mankind do nourish with their waters clear

The which, more eath[w] it were for mortal wight
To tell the sands, or count the stars on high,
Or ought more hard, than think to reckon right.
But well I wote that these, which I descry,
Were present at this great solemnity:

---

[t] Wrists.   [u] Her will.
[v] Perhaps a misprint for "both."   [w] Easy.

And there, amongst the rest, the mother was
Of luckless Marinel, Cymodoce ;
Which, for my muse herself now tired has,
Unto another Canto I will overpass.

Canto XII. (35 stanzas).—Still dwelling on the thought with which he had concluded the preceding Canto, the poet resumes :—

O what an endless work have I in hand,
To count the sea's abundant progeny,
Whose fruitful seed far passeth those in land,
And also those which won in the azure sky !
For much more eath to tell the stars on high
All be they endless seem in estimation,
Than to recount the sea's posterity :
So fertile be the floods in generation,
So huge their numbers, and so numberless their nation.

Therefore the antique wizards well invented
That Venus of the foamy sea was bred ;
For that the seas by her are most augmented.
Witness the exceeding fry which there are fed,
And wondrous shoals which may of none be read.
Then blame me not if I have erred in count
Of gods, of nymphs, of rivers, yet unread :
For, though their numbers do much more surmount,
Yet all those same were there which erst I did recount.

All those were there, and many others, filling the house of Proteus even to the door. And among the rest, as already mentioned, was the mother of Marinel, now, as we have seen, called Cymodoce (instead of Cymoent, as before). With her, too, had come Marinel himself,

—————————— to learn and see
The manner of the gods when they at banquet be.

But, being half mortal, he could not sit down and partake with them ; so after a little while he walked abroad to take a view of a dwelling-place so unlike anything he had ever seen on earth ; and, while so engaged,

Under the hanging of an hideous cliff
He heard the lamentable voice of one
That piteously complained her careful grief,
Which never she before disclosed to none,

But to herself her sorrow did bemoan :
So feelingly her case she did complain,
That ruth it moved in the rocky stone,
And made it seem to feel her grievous pain,
And oft to groan with billows beating from the main :

"Though vain I see my sorrows to unfold
And count my cares, when none is nigh to hear;
Yet, hoping grief may lessen being told,
I will them tell, though unto no man near:
For heaven, that unto all lends equal ear,
Is far from hearing of my heavy plight;
And lowest hell, to which I lie most near,
Cares not what evils hap to wretched wight;
And greedy seas do in the spoil of life delight."

He, she went on, who kept her in bondage was only hardened the more by her complaints and tears; yet would she never repent of her constancy to her own love, but rather rejoice at all she suffered for his sake. And, when she should be at rest in death at last, all she asked was that the lament she now made might then be borne to his ears, and he might know how hard she thought it that he, a knight professing arms, should let her die without attempting her deliverance. Then, after a pause, she began afresh :—

"Ye gods of seas, if any gods at all
Have care of right or ruth of wretches' wrong,
By one or other way me, woeful thrall,
Deliver hence out of this dungeon strong,
In which I daily dying am too long :
And, if ye deem [x] me death for loving one
That loves not me, then do it not prolong,
But let me die and end my days atone,[y]
And let him live unloved, or love himself alone.

But, if that life ye unto me decree,
Then let me live, as lovers ought to do,
And of my life's dear love beloved be :
And, if he should through pride your doom undo,
Do you by duress him compel thereto,

---

[x] Adjudge.   [y] At once.

> And in this prison put him here with me;
> One prison fittest is to hold us two:
> So had I rather to be thrall than free;
> Such thraldom or such freedom let it surely be.
>
> But O vain judgment, and conditions vain,
> The which the prisoner points unto the free!
> The whiles I him condemn, and deem his pain,
> He where he list goes loose, and laughs at me:
> So ever loose, so ever happy be!
> But whereso loose or happy that thou art,
> Know, Marinel, that all this is for thee!"
> With that she wept and wailed, as if her heart
> Would quite have burst through great abundance of her smart.

Hearing his own name thus pronounced in passion and agony, Marinel is for the first time touched with remorse and pity; he wishes that he could release poor Florimel, but knows no means by which to make the attempt:—

> Thus whilst his stony heart with tender ruth,
> Was touched, and mighty courage mollified,
> Dame Venus' son that tameth stubborn youth
> With iron bit, and maketh him abide
> Till like a victor on his back he ride,
> Into his mouth his maistering bridle threw,
> That made him stoop, till he did him bestride:
> Then gan he make him tread his steps anew,
> And learn to love by learning lover's pains to rue.

He has now no rest for thinking how he may deliver her: sometimes he thinks of humbly suing Proteus for her discharge; sometimes of forcing him "with sword and targe" to give her up; sometimes of stealing her away. But these plans are all manifestly vain and hopeless. Then he begins

> To damn himself by every evil name,
> And deem unworthy or of love or life,
> That had despised so chaste and fair a dame,
> Which him had sought through trouble and long strife;
> Yet had refused a god that her had sought to wife.

At length, however, the feast being over, he is obliged

to take his departure and return with his mother to her bower. Here, in solitude and silence, he remembers the state in which he has left Florimel, suffering day and night " for his dear sake :"—

> The thought whereof empierced his heart so deep,
> That of no worldly thing he took delight;
> Ne daily food did take, ne nightly sleep,
> But pined and mourned, and languished, and alone did weep;
>
> That in short space his wonted cheerful hue
> Gan fade, and lively spirits deaded quite:
> His cheek-bones raw, and eye-pits hollow grew,
> And brawny arms had lost their knowen might,
> That nothing like himself he seemed in sight.
> Ere long so weak of limb, and sick of love
> He wox, that lenger he note stand upright,
> But to his bed was brought, and laid above,
> Like rueful ghost, unable once to stir or move.

His mother, alarmed and unable to discover the cause of his illness, hastens again to Tryphon, who, revisiting his patient, assures her that it is not, as she suspected, his old wound insufficiently cured and rankling under the orifice, or scar; but some other malady, or hidden grief, which his skill is unable to detect. Faint and trembling, she then applies to Marinel himself, beseeching him, " now with fair speeches, now with threatenings stern," to tell her if anything lies heavy on his heart; " who still her answered there was nought."

> Nathless she rested not so satisfied;
> But leaving watery gods, as booting nought,
> Unto the shiny heaven in haste she hied,
> And thence Apollo, king of leeches, brought.
> Apollo came; who, soon as he had sought
> Through his disease, did by and by out find
> That he did languish of some inward thought,
> The which afflicted his engrieved mind;
> Which love he read to be, that leads each living kind.

Cymodoce is at first angry and chides her son; but, reassuring herself with the thought that it must be one of the sea-nymphs he had lately seen for whom he languished, and that love of nymphs could not be included in the " fatal read" which had warned him to beware of the love of women, she afterwards wooes him with fair entreaty to reveal to her who it is that moves his heart so sore. When, however, he tells her that it is Florimel, she begins to chafe afresh, and to " grieve in every vein." Yet, whatever the prophecy of Proteus may mean, or whether it be true or false, it is evident that her son will die at any rate if the only remedy be not instantly procured by the liberation of the lady. She feels that it is useless to make suit to Proteus, or " unto any meaner to complain;" but hieing her at once to great King Neptune himself, " and on her knee before him falling low," she humbly implores him to grant her the life of her son, whom his foe, a cruel tyrant, has iniquitously and presumptuously condemned to death. God Neptune, softly smiling, replies that the person of whom she complains has committed wrong against him as well as against her; for to condemn to death appertains to none but to " the sea's sole sovereign." " Read therefore," he says,

————— " who it is which thus hath wrought,
And for what cause; the truth discover plain:
For never wight so evil did or thought,
But would some rightful cause pretend, though rightly nought."

She informs him that it is Proteus; and that the pretence he alleges is her son having laid claim to a waift, which had come by chance upon the seas, and which in reality belonged to neither of them, but to Neptune himself, by his prerogative as sovereign: " Therefore," she adds,

——————— " I humbly crave your majesty
It to replevy,[y] and my son reprive:[z]
So shall you by one gift save all us three alive."

Her prayer is granted; a warrant is made out forthwith,

[y] Release, cause to be given up. [z] Reprieve.

"under the sea-god's seal autentical," commanding Proteus instantly to set at liberty the Maid he had lately taken captive while wandering on the seas; and Proteus, as soon as he reads the order, which Cymodoce straightway takes to him, is reluctantly compelled to obey, and to give up Florimel:—

> Whom she receiving by the lily hand,
> Admired her beauty much, as she mote well,
> For she all living creatures did excel,
> And was right joyous that she gotten had
> So fair a wife for her son Marinel.

As for Marinel himself, as "soon as he beheld that angel's face," his heart revived, even as a withered flower at the return of warm and genial weather

> Lifts up his head that did before decline,
> And gins to spread his leaf before the fair sunshine.

Nor did Florimel want her share of the blessedness:—

> Ne less was she in secret heart affected,
> But that she masked it with modesty,
> For fear she should of lightness be detected.

Book Fifth.

The Fifth Book of the Fairy Queen is entitled *The Legend of Artegal, or of Justice.* The introductory address is of greater length than usual, and is very fine. It begins,

> So oft as I with state of present time
> The image of the antique world compare,
> Whenas man's age was in his freshest prime,
> And the first blossom of fair virtue bare;
> Such odds I find twixt those, and these which are,
> As that, through long continuance of his course,
> Me seems the world is run quite out of square
> From the first point of his appointed source;
> And being once amiss grows daily worse and worse:

> For from the golden age, that first was named,
> It's now at erst [a] become a stony one;
> And men themselves, the which at first were framed
> Of earthly mould, and formed of flesh and bone,
> Are now transformed into hardest stone;
> Such as behind their backs (so backward bred)
> Were thrown by Pyrrha and Deucalion:
> And, if than those may any worse be read,
> They into that ere long will be degendered.

> Let none then blame me, if, in discipline
> Of virtue and of civil use's lore,
> I do not form them to the common line
> Of present days which are corrupted sore;
> But to the antique use which was of yore,
> When good was only for itself desired,
> And all men sought their own, and none no more:
> When justice was not for most meed outhired,
> But simple truth did reign, and was of all admired.

---

[a] At length.

For what all men then used to call virtue is now called vice, and the name of virtue is given to what was then esteemed vicious; right is now wrong, and wrong is right; and all other things are similarly changed. Nor, proceeds our author, is this to be wondered at, seeing that the revolving heavens themselves (he alludes to the precession of the equinoxes) are wandered far away from where they first were fixed, as plainly appears;

> For that same golden fleecy Ram, which bore
> Phryxus and Helle from their stepdame's fears,
> Hath now forgot where he was placed of yore,
> And shouldered hath the Bull which fair Europa bore:

> And eke the Bull hath with his bow-bent horn
> So hardly butted those two Twins of Jove,
> That they have crushed the Crab, and quite him borne
> Into the great Nemæan Lion's grove.

Even the Sun, in these fourteen hundred years that have elapsed since the time " that learned Ptolomy his height did take," is declined nigh thirty minutes to the south, so that it may be feared we shall in time lose his light altogether. Indeed, if credit may be given to the old Egyptian sages, he had, since they first began to take his height (a space, according to Herodotus, whose account is here referred to, of 11,340 years) four times changed his place, and twice risen where he now sets and set where he now rises.

> But most is Mars amiss of all the rest;
> And next to him old Saturn, that was wont be best.
> For during Saturn's ancient reign it's said
> That all the world with goodness did abound;
> All loved virtue, no man was afraid
> Of force, ne fraud in wight was to be found;
> No war was known, no dreadful trumpet's sound;
> Peace universal reigned mongst men and beasts:
> And all things freely grew out of the ground:
> Justice sat high adored with solemn feasts,
> And to all people did divide her dread beheasts:[b]

---

[b] Commands.

Most sacred virtue she of all the rest,
Resembling God in his imperial might;
Whose sovereign power is herein most exprest,
That both to good and bad he dealeth right,
And all his works with justice hath bedight.[c]
That power he also doth to princes lend,
And makes them like himself in glorious sight
To sit in his own seat, his cause to end,
And rule his people right, as he doth recommend.

This leads naturally to the customary appeal to Elizabeth, who is addressed as "dread sovereign goddess," and requested to pardon the boldness of her "basest thrall" who dares discourse of so high a theme as her great justice; "the instrument whereof," the eleven stanzas conclude, "lo, here thy Artegal."

Canto I. (30 stanzas).—It has already been stated that Sir Artegal (or Artheyal, as he is called in the earlier part of the poem) is understood to stand for Arthur Lord Grey of Wilton, who was sent over as Lord Lieutenant to Ireland in July 1580, when Spenser accompanied him as his secretary. In the present Book he appears more distinctly than heretofore in his historical character; and his Irish government, which lasted for about two years, and comprised the suppression of the great rebellion headed by the Earl of Desmond, is especially shadowed forth in the allegory.

The present Canto opens with the praise of Bacchus and Hercules, who first, we are told, in the ancient world gave example of the repression of wrong and the establishment of right under the rule and by the power of Justice, the former in the East, the latter in the West; and then we are carried back to the story of Artegal, and the great adventure upon which we left him proceeding after his marriage with Britomart, at the end of the Sixth Canto of the preceding Book. The object upon which he was bound was to succour a distressed lady, Irena (that is, Ireland, anciently Ierne), against the tyrant Grantorto, who withheld from her her heritage;

[c] Adorned.

Irena had come and besought redress from the Fairy Queen, and that mighty empress, whose glory it is to be the patroness and helper of all who are poor and oppressed, had selected Artegal for the enterprise. For he from his infancy had been brought up and instructed in all good and right by Astræa herself, who one day while she lived among men and walked about over the earth, "found this gentle child amongst his peers playing his childish sport," and, having allured him "with gifts and speeches mild to wend with her," brought him to a distant cave, where she nursed him till he came of years, "and all the discipline of justice there him taught." She taught him to weigh right and wrong in equal balance, and to measure out equity

> According to the line of conscience,
> Whenso it needs with rigour to dispense:
> Of all the which, for want there of mankind,
> She caused him to make experience
> Upon wild beasts, which she in woods did find,
> With wrongful power oppressing others of their kind.

Thus educated, when he came to the ripeness of his age he was both the terror of the brute creation and the admiration of men;

> Ne any lived on ground that durst withstand
> His dreadful hest,[d] much less him match in fight,
> Or bide the horror of his wreakful hand,
> Whenso he list in wrath lift up his steely brand.

This brand, or sword, she had procured for him "by her sleight and earnest search," from the eternal house of Jove, where it lay, "unwist of wight,"

> Since he himself it used in that great fight
> Against the Titans, that whilome rebelled
> Gainst highest heaven; Chrysaor it was hight;
> Chrysaor, that all other swords excelled,
> Well proved in that same day when Jove those giants quelled:

---

[d] Command.

> For of most perfect metal it was made,
> Tempered with adamant amongst the same,
> And garnished all with gold upon the blade
> In goodly wise, whereof it took his name,
> And was of no less virtue than of fame:
> For there no substance was so firm and hard,
> But it would pierce or cleave whereso it came;
> Ne any armour could his dint outward;
> But wheresoever it did light, it throughly shard.*

When Astræa returned to heaven—

> Where she hath now an everlasting place
> Mongst those twelve signs, which nightly we do see
> The heaven's bright-shining baudrick to enchase;
> And is the Virgin, sixth in her degree,
> And next herself her righteous Balance hanging be;—

she left also to Artegal, always to go with him and to perform whatever he commanded, an iron man, her faithful groom, or attendant, and executioner of her decrees:—

> His name was Talus, made of iron mould,
> Immoveable, resistless, without end:
> Who in his hand an iron flail did hold,
> With which he threshed out falsehood, and did truth unfold.

Artegal being Justice, Talus is Power, with which Justice, to be of any efficiency, must be attended or associated. Talus, according to the ancient mythologists, was a judge of the isle of Crete, who, partly from his severity, partly from carrying about with him the laws which he administered inscribed on brazen tablets, was called the Brazen Man, and came to have the popular reputation of being made of brass. "But how properly," observes Upton, "does Spenser depart from ancient mythology, having a mythology of his own! Spenser's Talus is no *judge*; therefore not a *brazen* man; but he is an *executioner*, an *iron* man, imaging his unfeeling and rigid character." Him Artegal accordingly takes with

---

* Shared, sheared, shore.

him on his present expedition; and now, as they are making their way along together, they came upon a startling sight—a squire, squalidly attired, lamenting grievously with many bitter tears, and lying beside him a headless lady wallowing in her blood. Greatly moved, Artegal asks the squire who it is that has done so foul a deed, himself or another. It were little loss, the miserable man replies, if he should admit the crime to be his own, that he might drink the cup whereof she has drunk; but he would not take to himself another's guilt. The murderer is a knight, "if knight he may be thought," who came to him a short time ago as he sate here solacing himself with a fair lady, his love; the knight was accompanied by this other lady, who now lies headless before them, and insisted upon exchanging her for the one who was with the squire; the squire and both ladies, as may be supposed, objected to this arrangement; but the knight, throwing down his own lady from the courser on which she rode along with him, snatched up the other and rode off with her; and, when the one he had abandoned ran after him and laid hold of him, praying that she might rather die by his hand than be so cast off,

—————— his sword he drew all wrathfully,
And at one stroke cropped off her head with scorn.

To Artegal's impatient inquiry which way he had gone, and how he might be known, the squire states that he bears for his ensign armorial a broken sword within a bloody field—but that he is now too far away over the plain to be overtaken.

No sooner said, but straight he after sent
His iron page, who him pursued so light,
As that it seemed above the ground he went:
For he was swift as swallow in her flight,
And strong as lion in his lordly might.

It is not long before the all-subduing Talus overtakes the ruffian, who is called Sir Sanglier (which name, it has been conjectured, may be designed to glance at *Shan* O'Neal, the leader of the Irish insurrection of 1567, who was notorious for his profligacy). To the call of the iron man, he answers by making the lady alight, and riding at him with all his force; but Talus, no more moved than is a rock when a stone is thrown at it,

— to him leaping lent him such a knock,
That on the ground he laid him like a senseless block;

and before he can recover himself he has him seized so firmly in his iron paw that when he comes to his senses he finds he cannot wag a limb. The lady, too, who flies in dread from the tremendous man, is quickly forced to stay. But, when they are brought back to Artegal and the squire, Sir Sanglier flatly denies all that he has been charged with, and defies his accuser to the proof. The squire, too weak to encounter such an antagonist, is inclined to give in; yet Artegal has no doubt that he has told the truth. It might seem that the most natural and most satisfactory plan would be to appeal to the lady; but she may not perhaps have been so much disinclined as she ought to have been to admit the claim of her bold reaver, with whom she appears both to have gone off somewhat readily and to have been riding along peaceably enough when they were overtaken by Talus; at any rate Artegal takes another method of settling the matter. Having requested them to allow him to decide the cause, and got both to swear to submit to his judgment, he proceeds to apply Solomon's famous test for the discovery of the truth in such cases, and proposes to have both the dead and the living lady divided equally between the two claimants. If either, he declares, should dissent from this proposal, he must bear about with him the dead lady's head for a year as a penance, and for a witness or confession to the world that he is her murderer.

> Well pleased with that doom was Sanglier,
> And offered straight the lady to be slain:
> But that same squire to whom she was more dear,
> Whenas he saw she should be cut in twain,
> Did yield she rather should with him remain
> Alive than to himself be shared dead;
> And, rather than his love should suffer pain,
> He chose with shame to bear that lady's head:
> True love despiseth shame when life is called in dread.

Artegal immediately pronounces his just judgment; but it requires the intervention of Talus to compel the discomfited Sir Sanglier to take up the head, which, however, he does at last, going off with it like a "rated spaniel." The squire, filled with adoration of his benefactor, would gladly become his squire, and accompany him on his adventure; but Sir Artegal will by no means consent, and, leaving him and his lady-love, of whose state of feeling nothing is said, he proceeds on his journey as before:—

> Ne wight with him but only Talus went;
> They two enough to encounter an whole regiment.

Canto II. (54 stanzas).—Proceeding along Sir Artegal now meets a dwarf hastening in the opposite direction; whom, having compelled him, much against his will, to stop and tell his news, he finds to be Dony, Florimel's dwarf, whom the reader may remember to have already encountered in the Fifth Canto of the Third Book, but of whom we have heard nothing since Arthur there promised never to forsake him till they should have found his mistress, whom the Prince had seen the day before making her escape from the foul foster, and had so long unsuccessfully attempted to overtake in her flight. When Arthur re-appears in the Eighth Canto of the Fourth Book the dwarf is not with him, and how they have been separated we are not informed. The account that Dony now gives of himself, or that is given of him by the poet, is, that, having found in his way her "scattered scarf" (of the loss of which we now hear for the first time), he had long feared that his mistress was dead; but he has now learned, and informs Artegal, much to that noble knight's gratification, that she has been found again, and is about to be espoused to Marinel, he himself being on his way to the bridal, although he doubts if he will be in time, for it is to take place at the Castle of the Strond (Marinel's precious strand, or shore) three days hence. In his way, besides, there is a bridge a little farther on, which is kept by a cruel Saracen, a man expert in arms, and made still bolder by the diabolical aid which he receives from his daughter, who is an enchantress. He has appropriated by force and oppression many great lordships and goodly farms; and he allows no one to pass over his bridge, be he rich or poor, " but he him makes his passage-penny pay."

> " Thereto he hath a groom of evil guise,
> Whose scalp is bare, that bondage doth bewray,
> Which polls and pills the poor in piteous wise;
> But he himself upon the rich doth tyrannize.
>
> His name is hight Pollente, rightly so,
> For that he is so puissant and strong,
> That with his power he all doth overgo,
> And makes them subject to his mighty wrong."

Some too he entraps by stratagem; his custom being to fight upon the bridge, which is very narrow, but of exceeding length, and pierced by many trap-falls, through which horse and rider drop into the swift river that flows underneath, upon which he instantly leaps into the water after them and easily overpowers and despatches both. All their spoils he brings to his daughter, who has thus heaped up her wicked treasury to such a height that her wealth exceeds that of many princes, and she has purchased all the country lying round. Her name is Munera (in allusion to the *gifts* of her father, upon which she subsists).

> " Thereto she is full fair, and rich attired,
> With golden hands and silver feet beside,
> That many lords have her to wife desired:
> But she them all despiseth for great pride."

On hearing this relation Artegal swears by his life that, with God to guide him, he will take no other road this day but by that bridge; and commands the dwarf to lead him thither. Having come to the place they see the Saracen waiting on the bridge, all ready armed; and, when they proceed to pass over, a villain comes up to them " with skull all raw "—the same groom, or slave, already described as testifying his bondage by his bald scalp—and demands their passage-money. Artegal's indignant answer is merely " Lo, there thy hire," and a blow of his sword which deprives the villain of life. The Pagan now rushes at him; but he is prepared: a trap-door opens at the moment when they are about to meet breast to breast; Pollente leaps down, counting upon finding his adversary, as usual, fallen and struggling in the water; but Artegal preserves his seat and his presence of mind.

> There being both together in the flood,
> They each at other tyrannously flew;
> Ne ought the water cooled their hot blood,
> But rather in them kindled choler new:
> But there the Paynim, who that use well knew
> To fight in water, great advantage had,
> That oftentimes him nigh he overthrew:
> And eke the courser whereupon he rad
> Could swim like to a fish whiles he his back bestrad.

Perceiving the advantage that the Pagan in this way has, Artegal suddenly closes with him, and gripes him so fast by his iron collar, that he nearly bursts his windpipe. The struggle is fierce and long. As, when a dolphin and a seal engage with one another in battle " in the wide champian of the ocean plain,"—

> They snuff, they snort, they bounce, they rage, they roar,
> That all the sea, disturbed with their train,
> Doth fry with foam above the surges hoar:
> Such was betwixt these two the troublesome uproar.

Artegal at length compels him to dismount; and now they are upon a par:—

> For Artegal in swimming skilful was,
> And durst the depth of any water sound.
> So ought each knight, that use of peril has,
> In swimming be expert, through waters' force to pass.

Yet the event is still for a time doubtful. Artegal, however, being better breathed, retains his strength the longest, and the other is forced to leave the water;—

> But Artegal pursued him still so near
> With bright Chrysaor in his cruel hand

That, as his head he gan a little rear
Above the brink to tread upon the land,
He smote it off, that tumbling on the strand
It bit the earth for very fell despite,
And gnashed with his teeth, as if he banned
High God, whose goodness he despaired quite,
Or cursed the hand which did that vengeance on him dight.

The corpse is carried down the blood-stained stream; but the blasphemous head the victor fixes high upon a pole,

Where many years it afterwards remained,
To be a mirror to all mighty men,
In whose right hands great power is contained,
That none of them the feeble over-ren,[f]
But always do their power within just compass pen.

Artegal now proceeds to the castle and demands entrance; but he is assailed by its numerous defenders, both with furious invectives and with stones thrown down upon him from the battlements; so that he is compelled to withdraw, and to desire Talus to interpose with his supernatural might.

Eftsoons his page drew to the castle gate,
And with his iron flail at it let fly,
That all the warders it did sore amate,[g]
The which ere-while spake so reproachfully,
And made them stoop, that looked erst so high.
Yet still he beat and bounced upon the door,
And thundered strokes thereon so hideously,
That all the piece[h] he shaked from the floor,
And filled all the house with fear and great uproar.

With noise whereof the lady forth appeared
Upon the castle wall; and, when she saw
The dangerous state in which she stood, she feared
The sad effect of her near overthrow;
And gan entreat that iron man below
To cease his outrage, and him fair besought;
Sith neither force of stones which they did throw,

---

[f] Overrun.　　[g] Affright.　　[h] Fortress.

Nor power of charms, which she against him wrought,
Might otherwise prevail, or make him cease for ought.

But, whenas yet she saw him to proceed
Unmoved with prayers or with piteous thought,
She meant him to corrupt with goodly meed;
And caused great sacks with endless riches fraught
Unto the battlement to be upbrought,
And poured forth over the castle wall,
That she might win some time, though dearly bought,
Whilst he to gathering of the gold did fall;
But he was nothing moved nor tempted therewithal:

But still continued his assault the more,
And laid on load with his huge iron flail,
That at the length he has yrent the door
And made way for his maister to assail:
Who being entered, nought did them avail
For wight against his power themselves to rear:
Each one did fly; their hearts began to fail;
And hid themselves in corners here and there
And eke their dame half dead did hide herself for fear.

It is thought at first that she has made her escape; but Talus, whose scent is no more to be eluded than his arm is to be resisted, finds her at length hidden under a heap of gold; whence he drags her forth by her beautiful locks so roughly, and with so little "pity of her goodly hue," that Artegal himself is touched with her unseemly plight. He will not, however, interfere with the proceedings of the stern iron man; who, while the fair lady kneels at his feet and holds up her hands in supplication, chops off those hands of gold and those feet of silver, that sold justice and sought unrighteousness, and nails them on high to be a spectacle and a warning to all. He then takes her up by the slender waist, and, heedless of her loud cries for mercy, casts her over the castle wall into the muddy flood below; and after that he takes all her vast treasure, the spoil which her father had scraped together by hook and crook, and, burning all to ashes, pours it down the stream. Lastly, he razes the castle to the foundation; and Artegal, having then abolished the evil customs of that bridge, proceeds on his journey.

The remainder of the Canto is very remarkable. After travelling a long way, Artegal and Talus come to the sea-shore, and there see before them a vast assembly of people, towards whom they advance to learn what such a gathering may mean. The sequel we give without curtailment :—

There they beheld a mighty giant stand
Upon a rock, and holding forth on high
An huge great pair of balance in his hand,
With which he boasted in his surquedry [i]
That all the world he would weigh equally,
If ought he had the same to counterpoise:
For want whereof he weighed vanity,
And filled his balance full of idle toys:
Yet was admired much of fools, women, and boys.

He said that he would all the earth uptake
And all the sea, divided each from either:
So would he of the fire one balance make,
And one of the air, without or wind or weather:
Then would he balance heaven and hell together,
And all that did within them all contain;
Of all whose weight he would not miss a feather:
And look, what surplus did of each remain,
He would to his own part restore the same again.

For why, he said, they all unequal were,
And had encroached upon other's share;
Like as the sea (which plain he shewed there)
Had worn the earth; so did the fire the air;
So all the rest did others parts impair:
And so were realms and nations run awry.
All which he undertook for to repair,
In sort as they were formed anciently;
And all things would reduce into equality.

Therefore the vulgar did about him flock,
And cluster thick unto his leasings [k] vain;
Like foolish flies about an honey-crock;
In hope by him great benefit to gain,
And uncontrolled freedom to obtain.

     Pride, presumption.   [k] Lies.

All which when Artegal did see and hear,
How he misled the simple people's train,
In sdainful wise he drew unto him near,
And thus unto him spake, without regard or fear;

"Thou, that presum'st to weigh the world anew,
And all things to an equal to restore,
Instead of right me seems great wrong dost shew,
And far above thy force's pitch to soar:
For, ere thou limit what is less or more
In everything, thou oughtest first to know
What was the poise of every part of yore:
And look then, how much it doth overflow
Or fail thereof, so much is more than just to trow.[l]

For at the first they all created were
In goodly measure by their Makers' might;
And weighed out in balances so near,
That not a dram was missing of their right:
The earth was in the middle centre pight,[m]
In which it doth immoveable abide,
Hemmed in with waters like a wall in sight,
And they with air, that not a drop can slide:
All which the heavens contain, and in their courses
    guide.

" Such heavenly justice doth among them reign,
That every one do know their certain bound;
In which they do these many years remain,
And mongst them all no change hath yet been found:
But, if thou now shouldst weigh them new in pound,[n]
We are not sure they would so long remain:
All change is perilous, and all chance unsound.
Therefore leave off to weigh them all again,
Till we may be assured they shall their course retain."

" Thou foolish elf," said then the giant wroth,
" Seest not how badly all things present be,
And each estate quite out of order go'th?
The sea itself dost thou not plainly see
Encroach upon the land there under thee?
And the earth itself how daily it's increased
By all that dying to it turned be?

---

[l] To wit.   [m] Fixed.   [n] Weight.

Were it not good that wrong were then surceast,
And from the most that some were given to the least?

Therefore I will throw down these mountains high,
And make them level with the lowly plain;
These towering rocks, which reach unto the sky,
I will thrust down into the deepest main,
And, as they were, them equalize again.
Tyrants, that make men subject to their law,
I will suppress, that they no more may reign;
And lordings curb that commons overawe;
And all the wealth of rich men to the poor will draw."

" Of things unseen how canst thou deem aright,"
Then answered the righteous Artegal,
" Sith thou misdeem'st so much of things in sight?
What though the sea with waves continual
Do eat the earth, it is no more at all;
Ne is the earth the less, or loseth ought:
For whatsover from one place doth fall
Is with the tide unto another brought:
For there is nothing lost, that may be found if sought.

Likewise the earth is not augmented more
By all that dying into it do fade;
For of the earth they formed were of yore:
However gay their blossom or their blade
Do flourish now, they into dust shall vade.
What wrong then is it if that when they die
They turn to that whereof they first were made?
All in the power of their great Maker lie:
All creatures must obey the voice of the Most High.

They live, they die, like as He doth ordain,
Ne ever any asketh reason why.
The hills do not the lowly dales disdain;
The dales do not the lofty hills envy.
He maketh kings to sit in sovereignty;
He maketh subjects to their power obey:
He pulleth down, He setteth up on high;
He gives to this, from that He takes away:
For all we have is His: what He list do, He may

Whatever thing is done, by Him is done,
Ne any may His mighty will withstand;

Ne any may His sovereign power shun,
Ne loose that He hath bound with stedfast band:
In vain therefore dost thou now take in hand
To call to count or weigh His works anew,
Whose counsel's depth thou canst not understand;
Sith of things subject to thy daily view
Thou dost not know the causes nor their courses due.

For take thy balance, if thou be so wise,
And weigh the wind that under heaven doth blow;
Or weigh the light that in the east doth rise;
Or weigh the thought that from man's mind doth flow
But, if the weight of these thou canst not show,
Weigh but one word which from thy lips doth fall:
For how canst thou those greater secrets know,
That dost now know the least thing of them all?
Ill can he rule the great that cannot reach the small."

Therewith the giant much abashed said,
That he of little things made reckoning light;
Yet the least word that ever could be laid
Within his balance he could weigh aright.
"Which is," said he, "more heavy, than, in weight,
The right or wrong, the false or else the true?"
He answered that he would try it straight:
So he the words into his balance threw;
But straight the winged words out of his balance flew.

Wroth wexed he then, and said that words were light,
Ne would within his balance well abide:
But he could justly weigh the wrong or right.
"Well then," said Artegal, "let it be tried:
First in one balance set the true aside."
He did so first, and then the false he laid
In the other scale; but still it down did slide,
And by no mean could in the weight be staid:
For by no means the false will with the truth be
    weighed.

"Now take the right likewise," said Artegale,
"And counterpoise the same with so much wrong,"
So first the right he put into one scale;
And then the giant strove with puissance strong
To fill the other scale with so much wrong:

But all the wrongs that he therein could lay
Might not it poise; yet did he labour long,
And swate, and chafed, and proved every way:
Yet all the wrongs could not a little right down weigh.

Which when he saw, he greatly grew in rage,
And almost would his balances have broken:
But Artegal him fairly gan assuage,
And said, "Be not upon thy balance wroken;
For they do nought but right or wrong betoken;
But in the mind the doom of right must be:
And so likewise of words, the which be spoken,
The ear must be the balance, to decree
And judge, whether with truth or falsehood they agree.

But set the truth and set the right aside,
For they with wrong or falsehood will not fare,
And put two wrongs together to be tried,
Or else two falses of each equal share,
And then together do them both compare;
For truth is one, and right is ever one."
So did he; and then plain it did appear,
Whether of them the greater were attone;
But right sat in the midest of the beam alone.

But he the right from thence did thrust away
For it was not the right which he did seek:
But rather strove extremities to weigh,
The one to diminish, the other for to eke:
For of the mean he greatly did misleak.
Whom when so lewdly minded Talus found,
Approaching nigh unto him cheek by cheek,
He shouldered him from off the higher ground,
And down the rock him throwing in the sea him drowned.

Like as a ship, whom cruel tempest drives
Upon a rock with horrible dismay,
Her shattered ribs in thousand pieces rives
And, spoiling all her gears and goodly ray,
Does make herself misfortune's piteous prey:
So down the cliff the wretched giant tumbled;
His battered balances in pieces lay,
His timbered bones all broken rudely rumbled:
So was the high-aspiring with huge ruin humbled.

That when the people, which had there about
Long waited, saw his sudden desolation,
They gan to gather in tumultous rout,
And mutining to stir up civil faction
For certain loss of so great expectation:
For well they hoped to have got great good,
And wondrous riches by his innovation:
Therefore, resolving to revenge his blood,
They rose in arms, and all in battle order stood.

Which lawless multitude him coming to
In warlike wise when Artegal did view,
He much was troubled, ne wist what to do:
For loth he was his noble hands to embrue
In the base blood of such a rascal crew;
And otherwise, if that he should retire,
He feared lest they with shame would him pursue:
Therefore he Talus to them sent to inquire
The cause of their array, and truce for to desire.

But, soon as they him nigh approaching spied,
They gan with all their weapons him assay,
And rudely strook at him on every side;
Yet nought they could him hurt, ne ought dismay:
But, when at them he with his flail gan lay,
He like a swarm of flies them overthrew:
Ne any of them durst come in his way,
But here and there before his presence flew,
And hid themselves in holes and bushes from his view;

As when a falcon hath with nimble flight
Flown at a flush of ducks foreby° the brook,
The trembling fowl dismayed with dreadful sight
Of death, the which them almost overtook,
Do hide themselves from her astonying look
Amongst the flags and covert round about.
When Talus saw they all the field forsook,
And none appeared of all that rascal rout,
To Artegal he turned and went with him throughout.

If this had been published in the end of the eighteenth instead of in the end of the sixteenth century—in the year 1796 instead of in the year 1596—the allegory could not have been more perfect, taken as a poetical represen-

° Near to.

tation or reflection of recent events, and of a passage in the political and social history of the world generally held to be not more memorable than entirely novel and unexampled. Here is the Liberty and Equality system of philosophy and government—the portentous birth of the French Revolution—described to the life two hundred years before the French Revolution broke out; described both in its magnificent but hollow show, and its sudden explosion or evaporation. This is probably one of the instances in which we overrate the advance of modern speculation; the system in question was never indeed before attempted to be carried into practice on so large a scale, or so conspicuous a platform, as in the end of the last century in France; but its spirit, though not perhaps its distinct shape, had appeared before in many popular outbreaks, and as an idea it must long have been familiar to thinking men. The principles not only of political philosophy but even of what is called political economy, generally assumed to be almost wholly a modern science, were the subject of much more attention, and were much more profoundly investigated, in Spenser's age than is commonly supposed.

Our attention has been directed by a correspondent to a close resemblance between part of Artegal's refutation of the giant's pretensions and the discourse of the angel Uriel in the Fourth Chapter of the Second Book of Esdras in exposure of the ignorance of that prophet. Our correspondent remarks that the present passage may furnish a notion of what Spenser's lost version of the Book of Ecclesiastes may have been.*

It is remarkable that no notice is taken in the summary at the head of the Canto of this exploit of Artegal's, with which it is principally occupied, nor, it will be observed, is the name of the vaunting giant any where mentioned. In the case of an ancient author the circumstances would be thought by the critics almost sufficient to condemn the whole episode as an interpolation by another hand.

* See Vol. I. p. 31.

Canto III. (40 stanzas).—We now come at last to the marriage of Marinel and Florimel :—

> After long storms and tempests overblown
> The sun at length his joyous face doth clear:
> So whenas fortune all her spite hath shown,
> Some blissful hours at last must needs appear;
> Else should afflicted wights oft-times despair.
> So comes it now to Florimel by turn,
> After long sorrows suffered whylere,
> In which captived she many months did mourn,
> To taste of joy, and to wont pleasures to return :

She was brought by Marinel to Fairy Land, there to be made his joyous bride :

> The time and place was blazed far and wide,
> And solemn feasts and jousts ordained therefore,
> To which there did resort from every side
> Of lords and ladies infinite great store;

But we are not to expect all that took place to be recounted. That, the poet warns us, is more than either his knowledge or his subject warrants him to undertake :—

> To tell the glory of the feast that day,
> The goodly service, the deviceful [p] sights,
> The bridegroom's state, the bride's most rich array,
> The pride of ladies, and the worth of knights,
> The royal banquets, and the rare delights,
> Were work fit for an herald, not for me :
> But for so much as to my lot here lights,
> That with this present treatise doth agree,
> True virtue to advance, shall here recounted be.

The feast being over, all prepare for the jousting; and first Sir Marinel issues forth, accompanied by six other knights, all ready to maintain in fight against all comers that the beauty of Florimel excels that of all other women.

> The first of them was hight Sir Orimont,
> A noble knight, and tried in hard assays:
> The second had to name Sir Bellisont,
> But second unto none in prowess' praise :

---

[p] Full of devices.

> The third was Brunel, famous in his days:
> The fourth Ecastor, of exceeding might:
> The fifth Armeddan, skilled in lovely lays:
> The sixth was Lansack, a redoubted knight:
> All six well seen in arms, and proved in many a fight.

Against them come many "from every coast and country under sun;" and many passages of arms take place; yet after all on this first day little is either lost or won; but the name that gains the greatest glory is that of Marinel. And so it is likewise on the second day. On the third also the redoubted Lord of the Precious Strand

> —— through the thickest like a lion flew,
> Rashing off helms, and riving plates asunder;
> That every one his danger did eschew:
> So terribly his dreadful strokes did thunder,
> That all men stood amazed, and at his might did wonder.

But, venturing in his impetuous courage too far among the thick of his enemies, he is overpowered, and, having been bound by them, is about to be carried away captive, forsaken by all, when unexpected succour arrives. Sir Artegal comes into the tilt-yard, accompanied by Braggadoccio and the snowy lady, whom he has chanced to meet as he rode along. As soon as he learns what has befallen Marinel, not wishing to be known, he desires Braggadoccio to change shields with him; and then, rushing among the captors of Marinel, soon rescues him, although he has first to overcome fifty knights by whom his onset is opposed, and then to get the prisoner out of the hands of as many more who have staid behind to guard him. When Marinel is unbound and at liberty, he and Artegal turn round, and quickly drive the whole force of the enemy from the field. Artegal then restores his borrowed shield to its owner. It now falls to be determined to whom the prize of valour for the day belongs; all call for the strange knight, with the shield "which bore the sun broad blazed in a golden field;" Braggadoccio comes forward; and to him the honour is adjudged by acclamation—the trumpets three times shrilly sounding the name of Don Braggadoccio, and goodly greetings and a thousand thanks being bestowed upon him by the lips of the fairest Florimel herself. But she is confounded with astonishment and shame when the boaster, instead of the usual courteous acknowledgment, answers her rudely and scornfully, that what he has done that day he has done not for her but for his own dear lady's sake, whom he will at his peril maintain to excel in beauty both her and all others whatsoever. And then he brings forth his snowy Florimel, who has been standing by all this while in charge of Trompart, and covered with a veil, which is now uplifted. The crowd are stupified with amazement; some say it is surely the true Florimel, others declare that Florimel herself is not so fair—"so feeble skill of perfect things the vulgar has."

>Which whenas Marinel beheld likewise,
>He was therewith exceedingly dismayed;
>Ne wist he what to think, or to devise;
>But, like as one whom fiends had made afraid,
>He long astonished stood, ne ought he said,
>Ne ought he did, but with fast fixed eyes
>He gazed still upon that snowy maid,
>Whom, ever as he did the more avise,
>The more to be true Florimel he did surmise.
>
>As when two suns appear in the azure sky,
>Mounted in Phœbus' chariot fiery bright,
>Both darting forth fair beams to each man's eye,
>And both adorned with lamps of flaming light;
>All that behold so strange prodigious sight,
>Not knowing nature's work, nor what to ween,
>Are rapt with wonder and with rare affright,
>So stood Sir Marinel when he had seen
>The semblant of this false by his fair beauty's queen.

Artegal, however, now steps forward. "Thou losel base," he begins, addressing the Boaster,

>That hast with borrowed plumes thyself endued,
>And other's worth with leasings dost deface,
>When they are all restored thou shalt rest in disgrace.
>
>"That shield, which thou dost bear, was it indeed
>Which this day's honour saved to Marinel;

But not that arm, nor thou the man, I read,
Which didst that service unto Florimel:"

He then calls upon him to show the marks of fight either upon his sword or upon his person;—proceeding

"But this the sword which wrought those cruel stounds,
And this the arm the which that shield did bear,
And these the signs," (so shewed forth his wounds,)
"By which that glory gotten doth appear."

As for the lady, he believes her, he declares, to be only "some fair franion," or light character, "fit for such a fere," or companion, who has chanced to fall into his hands. And for proof he desires that Florimel may be called.

So forth the noble lady was ybrought,
Adorned with honour and all comely grace:
Whereto her bashful shamefacedness ywrought
A great increase in her fair blushing face;
As[q] roses did with lilies interlace:
For of those words, the which that boaster threw,
She inly yet conceived great disgrace:
Whom whenas all the people such did view,
They shouted loud, and signs of gladness all did shew.

Then did he set her by that snowy one,
Like the true saint beside the image set;
Of both their beauties to make paragon
And trial, whether should the honour get.
Straightway, so soon as both together met,
The enchanted damsel vanished into nought:
Her snowy substance melted as with heat,
Ne of that goodly hue remained ought,
But the empty girdle which about her waist was wrought.

As when the daughter of Thaumantes fair[r]
Hath in a watery cloud displayed wide

---

[q] As if.
[r] Iris (the Rainbow) daughter of Thaumas (not Thaumantes).

> Her goodly bow, which paints the liquid air,
> That all men wonder at her colour's pride;
> All suddenly, ere one can look aside,
> The glorious picture vanisheth away,
> Ne any token doth thereof abide:
> So did this lady's goodly form decay,
> And into nothing go, ere one could it bewray.

While all are transfixed with astonishment, and Braggadoccio in particular stands "like a lifeless corse immoveable," Artegal taking up the golden belt, Florimel's own girdle, presents it to her, and she puts it about her tender waist, which, in evidence of her perfect purity, it perfectly fits. Another claimant upon Braggadoccio's borrowed plumes now comes forward, our old friend Sir Guyon, the champion of Temperance, the appropriation of whose horse by the losel was, it will be remembered, the exploit which first introduced him to our notice, in the Third Canto of the Second Book. It is the same upon which he is still mounted; and Guyon, seizing with one hand on the golden bit, with the other draws his sword and is going to kill the thief at once. He is however held back; and

> Thereof great hurly burly moved was
> Throughout the hall for that same warlike horse;

that is to say, apparently, there is a general desire among the knights to get possession of the noble animal, as well as a strong disposition to retain him on the part of Braggadoccio. As, however, that boasting coward will not accept Guyon's challenge to try his right in arms, Artegal asks Guyon if he can mention any private mark about the horse by which he knows him to be his.

> "If that," said Guyon, "may you satisfy,
> Within his mouth a black spot doth appear,
> Shaped like a horse's shoe, who list to seek it there."

The first that attempts to look into his mouth the horse settles by such a kick in the ribs that he never speaks more; another, who, with more caution, takes hold of him "by the bright embroidered headstall," he rids himself of as effectually by biting him through the shoulder-bone. Nor will he allow any one to approach him till Guyon himself speaks to him, and calls him by his name, Brigadore; as soon as he hears that well-known voice he stands as still as a stake,

> And, whenas he him named, for joy he brake
> His bands, and followed him with gladful glee,
> And frisked, and flung aloft, and louted low on knee.

Artegal now pronounces judgment; the steed is made over to Sir Guyon, arrayed in golden saddle as he stands; and Braggadoccio is commanded to be gone, and " fare on foot till he an horse have gained." But the proud boaster still reclaims with foul and insolent language against Artegal's decision. The latter is so incensed that he thrice lays his hand on his sword to kill him, and is only prevented by the interference of Guyon. Talus, however, takes him up by the back, and, carrying him forth, inflicts on him a suitable chastisement;—

> First he his beard did shave, and foully shent;[s]
> Then from him reft his shield, and it renversed,
> And blotted out his arms with falsehood blent;
> And himself baffled,[t] and his arms unhersed;[u]
> And broke his sword in twain, and all his armour spersed.[v]

Trompart too, although he has taken to his heels, the inevitable iron man catches, and gives him a whipping. And " now," says the poet, concluding the Canto,

> —— when these counterfeits were thus uncased
> Out of the foreside of their forgery,
> And in the sight of all men clean disgraced,
> All gan to jest and gibe full merrily
> At the remembrance of their knavery:
> Ladies can laugh[w] at ladies, knights at knights,
> To think with how great vaunt of bravery
> He them abused through his subtile sleights,
> And what a glorious shew he made in all their sights.

---

[s] Disfigured. [t] Disgraced.
[u] Took down from the place where they hung.
[v] Dispersed, scattered. [w] Laughed.

There leave we them in pleasure and repast,
Spending their joyous days and gladful nights,
And taking usury of time forepast,
With all dear delices and rare delights,
Fit for such ladies and such lovely knights:
And turn we here to this fair furrow's end
Our weary yokes, to gather fresher sprites,
That, whenas time to Artegal shall tend,
We on his first adventure may him forward send.

Canto IV. (51 stanzas).—The history of Artegal is now resumed as follows:—

Whoso upon himself will take the skill
True justice unto people to divide,
Had need have mighty hands for to fulfil
That which he doth with righteous doom decide,
And for to maister wrong and puissant pride:
For vain it is to deem[x] of things aright,
And makes wrong-doers justice to deride,
Unless it be performed with dreadless might:
For Power is the right hand of Justice truly hight.

Therefore whilome to knights of great emprise
The charge of justice given was in trust,
That they might execute her judgments wise,
And with their might beat down licentious lust,[y]
Which proudly did impugn her sentence just
Whereof no braver precedent this day
Remains on earth, preserved from iron rust
Of rude oblivion and long time's decay.
Than this of Artegal, which here we have to say.

Leaving the Castle of the Strond, accompanied as before only by "that great iron groom," Artegal as he passes along the sea shore comes upon two comely squires on the point of engaging with one another in fight, apparently for a strong iron-bound coffer,—much injured either from having been tossed about in the sea, or brought from some far country,—which stands before them; while by them are two seemly damsels striving with all earnestness to pacify them, sometimes with

---

[x] Pass judgment upon.   [y] Wilfulness.

entreaty, sometimes with threats. To Artegal's inquiries the elder, Bracidas, informs him, that they are two brethren between whom their father, Milesio, had at his death made an equal partition of his lands, leaving to each one of the two islands lying in sight, which were then of equal size; but that the sea had since carried away the greater part of his island, and added it to the other belonging to his younger brother Amidas; that at first, moreover, he himself loved the maid standing furthest off, the fair Philtra, or Philtera, with whom he would have got a goodly fortune, while Amidas loved the other called Lucy, who had little dower except her beauty and her virtue; but now, since the diminution of his lands, Philtra had gone over to his brother, who on his part had taken her for his love and left Lucy. Upon this that unhappy maid had in her despair thrown herself into the sea; but, the desire of life, or dread of death, reviving in her as she was tossed about by the waves, she had there caught hold of the chest now standing before them, and she and it had been cast ashore together upon the smaller island, where he, Bracidas, had found her, and saved her from perishing. In return she had bestowed upon him all she had to give, the chest and herself—"both goodly portions, but of both the better she," although the chest, too, upon being examined was found to contain a large amount of treasure. Now, however, the whole was claimed by Philtra and her husband, on the pretence that it was property of her's which had been lost at sea. "Whether it be so or no," concludes Bracidas, "I cannot say;"—

"But, whether it indeed be so or no,
This do I say, that whatso good or ill
Or God, or fortune, unto me did throw
(Not wronging any other by my will,)
I hold mine own, and so will hold it still.
And though my land he first did win away,
And then my love, (though now it little skill,[z])
Yet my good luck he shall not likewise prey[a];
But I will it defend whilst ever that I may."

---

[z] Matter.   [a] Make prey of.

All the rejoinder that Amidas makes is merely, that the
money can certainly be proved to be part of the estate of
Phil*'a, and that therefore it ought to be given up to her
without more ado. Confident, however, as each is in the
justice of his own view of the matter, they agree to leave
Artegal to decide between them, and, as a pledge that
they will submit to the judgment he shall pronounce,
they both place their swords under his foot.

> Then Artegal thus to the younger said;
> "Now tell me, Amidas, if that ye may,
> Your brother's land the which the sea hath laid
> Unto your part, and plucked from his away,
> By what good right do you withhold this day?"
> "What other right," quoth he, "should you esteem,
> But that the sea it to my share did lay?"
> "Your right is good," said he, "and so I deem
> That what the sea unto you sent your own should seem."
>
> Then turning to the elder, thus he said:
> "Now, Bracidas, let this likewise be shown;
> Your brother's treasure, which from him is strayed,
> Being the dowry of his wife well known,
> By what right do you claim to be your own?"
> "What other right," quoth he, "should you esteem,
> But that the sea hath it unto me thrown?"
> "Your right is good," said he, "and so I deem
> That what the sea unto you sent your own should seem.
>
> "For equal right in equal things doth stand:
> For what the mighty sea hath once possessed,
> And plucked quite from all possessor's hand,
> Whether by rage of waves that never rest,
> Or else by wrack that wretches hath distressed,
> He may dispose by his imperial might,
> As thing at random left, to whom he list.
> So, Amidas, the land was yours first hight;
> And so the treasure yours is, Bracidas, by right."

Bracidas and Lucy immediately seize on the treasure,
and, though Amidas and Philtra do not profess to approve
of the sentence, they do not dispute it.

> So was their discord by this doom appeased,
> And each one had his right.

Artegal then departs on his way, "to follow his old quest."

As he and Talus are travelling along they see at a distance a great rout, or throng, of people, whom, upon coming up to them, they find to their surprise to be a troop of women, all clad in armour and with weapons in their hands. In the midst of them is a knight, with both his hands tied behind him, and a halter about his neck, whom they are evidently dragging along to the gallows; his head is bare, but his face is covered, and he is groaning inwardly in bitter vexation and shame "that he of women's hands so base a death should die;" while they, "like tyrants merciless," are taunting and reviling him, and triumphing over his misery. When Artegal comes up, they begin to swarm about him, thinking to get him also into their power. He is ashamed himself "on womankind his mighty hand to shend," or dishonour; but, having drawn back, he sends Talus among them, who "with few souces of his iron flail," disperses them in a moment. When the captive knight is brought to Artegal, he immediately recognises him as Sir Turpin, or Terpin. The account that Terpin gives of himself is, that, having heard of a defiance lately published against all knights of the order of Maidenhead by Radigund, the proud Queen of the Amazons,—infuriated, it was said, by her hatred to Bellodant the Bold, who had rejected her love,—he had encountered her in fight, and, having been overcome, was, when he was rescued by Artegal, about to be put to death because he would not quietly submit to the degrading life she imposed upon whosoever thus fell into her power:—

"For all those knights, the which by force or guile
She doth subdue, she foully doth entreat:
First, she doth them of warlike arms despoil,
And clothe in women's weeds; and then with threat
Doth them compel to work to earn their meat,
To spin, to card, to sew, to wash, to wring;
Ne doth she give them other thing to eat
But bread and water or like feeble thing;
Them to disable from revenge adventuring.

But, if through stout disdain of manly mind
Any her proud observance will withstand

> Upon that gibbet, which is there behind,
> She causeth them be hanged up out of hand."

Sir Artegal, on hearing all this, of course burns to avenge the cause of the noble order to which he belongs; and Terpin forthwith conducts him to the residence of the Amazonian queen, which is not more than a mile or two distant;

> A goodly city and a mighty one,
> The which, of her own name, she called Radegone.

Warned by the watchmen, the people run to arms, swarming in clusters like bees; and ere long the queen herself, "half like a man," comes forth among the warlike multitude and proceeds to arrange the lines. The knights beat a peal upon the gates, demanding entrance, and to the contemptuous refusal of the porter, who laughs at the presumption of three individuals attempting to storm a populous city, they reply with many threats, if they win the place, "to tear his flesh in pieces for his sins;" till provoked by their bold words Queen Radigund orders the gates to be unbarred. They press forward, but are immediately staid by a shower of arrows, their numerous enemies at the same time rushing upon them from all sides and heaping strokes upon them with theirs words. In the furious fight that ensues, Radigund, seeing Terpin, inspired by revenge, doing powerful execution among her maids, flies at him like a lioness, and, dealing him a tremendous blow on his headpiece, strikes him senseless to the earth.

> Soon as she saw him on the ground to grovel,
> She lightly to him leapt; and, in his neck
> Her proud foot setting, at his head did level,
> Weening at once her wrath on him to wreak,
> And his contempt, that did her judgment break:
> As when a bear hath seized her cruel claws
> Upon the carcase of some beast too weak
> Proudly stands over, and awhile doth pause
> To hear the piteous beast pleading her plaintive cause.

But now Artegal, leaving the bloody slaughter in which he swims, runs to save his friend:—

There her assailing fiercely fresh he raught her
Such an huge stroke, that it of sense distraught her
And, had she not it warded warily,
It had deprived her mother of a daughter:
Nathless for all the power she did apply
It made her stagger oft, and stare with ghastly eye;

Like to an eagle, in his kingly pride
Soaring through his wide empire of the air,
To weather his broad sails, by chance hath spied
A goshawk, which hath seized for her share
Upon some fowl, that should her feast prepare,[b]
With dreadful force he flies at her belive[c]
That with his sonce, which none enduren dare,
Her from the quarry he away doth drive,
And from her griping pounce the greedy[d] prey doth rive.

She soon, nevertheless, recovers her senses, and, frantic with rage and mortified pride, eagerly seeks to renew the encounter; her maids, however, flock about her, and bear her off before she and Artegal can meet again. But among the rest the fight lasts till the evening;

And every while that mighty iron man,
With his strange weapon, never wont[e] in war,
Them sorely vexed, and coursed, and over-ran,
And broke their bows, and did their shooting mar,
That none of all the many once did darre[f]
Him to assault nor once approach him nigh;
But like a sort[g] of sheep dispersed far,
For dread of their devouring enemy,
Through all the fields and valleys did before him fly.

When it becomes dark, Radigund with sound of trumpet recals her troops within the walls; and Artegal, pitching his pavilion before the city-gate, prepares to rest therein along with Terpin, Talus, as he is wont, keeping watch. But Radigund now determines to offer to decide the quarrel in her own person in single combat with the

[b] To make a feast for her.
[c] Forthwith. [d] Greedily caught.
[e] Used. [f] Dare. [g] Flock.

Fairy Knight; and, calling to her a trusty maid named Clarin, charges her with a message to that effect. "But," she adds,

> ———"conditions do to him propound;
> That, if I vanquish him, he shall obey
> My law, and ever to my lore be bound;
> And so will I, if me he vanquish may;
> Whatever he shall like to do or say:
> Go straight, and take with thee to witness it
> Six of thy fellows of the best array,
> And bear with you both wine and junkets fit,
> And bid him eat: henceforth he oft shall hungry sit."

The damsel accordingly proceeds to the gate, and there sounds a trumpet from the wall, which immediately brings Talus forth from the tent, "to weeten what that trumpet's sounding meant." She informs the iron man that she would speak with his lord; and, being conducted, with her six companions to Artegal, she delivers her message;

> Which he accepting, well as he could weet,[h]
> Them fairly entertained with courtsies meet,
> And gave them gifts and things of dear delight:
> So back again they homeward turned their feet;
> But Artegal himself to rest did dight,
> That he mote fresher be against the next day's fight.

Canto V. (57 stanzas).—As soon as it is dawn the Knight and the Amazonian Queen both proceed to array themselves for the coming fight; the latter,

> All in a camis[i] light of purple silk
> Woven upon with silver, subtly wrought,
> And quilted upon satin white as milk;
> Trailed with ribands diversly distraught,
> Like as the workman had their courses taught;
> Which was short tucked for light motion
> Up to her ham; but, when she list, it raught
> Down to her lowest heel, and thereupon
> She wore for her defence a mailed habergeon.

---

[h] As he well knew how.   [i] Thin gown.

> And on her legs she painted buskins wore,
> Basted[k] with bands of gold on every side,
> And mails between, and laced close afore;
> Upon her thigh her scymitar was tied
> With an embroidered belt of mickle pride;
> And on her shoulder hung her shield, bedecked
> Upon the boss with stones that shined wide,
> As the fair moon in her most full aspect;
> That to the moon it mote be like in each respect.

Thus attired, she issues from the city gate, in the midst of a numerous guard of damsels,

> Playing on shalms and trumpets, that from hence
> Their sound did reach unto the heavens' height,

and retires to a rich pavilion prepared for her reception. Artegal first enters the lists; and now, in the midst of a vast expecting multitude, the trumpets sound, and the combat begins. "With bitter strokes it both began and ended." Radigund at first rushes on with furious rage; but she is received by Artegal with a firmness upon which she can make no impression, and, as soon as her strength begins somewhat to abate, he becomes the assailant.

> Like as a smith that to his cunning feat
> The stubborn metal seeketh to subdue,
> Soon as he feels it mollified with heat,
> With his great iron sledge doth strongly on it beat;
>
> So did Sir Artegal upon her lay,
> As if she had an iron anvil been,
> That flakes of fire, bright as the sunny ray,
> Out of her steely arms were flashing seen,
> That all on fire ye would her surely ween.

With a blow of his trenchant blade he slices off the half of her shield; and she with her sharp scymitar wounds him in the thigh. Another of his puissant strokes shatters the remainder of her shield to pieces; and then with a blow upon her helmet he fells her to the ground. But when he has unlaced her helmet, intending to cut

[k] Sewed slightly.

off her head, such a miracle of nature's fairest workmanship blazes out upon him from her face, bathed as it is in blood and sweat—

> Like as the moon, in foggy winter's night,
> Doth seem to be herself, though darkened be her light—

that his astonished heart is pierced with pity, and he throws his sword from him,

> Cursing his hand that had that visage marred:
> No hand so cruel, nor no heart so hard,
> But ruth of beauty will it mollify.

Meanwhile the lady, recovering from her swoon, suddenly starts up, and, seeing her adversary weaponless, not very generously assails him again as fiercely as ever. He defends himself as well as he can from her pitiless storm of blows, and also earnestly entreats her to discontinue her fury; but, as a puttock, or kite, that may have seen a gentle falcon sitting on a hill with one of its wings broken, will attack and persist in annoying it, so does she continue to lay on for all that he can do or say. At last, as he has no means of either returning or staying her strokes, nothing is left for him but to deliver up his shield, and yield himself to her mercy. Thus is he condemned by doom of his own mouth to be her thrall; having by abandoning his sword lost the victory he at first had won. Radigund merely strikes him with the flat of her sword, in sign of his vassalage, while the more unfortunate Terpin is at once attached and swung up on the gallows, from which he had so lately escaped in vain.

> But, when they thought on Talus hands to lay,
> He with his iron flail amongst them thundered,
> That they were fain to let him scape away,
> Glad from his company to be so sundered;
> Whose presence all their troops so much encumbered,
> That the heaps of those which he did wound and slay,
> Besides the rest dismayed, might not be numbered:
> Yet all that while he would not once essay
> To rescue his own lord, but thought it just to obey.

Then the Amazon, taking Artegal, causes him to be stripped of all his knightly ornaments, and to be shamefully arrayed instead in woman's weeds, with a white apron before him in place of "curiets and bases," or cuirasses and cuisses. Then she brings him into "a long large chamber," where she makes his arms be suspended aloft, and breaks his sword, and where he sees all around him

> Many brave knights whose names right well he knew,
> There bound to obey that Amazon's proud law,
> Spinning and carding all in comely rew,[1]
> That his big heart loathed so uncomely view:
> But they were forced, through penury and pine,
> To do those works to them appointed due:
> For nought was given them to sup or dine,
> But what their hands could earn by twisting linen twine.

The noble Artegal is placed the lowest of all, and a distaff is given him on which to spin flax and tow;

> A sordid office for a mind so brave:
> So hard it is to be a woman's slave!

Yet, having plighted his faith to obey his conqueror as a vassal, he submits. As may be expected, the poet does not forget to compare him to Hercules, when, "for Iola's sake," as he has it—putting Iola, or Iole, by mistake for Omphale—he had exchanged his club for a distaff, and his lion's skin for a pall of gold;

> In which, forgetting wars, he only joyed
> In combats of sweet love, and with his mistress toyed.

Such, it is added, is the cruelty of womankind whenever they shake off the wise law of nature which binds them "to obey the hests of man's well-ruling hand;"

> For virtuous women wisely understand,
> That they were born to base humility,
> Unless the heavens them lift to lawful sovereignty—

the last line being, of course, a salvo to prevent offence being taken by Elizabeth.

Artegal long remains thus in subjection to the proud

---

[1] Row.

queen; meanwhile her wandering fancy is taken captive by her captive; for a long time her love struggles with her pride; but at last she secretly calls to her her most trusted handmaid, Clarinda (the same who has already been mentioned as Clarin), and, after for a moment turning away her head,

> ——————————— as half abashed,
> To hide the blush which in her visage rose
> And through her eyes like sudden lightning flashed,
> Decking her cheek with a vermilion rose,

composes her countenance, and confesses that she has that to disclose in regard to which through dread of shame she would fain be silent. Clarinda urges her to speak with soothing, encouraging words:—

> Say on, my sovereign lady, and be bold:
> Doth not your handmaid's life at your foot lie?

and then she tells her all; and engages her to endeavour, by any way she can devise, to win Artegal to feelings answering to her own, yet without discovering to him that he is himself loved. That her confidante may the better bring this to pass, she gives her a ring, which will be, she tells her, a warrant to old Eumenias, the keeper of the place where Artegal is confined, to afford her free passage in and out whenever she chooses. And "Go now," she says,

> ——— Clarinda, well thy wits advise,
> And all thy forces gather unto thee,
> Armies of lovely looks, and speeches wise,
> With which thou canst even Jove himself to love entise.

Clarinda accordingly proceeds with all zeal to execute her delicate commission, beginning by trying, by all the means she may, "to curry favour with the elfin knight, her lady's best beloved." After some time she one day takes an opportunity of suggesting to him that there is a way in which he might very probably succeed in rescuing himself from his unhappy state:—why should he not try what he can do to move Radigund by fair entreaty to give him his liberty? Although she has spent her days in war, yet she was not born of bears and tigers; nor, although she scorn all love of men, is she for that more secure than others of her sex against the all-conquering power. Excited by the thoughts she has put into his head, Artegal admits that as "a queen, and come of queenly kind," Radigund is abundantly worthy to be sued unto, especially by one whose life is in her hands by right as well as in fact; and he adds that if by Clarinda's good offices he could procure the necessary means he certainly would make the attempt.

> She feeling him thus bite upon the bait,
> Yet, doubting lest his hold was but unsound
> And not well fastened, would not strike him straight,
> But drew him on with hope, fit leisure to await.

Poor Clarinda, however, too heedless herself of the hook, ere long loses her own footing, and, slipping into the water, is caught with the bait she lays for another; wounded "with her deceit's own dart," the foolish maid finds that she has herself fallen in love with Artegal. She does not dare to reveal her affection either to himself or any other; but when her mistress one day sends for her, and asks her what tidings she has of good success, she pretends that she has found the Fairy Knight quite obstinate and stern, and determined rather to die than entertain a thought of love for his enemy: "his body was her thrall, his heart was freely placed,"—that was his immoveable determination.

> Which when the cruel Amazon perceived,
> She gan to storm, and rage, and rend her gall,
> For very fell despite, which she conceived,
> To be so scorned of a base-born thrall,
> Whose life did lie in her least eye-lid's fall.

Of that life she vows, with many a menacing curse, he shall soon be deprived. When her heat is over, however, she sees matters in another light—and desires Clarinda to try the stubborn knight again with more various and more searching temptations:—

> "Say and do all that may thereto prevail;
> Leave nought unpromised that may him persuade,

> Life, freedom, grace, and gifts of great avail,
> With which the gods themselves are milder made:
> Thereto add art, even women's witty trade,
> The art of mighty words that men can charm;
> With which in case thou canst him not invade,
> Let him feel hardness of thy heavy arm:
> Who will not stoop with good shall be made stoop with harm.
>
> "Some of his diet do from him withdraw,
> For I him find to be too proudly fed:
> Give him more labour, and with straiter law,
> That he with work may be forwearied:
> Let him lodge hard, and lie in strawen bed,
> That may pull down the courage of his pride;
> And lay upon him, for his greater dread,
> Cold iron chains with which let him be tied;
> And let whatever he desires be him denied."

Thus charged, the false maiden returns to the prison.

> There all her subtile nets she did unfold,
> And all the engines of her wit display;

so that she deceived and betrayed at once her lady, the knight, and herself. Radigund she beguiles, even as a wicked nurse, who, pretending to feed her child out of her mouth, swallows what she receives therein herself, and leaves the child unnourished; for she pretends to Artegal that she has made earnest suit for his freedom in vain; that, on the contrary, her mistress's orders are that she shall augment his sufferings and load him with iron fetters; all which, nevertheless, she forbears to do for the love she bears him—"so praying him to accept her service evermore." She even promises that, "in case she might find favour in his eye," she will devise some way of setting him at liberty. Artegal, tempted by this prospect, warmly thanks her for her courtesy,

> And, with fair words, fit for the time and place,
> To feed the humour of her malady,

promises that, if she will indeed do for him what she says, he will do what he can to merit such grace. Yet for all this, never, we are assured, does he mean in his noble mind "to his own absent love to be untrue." Neither does Clarinda for her part mean ever to procure him his liberty, but rather to fix him in faster bondage. Yet in the meantime she somewhat amends his scanty fare, and also lessens his work, in the hope that his love may thereby grow. And thus he long remains in the hands of the mistress and the maid—" of both beloved well, but little friended ;" till at last his deliverance is achieved by his own Britomart. But that will be best related in another Canto.

Canto VI. (40 stanzas).—Some, the poet begins by observing, will, he knows, deem it great weakness in Artegal to have so yielded himself up "to the insolent command of women's will;" but let the man who so judges take good heed that he himself stand steadfast;

> For never yet was wight so well aware,
> But he at first or last was trapped in women's snare.

Yet Artegal amid all the temptations to which he was exposed still preserved his loyalty to his own love ;

> Whose character in the adamantine mould
> Of his true heart so firmly was engraved,
> That no new love's impression ever could
> Bereave it thence.

Not quite sure of this, however, does Britomart feel when, after she has been long expecting his return, the account of what has befallen him is brought to her by Talus—" brought in untimely hour, ere it was sought." She has been already tormenting herself with various apprehensions; sometimes she dreaded that he had been overtaken by some misfortune or treachery ;

> But most she did her troubled mind molest,
> And secretly afflict with jealous fear,
> Lest some new love had him from her possessed ;
> Yet loth she was, since she no ill did hear,
> To think of him so ill ; yet could she not forbear.

Hearing nothing of him long after the utmost date assigned

for his return, she has at last almost determined to set out in quest of him:—

> Now she devised, amongst the warlike rout
> Of errant knights, to seek her errant knight;
> And then again resolved to hunt him out
> Amongst loose ladies lapped in delight:
> And then both knights envied, and ladies eke did spite.

At last one day as she is standing at a window that opens to the west, in which direction Artegal had gone, and sending

> ——— her winged thoughts more swift than wind
> To bear unto her love the message of her mind,

after looking long she at last espies one coming towards her in haste:—

> Well weened she then, ere she him plain descried,
> That it was one sent from her love indeed.

When he approaches, she sees that it is Talus. With her heart filled with hope and dread, she runs forth.

> Even in the door him meeting, she begun;
> "And where is he thy lord, and how far hence?
> Declare at once: and hath he lost or won?"

Talus, who, although without the sense of sorrow, yet with the consciousness of the ill tidings he brings, inly chills and quakes, stands silent. She desires him to be bold, and tell her what has happened, be it good or evil. Has his lord, she asks, been vanquished by his tyrant enemy?

> "Not by that tyrant, his intended foe;
> But by a tyranness," he then replied,
> "That him captived hath in hapless woe."
> "Cease thou, bad newsman; badly dost thou hide
> Thy maister's shame, in harlot's bondage tied:
> The rest myself too readily can spell."

And then she turns from him in rage, suffering him to say no more, and, shutting herself up in her chamber, she is there torn by a tempest of contending emotions. She blames and bitterly regrets her own facility in yielding herself so lightly to a stranger's love—one of whose life and manners she knew nothing. Sometimes in her rage she burns to blot out that stain upon her honour by compelling him to fight with her, and so finding for herself an honourable death.

> A while[m] she walked, and chafed; a while she threw
> Herself upon her bed, and did lament:
> Yet did she not lament with loud alew,[n]
> As women wont, but with deep sighs and singulfs[o] few.

> Like as a wayward child, whose sounder sleep
> Is broken with some fearful dream's afright,
> With froward will doth set himself to weep,
> Ne can be stilled for all his nurse's might,
> But kicks, and squalls, and shrieks for fell despite;
> Now scratching her, and her loose locks misusing,
> Now seeking darkness, and now seeking light,
> Then craving suck, and then the suck refusing:
> Such was this lady's fit in her love's fond accusing.

At length, however, she sends for Talus again, and asks him in what circumstances Artegal was, how he was employed, "and whether he did woo, or whether he were wooed." "Ah wellaway!" replies the iron man; "he is not the while in state to woo;" and then he explains to her that he "lies in wretched thraldom, weak and wan," although indeed compelled thereunto not by strong hand but by "his own doom, that none can now undo." Is not this, she rejoins, the very thing she has asserted? Talus is in a compact with his lord to hide the truth from her and to deceive her. On this Talus relates the whole story of Artegal's captivity, as it has already been told in the two last Cantos. Agitated with wrath and grief, we are told, she heard him to the end; then she lost not another moment, or answered a word;

> But straight herself did dight, and armour don,
> And mounting to her steed bade Talus guide her on.

Forthwith, accordingly, they set out together:

---

[m] One while.   [n] Halloo, howling.   [o] Sobs.

> Sadly she rode and never word did say
> Nor good nor bad, ne ever looked aside,
> But still right down ; and in her thought did hide
> The fellness of her heart, right fully bent
> To fierce avengement of that woman's pride,
> Which had her lord in her base prison pent,
> And so great honour with so foul reproach had blent.

Thus proceeding on her way, she meets toward the eventide

> A knight, that softly paced on the plain,
> As if himself to solace he were fain :
> Well shot in years he seemed, and rather bent
> To peace than needless trouble to constrain ;
> As well by view of that his vestiment,
> As by his modest semblant, that no evil meant.

He gently salutes Britomart, whose sex, of course, he does not suspect ; and, possessed as her mind is by one only thought, she is yet not so discourteous as to refuse to enter into talk with him. At length he invites her to take up her lodging with him for the night, which she agrees to do.

> Not far away, but little wide by west,
> His dwelling was, to which he him addressed ;
> Where soon arriving they received were
> In seemly wise, as them beseemed best ;
> For he their host them goodly well did cheer,
> And talked of pleasant things the night away to wear.

When the time of rest arrives Britomart is conducted to a chamber, where grooms are awaiting to undress her ; but she declines to doff either garments or armour, excusing herself by a vow she has made never to do so till she has achieved her revenge on her foe. All night she lies,

> Restless, recomfortless, with heart deep grieved,
> Not suffering the least twinkling sleep to start
> Into her eye, which the heart mote have relieved ;
> But if the least appeared, her eyes she straight reprieved.[p]

---

[p] Reproved.

> "Ye guilty eyes," said she, "the which with guile
> My heart at first betrayed, will ye betray
> My life now too, for which a little while
> Ye will not watch? false watches, wellaway!
> I wote when ye did watch both night and day
> Unto your loss; and now needs will ye sleep?
> Now ye have made my heart to wake alway,
> Now will ye sleep? ah! wake, and rather weep
> To think of your night's want, that should ye waking keep."

And thus she spends the weary hours, sometimes sitting up, sometimes walking softly about the room, while Talus also, watching without the door, never suffers sleep "to seize his eyelids sad." Suddenly, however,

> What time the native bellman of the night,
> The bird that warned Peter of his fall,
> First rings his silver bell to each sleepy wight,
> That should their minds up to devotion call,

she hears a noise below, and all at once the bed on which it was intended she should lie is let down through a trap-door into a lower apartment, after which the opening is again closed. Alarmed by this treachery she nevertheless stirs not nor calls out. Soon after she hears the sound of armed men approaching, on which she quickly seizes her sword and shield. Two knights all ready for fight now present themselves at the chamber door, and at their heels many more, "a rascal rout, with weapons rudely dight." As soon as Talus sees them by the glimmering light (his ear does not appear to have been so acute as that of his mistress, or indeed to have been of ordinary sharpness), he starts up, with his "thresher" ready for action in his hand; they press about him and let drive at him from all sides;

> But, soon as he began to lay about
> With his rude iron flail, they gan to fly,
> Both armed knights, and eke unarmed rout.

Yet he pursues them, and knocks them down wherever he can find them in the dark, so that they lie in all directions like scattered sheep.

The meaning of all this is now explained. The "goodman of the house" is named Dolon—"a man of subtile wit and wicked mind," who in his youth had been a knight and borne arms, but, never valorous, had worked always by sly shifts and wiles, and brought many noble knights to shame by treason and treachery. He had three sons, all of dispositions like his own, of whom the eldest was that Guizor, the groom or porter of the Saracen Pollente, lord of the perilous bridge, who had been put out of existence with so little ceremony by Artegal, when he came up and made his demand for the customary passage penny, as related in the Second Canto of this Book. [Upton, we may here mention by the bye, hazards a conjecture that Pollente with his trapfalls may be designed for Charles IX. of France, infamous for the treacherous massacre of the Protestants on the day of St. Bartholomew, and that Guizor, his "groom of evil guise," may be the great head of the Popish party, the Duke of Guise]. Ever since the loss of his son, Dolon has been devising how to be avenged; and Britomart owes the danger she has just encountered to her having been mistaken by him for Artegal, principally from her being accompanied by "that iron page."

As soon as the day breaks she leaves her chamber with the intention of punishing Dolon as he deserves; but both sire and sons have fled. The sons, it is to be supposed, were the two armed knights, who headed the "rascal rout" dispersed by Talus. So, taking her steed "and thereon mounting light," she proceeds on her journey. But she has not "rid the mountenance of a flight," that is, the amount or length of an arrow-flight, when she sees the two brothers before her occupying the same long narrow bridge on which Artegal had fought with Pollente. They receive her with insult and defiance, accusing her of the murder of Guizor by guile, and affirming that she is no knight, but a recreant false traitor, that with loan of arms had knighthood stolen. Their words are strange and unintelligible to her, but, heeding them not, she continues to ride forward. Talus wishes to go before her to prepare the way, and scare those two losels; but that she will not allow: in her wrath at the proposal, we are told,

> The glancing sparkles through her beaver glared,
> And from her eyes did flash out fiery light,
> Like coals that through a silver censer sparkled bright.

Spurring on, she bears one of the brothers on her spear before her to the further end of the bridge; the other, as she passes, she brushes over the side into the river, where he drinks " his deadly last:"—

> As when the flashing levin ⁱ haps to light
> Upon two stubborn oaks, which stand so near
> That way betwixt them none appears in sight;
> The engine, fiercely flying forth, doth tear
> The one from the earth, and through the air doth bear;
> The other it with force doth overthrow
> Upon one side, and from his roots doth rear:
> So did the championess these two there strow,
> And to their sire their carcases left to bestow.

Canto VII. (45 stanzas).—" Nought is on earth," observes the poet, in beginning this new Canto,

> ——————————— more sacred or divine
> That gods and men do equally adore,
> Than this same virtue that doth right define:

the very heavens themselves are ruled by it;

> Well therefore did the antique world invent
> That Justice was a god of sovereign grace,
> And altars unto him and temples lent,
> And heavenly honours in the highest place;
> Calling him great Osiris, of the race
> Of the old Ægyptian kings that whilome were;
> With feigned colours shading a true case;
> For that Osiris, whilst he lived here,
> The justest man alive and truest did appear.

The wife of Osiris was Isis, and her also they made a goddess of great power and sovereignty, shadowing forth in her person that part of Justice called Equity, which is the thing to be now here treated of.

ⁱ Lightning.

Britomart, having come to the Temple of Isis, enters in with great humility by herself, for Talus may not be admitted; and there she will abide all the night:—

> There she received was in goodly wise
> Of many priests, which duly did attend
> Upon the rites and daily sacrifice,
> All clad in linen robes with silver hemmed;
> And on their heads with long locks comely kemd [r]
> They wore rich mitres shaped like the moon,
> To show that Isis doth the moon portend;
> Like as Osiris signifies the sun:
> For that they both like race in equal justice run.
>
> The championess them greeting, as she could, [s]
> Was thence by them into the temple led;
> Whose goodly building when she did behold
> Borne upon stately pillars, all bespread
> With shining gold, and arched over head,
> She wondered at the workman's passing skill,
> Whose like before she never saw nor read;
> And thereupon long while stood gazing still,
> But thought that she thereon could never gaze her fill.
>
> Thenceforth unto the idol they her brought;
> The which was framed all of silver fine,
> So well as could with cunning hand be wrought,
> And clothed all in garments made of line, [t]
> Hemmed all about with fringe of silver twine:
> Upon her head she wore a crown of gold;
> To show that she had power in things divine:
> And at her feet a crocodile was rolled,
> That with her wreathed tail her middle did enfold.
>
> One foot was set upon the crocodile,
> And on the ground the other fast did stand;
> So meaning to suppress both forged guile
> And open force: and in her other hand
> She stretched forth a long white slender wand.
> Such was the goddess: whom when Britomart
> Had long beheld, herself upon the land [u]

---

[r] Combed.
[s] As she well knew how to do.
[t] Linen.
[u] Ground.

She did prostrate, and with right humble heart
Unto herself her silent prayers did impart.

To which the idol as it were inclining
Her wand did move with amiable look,
By outward show her inward sense designing:
Who, well perceiving how her wand she shook,
It as a token of good fortune took.

But it now grows dark; whereupon she unlaces her helmet, and lays herself down to slumber by the altar's side, for the priests here use no other beds but the lap of their mother earth, thereby enuring themselves to sufferance and mortification; being all besides bound by vows to stedfast chastity and continence:—

Therefore they mote not taste of fleshly food,
Ne feed on ought the which doth blood contain,
Ne drink of wine; for wine they say is blood,
Even the blood of giants, which were slain
By thundering Jove in the Phlegrean plain:
For which the Earth (as they the story tell)
Wroth with the gods, which to perpetual pain
Had damned her sons which gainst them did rebel,
With inward grief and malice did against them swell:

And of their vital blood, the which was shed
Into her pregnant bosom, forth she brought
The fruitful vine; whose liquor bloody red,
Having the minds of men with fury fraught,
Mote in them stir up old rebellious thought
To make new war against the gods again:
Such is the power of that same fruit, that nought
The fell contagion may thereof restrain,
Ne within reason's rule her madding mood contain.

There did the warlike maid herself repose,
Under the wings of Isis all that night;
And with sweet rest her heavy eyes did close,
After that long day's toil and weary plight:
Where, whilst her earthly parts with soft delight
Of senseless sleep did deeply drowned lie,
There did appear unto her heavenly sprite
A wondrous vision, which did close imply
The course of all her fortune and posterity.

> Her seemed, as she was doing sacrifice
> To Isis, decked with mitre on her head
> And linen stole after those priestes guise,
> All suddenly she saw transfigured
> Her linen stole to robe of scarlet red,
> And moon-like mitre to a crown of gold;
> That even she herself much wondered
> At such a change, and joyed to behold
> Herself adorned with gems and jewels manifold.

While she is thus wondering and happy, suddenly a tempest seems to fill the temple, blowing the holy fire all about the altar and strewing the embers on the ground, so that flames break out in many places, and both the temple and she herself are in danger of being set on fire and consumed.

> With that the crocodile, which sleeping lay
> Under the idol's feet in fearless bower,
> Seemed to awake in horrible dismay,
> As being troubled with that stormy stour;
> And gaping greedy wide did straight devour
> Both flames and tempest; with which growen great,
> And swollen with pride of his own peerless power,
> He gan to threaten her likewise to eat:
> But that the goddess with her rod him back did beat.

The sacred beast then turning all his pride to meekness and humility, seems to throw himself at her feet and to sue for grace and love; which she accepting, conceives by him and brings forth a lion, that speedily subdues all other beasts. With this she awakens in great terror, and

> — thereupon long while she musing lay,
> With thousand thoughts feeding her fantasy;
> Until she spied the lamp of lightsome day
> Up-lifted in the porch of heaven high:
> Then up she rose fraught with melancholy,
> And forth into the lower parts did pass,
> Whereas the priests she found full busily
> About their holy things for morrow mass;
> Whom she saluting fair, fair re-saluted was.

But they perceive by her looks that she is not well

either bodily or mentally; and, one of them, who appears to be the chief, expressing his fears that something ails her, she tells them what she had seen in her vision. The priest is overpowered with astonishment by what he hears; and, addressing her now no longer as "Sir Knight," but recognising her true sex, filled with heavenly fury, he breaks out:—

> "Magnific virgin, that in quaint disguise
> Of British arms dost mask thy royal blood,
> So to pursue a perilous emprise;
> How couldst thou ween, through that disguised hood
> To hide thy state from being understood?
> Can from the immortal gods ought hidden be?
> They do thy lineage, and thy lordly brood,
> They do thy sire lamenting sore for thee,
> They do thy love forlorn in women's thraldom see."

The crocodile, he goes on to declare, is her faithful lover—

> "Like to Osiris in all just endeavour;
> For that same crocodile Osiris is,
> That under Isis' feet doth sleep for ever."

The knight shall subdue all her enemies, and restore her to the just heritage of her father's crown; and after that she shall bear him a son, who shall be like the lordly lion in eminence and power. And "So," says the seer, ending his address,

> "So bless thee God, and give thee joyance of thy dream!"

Much relieved by what has been told her, Britomart, after presenting rich presents to the priests and royal gifts of gold and silver to their goddess, takes her leave, and, continuing her journey, rests nowhere again till she comes to the land of the Amazons. Pitching her pavilion without the gate, even as had been done by Artegal, she spends the night, as he also had done, under the secure guardianship of Talus; while the Amazons, whose queen has heard of her arrival not with the terror natural to a woman, but with the composure and joyous expectation of a warrior, keep watch and ward on their city walls. On the morrow as soon as it is dawn both ladies come forth to the encounter. Before they begin the Amazon proposes her usual condition, that her adversary shall become bound, if beaten, to serve and obey her in whatever she may command; but Britomart indignantly refuses to bind herself to any other terms than those prescribed by the laws of chivalry. The fight is a very furious one; they hack and hew at one another with no regard to the better uses for which the loveliness they are defacing and mangling was made, struggling together, and wasting one another's blood, like a tiger and lioness over a disputed prey; Britomart is severely wounded in the shoulder; but in return she smites Radigund so fiercely on the helmet that the weapon pierces to the very brain, and the Amazon falls prostrate; on which the wrathful Britoness, giving her no time to come to herself again, with one more stroke cuts off her head. On seeing this all her followers fly into the town; yet not so fast

> But that swift Talus did the foremost win;
> And, pressing through the preace[v] unto the gate,
> Pelmell with them at once did enter in:
> There then a piteous slaughter did begin;
> For all that ever came within his reach
> He with his iron flail did thresh so thin,
> That he no work at all left for the leach.

Even " the noble conqueress," when she follows him into the place, and sees the heaps of slaughtered carcases, is touched with pity, and desires him to slack his fury; otherwise, we are assured, he would not have left a soul alive. Then, inquiring for the prison in which her lord is confined, she angrily breaks open the door and enters. The sight of the disguised knights fills her noble heart with indignation and shame; and especially when she comes to her own love so disfigured and degraded she turns her head aside, unable to endure the hateful spectacle. Then every other feeling is swallowed up in pity, and, looking upon him with more wonder and asto-

[v] Press.

nishment than Penelope on her Ulysses when he came home to her so worn by his twenty years' wandering, that she did not know him,

> "Ah! my dear lord, what sight is this," quoth she,
> "What May-game hath misfortune made of you?
> Where is that dreadful manly look? where be
> Those mighty palms, the which ye wont to embrue
> In blood of kings, and great hosts to subdue?
> Could ought on earth so wondrous change have wrought
> As to have robbed you of that manly hue?
> Could so great courage stooped have to ought?
> Then farewell, fleshly force; I see thy pride is nought!"

Then bringing him without further delay into a chamber she makes him doff "those uncomely weeds," and array himself in other raiment and armour bright, of which abundance is found in the palace of the Amazonian queen.

> So there awhile they afterwards remained,
> Him to refresh, and her late wounds to heal:
> During which space she there as princess reigned;
> And, changing all that form of common-weal,
> The liberty of women did repeal,
> Which they had long usurped; and, them restoring
> To men's subjection, did true justice deal:
> That all they, as a goddess, her adoring,
> Her wisdom did admire, and hearkened to her loring.[w]

The captive knights she appoints all magistrates of the city, making them swear fealty to Artegal, and endowing each of them with "great living and large fee."

But Artegal must now set out again upon his original adventure; and Britomart, although his departure brings back her sorrow, is too tender of his honour and her own to oppose his going. For a space she remains where he has left her; but at last she too takes her departure from the city of the Amazons—in the hope that the change of air and place may "change her pain, and sorrow somewhat ease."

Canto VIII. (51 stanzas).—This new Canto opens with the following fine lines:—

---

[w] Teaching.

Nought under heaven so strongly doth allure
The sense of man, and all his mind possess,
As Beauty's lovely bait, that doth procure
Great warriors oft their rigour to repress,
And mighty hands forget their manliness;
Drawn with the power of an heart-robbing eye,
And wrapt in fetters of a golden tress,
That can with melting pleasance mollify
Their hardened hearts enured to blood and cruelty.

So whilome learned that mighty Jewish swain,
Each of whose locks did match a man in might,
To lay his spoils before his leman's train:
So also did that great Oetean knight
For his love's sake his lion's skin undight;
And so did warlike Antony neglect
The world's whole rule for Cleopatra's sight.
Such wondrous power hath women's fair aspect
To captive men, and make them all the world reject.

Yet can it not detain Artegal from proceeding on the enterprize to which he has devoted himself; but, leaving his love, fair Britomart, he rides forward, Talus only accompanying him.

So travelling, he chanced far off to heed
A damsel flying on a palfrey fast
Before two knights that after her did speed
With all their power, and her full fiercely chased
In hope to have her overhent[x] at last:
Yet fled she fast, and both them far outwent,
Carried with wings of fear, like fowl aghast,
With locks all loose, and raiment all to rent;
And ever as she rode her eye was backward bent.

Presently a third knight appears pursuing the other two, and, while he holds his spear in rest, or ready for attack, urges his horse to its utmost speed. He soon overtakes one of the two and forces him to turn round. Artegal, to whom the lady as soon as she sees him flies for protection, throws himself between her and the other; and on the encounter the stranger knight is pitched more

---

[x] Overtaken.

than two spears' length out of his saddle, and, falling on
his head, breaks his neck. Meanwhile his companion
has been despatched by the third knight; who, however,
as soon as he has achieved that good work, dashes forward in pursuit of the other pagan, but, meeting Artegal, at once attacks him instead, as if he cared not at
whom he ran. They have both broken their spears,
and then drawn their swords, when the lady runs up,
and, crying and tearing her hair, prevails on them to
desist by pointing out to them that their two foes, and
hers, lie both dead enough on the ground. The stranger
knight is Prince Arthur; and he and Artegal, when
they have raised their visors and beheld each other's
faces, are struck with reciprocal admiration and respect,
and exchange courteous apologies and pardons. The
lady, whose name turns out to be Samient, now explains
to them (for Arthur knows no more about her and the
two slain knights than Artegal does) that she serves a
queen residing at no great distance from where they
are—

 A princess of great power and majesty,
 Famous through all the world and honoured far and
  nigh—

a Maiden Queen, moreover, her name Mercilla. This
is plainly Queen Elizabeth. Among the many enemies
who envy and endeavour to disturb the felicity of her
realm, and to subvert her crown and dignity, Samient goes
on to relate, is her powerful neighbour, the Soldan (supposed to mean Philip King of Spain), who is continually
either bribing and seducing her good knights, or attacking and despoiling them if they loyally resist his allurements; nay, even plotting against and seeking to destroy
her sacred person; being stirred up to all this, it is said,
by his bad wife Adicia—by whom must, however, be
understood, as the name signifies, merely the principle
of Injustice as animating and instigating the hostility of
the Spanish king. Or perhaps the Roman Catholic religion and interest may be more especially indicated by
this female figure. Thinking it best for herself and her

kingdom to deal amicably with Adicia, Mercilla had sent Samient to her to negotiate a peace between them; but Adicia, disdaining all agreement, and setting at nought the rights and privileges which all times have accorded to ambassadors, not only received her message with the utmost scorn and contumely, but thrust her out of doors like a dog, and, finally, sent after her, to abuse and dishonour her, the two false knights from whom she has just been so providentially delivered. The allusion here is supposed to be to King Philip's detention of the deputies of the States of Holland when they came to him to complain of and to beg the redress of their grievances.

On hearing this relation, the prince and Artegal agree instantly to join in revenging the wrongs of Samient and her mistress on the Soldan and his lady; but, deeming it prudent not in such a case to despise the aid of tactics, or stratagem, they arrange that Artegal shall array himself in the armour of one of the dead knights, and, taking Samient with him to present her as his conquered prize to Adicia, find in this way admission into the Soldan's court. Accordingly, as soon as Adicia sees him from her window, she sends a page to conduct him, and he is admitted into the palace, where, however, he declines to allow himself to be disarmed. Presently comes a challenge to the Soldan from the prince, demanding "that damsel whom he held as wrongful prisoner."

> Wherewith the Soldan all with fury fraught,
> Swearing and banning most blasphemously,
> Commanded straight his armour to be brought;
> And, mounting straight upon a chariot high,
> (With iron wheels and hooks armed dreadfully,
> And drawn of cruel steeds which he had fed
> With flesh of men, whom through fell tyranny
> He slaughtered had, and ere they were half dead
> Their bodies to his beasts for provender did spread),
>
> So forth he came all in a coat of plate
> Burnished with bloody rust.

This description has been ingeniously interpreted as shadowing forth the famous Armada. "The Soldan," observes Upton, "is the King of Spain: his *swearing and banning most blasphemously* may be supposed to hint at those many pious cursings, and papistical excommunications, so liberally thundered out against the Queen and her faithful subjects. Next the Soldan is described *mounting straight upon a chariot high.* Camden more than once mentions the great height of the Spanish ships, built with lofty turrets on their decks like castles. He [Spenser] says, *with iron wheels and hooks armed dreadfully.* The Prince of Parma likewise in the Netherlands built ships, says Camden, and prepared piles sharpened at the nether end, *armed with iron and hooked on the sides.* Let it be added, however, that 'twas reported that this Armada carried various instruments of torture, and thus literally was so armed. *And drawn of cruel steeds which he had fed with flesh of men:* What were the captains and soldiers of this Armada but persecutors, or those who acted under the command of persecutors, inquisitors, *devourers of men?* There were four engagements, the learned con*siders* further remarks, between the two fleets; and these he supposes to be successively imaged in the progress of the fight that fills the remainder of the Canto.

The Briton prince in his bright armour awaits the Soldan on the green (the commentators have omitted to remark the propriety of this term as indicating the sea, the scene of the real conflict); and Talus, so directed by his lord, attends at his stirrup as his page.

> Like to the Thracian tyrant, who they say
> Unto his horses gave his guests for meat,
> Till he himself was made their greedy prey,
> And torn in pieces by Alcides great;
> So thought the Soldan, in his folly's threat,
> Either the prince in pieces to have torn
> With his sharp wheels in his first rage's heat,
> Or under his fierce horses' feet have borne,
> And trampled down in dust his thought's disdained scorn.

But "the bold child," moving to the side, allows the chariot to fly past, and also dexterously avoids a dart which the pagan throws at him, and which otherwise would certainly have demolished either himself or his horse. The elevation, however, on which the Soldan is placed and the speed of his wing-footed coursers for a long time baffle all Arthur's efforts to get a blow at him; and at length the pagan lanches at him another of the many darts with which he is provided, when

> The wicked shaft, guided through the airy wide
> By some bad spirit that it to mischief bore,
> Stayed not, till through his cnrat[y] it did glide,
> And made a grisly wound in his enriven side.

Only more infuriated, the prince redoubles his efforts to get near his adversary, but the rushing chariot still drives him back, and even his good steed, renowned as he is "for noble courage and for hardy race," flies in dread from the carrion-eating horses of the pagan. At last, finding all other methods and forces vain against these animals, Arthur uncovers his shield—for the first time, it has been remarked, that he does so voluntarily in the course of the poem—and holds it up full in their view. The effect is instantaneous:—

> Like lightning flash that hath the gazer burned,
> So did the sight thereof their sense dismay,
> That back again upon themselves they turned,
> And with their rider ran perforce away:
> Ne could the Soldan them from flying stay
> With reins or wonted rule, as well he knew:
> Nought feared they what he could do or say,
> But the only fear that was before their view:
> From which like mazed deer dismayfully they flew.
>
> Fast did they fly as them their feet could bear
> High over hills, and lowly over dales,
> As they were followed of their former fear:
> In vain the pagan bans, and swears, and rails,
> And back with both his hands unto him hales
> The resty[z] reins, regarded now no more:
> He to them calls and speaks, yet nought avails;
> They hear him not, they have forgot his lore;
> But go which way they list: their guide they have forlore.

---

[y] Cuirass.   [z] Restiff.

As when the fiery-mouthed steeds, which drew
The sun's bright wane to Phaëton's decay,
Soon as they did the monstrous Scorpion view
With ugly craples[a] crawling in their way,
The dreadful sight did them so sore affray,
That their well-knowen courses they forwent;
And, leading the ever burning lamp astray,
This lower world nigh all to ashes brent,
And left their scorched path yet in the firmament:

Such was the fury of these headstrong steeds,
Soon as the infant's sunlike shield they saw,
That all obedience both to words and deeds
They quite forgot, and scorned all former law.
Through woods, and rocks, and mountains they did draw
The iron chariot, and the wheels did tear,
And tossed the paynim without fear or awe;
From side to side they tossed him here and there,
Crying to them in vain that nould his crying hear.

Yet still the prince pursued him close behind,
Oft making offer him to smite, but found
No easy means according to his mind:
At last they have all overthrown to ground
Quite topside turvy, and the pagan hound
Amongst the iron hooks and graples keen
Torn all to rags, and rent with many a wound;
That no whole piece of him was to be seen,
But scattered all about, and strewed upon the green.

Like as the cursed son of Theseüs,
That following his chase in dewy morn,
To fly his stepdame's love outrageous,
Of his own steeds was all to pieces torn,
And his fair limbs left in the woods forlorn;
That for his sake Diana did lament,
And all the woody nymphs did wail and mourn:
So was this Soldan rapt and all to rent,
That of his shape appeared no little moniment.

The conquest of the Soldan has therefore been achieved only by supernatural means. Have we not here a covert acknowledgment that the defeat of the Ar-

---

[a] Claws.

mada was in truth the work rather of the tempest than of any human exertion—as it was expressed on the medal struck at the time with the inscription *Flavit Jehovah et dissipati sunt* (Jehovah blew and they were scattered)?

Only the tyrant's shield and armour are left, which, that they may

>——— remain for an eternal token
> To all, mongst whom this story should be spoken,
> How worthily, by Heaven's high decree,
> Justice that day of wrong herself had wroken,

the prince orders to be suspended on a tree before the door of their late vanquished owner. At this sign Adicia, burning to be revenged, comes running down from the castle with knife in hand, designing to plunge it into the heart of Samient, whom she thinks secure in the keeping of her own knight;—

> Like raging Ino, when with knife in hand
> She threw her husband's murdered infant out;
> Or fell Medea, when on Colchic strand
> Her brother's bones she scattered all about;
> Or as that madding mother, mongst the rout
> Of Bacchus' priests, her own dear flesh did tear:
> Yet neither Ino, nor Medea stout,
> Nor all the Mœnades so furious were,
> As this bold woman when she saw that damsel there.

When she is stopped, and the weapon wrested from her, by Artegal, she rushes from the place in ungovernable frenzy, and, breaking forth by a postern door, makes for the woods, where it is said she was soon after transformed to a tigress. Meanwhile, Artegal, discovering himself, has attacked and put to utter rout all the followers of the Soldan, although there were of them " nigh an hundred knights of name;" after which he commands the gates to be opened wide, when the prince enters in triumph, and takes possession as the Soldan's conqueror of all the immense treasure and spoil found within the castle.

Canto IX. (50 stanzas).—Adicia, as has been said,

has fled to the woods, and been metamorphosed into a tiger; but

> What tiger, or what other salvage wight,
> Is so exceeding furious and fell
> As Wrong, when it hath armed itself with Might?
> Not fit mongst men that do with reason mell,
> But mongst wild beasts, and salvage woods, to dwell;
> Where still the stronger doth the weak devour,
> And they that most in boldness do excel
> Are dreaded most, and feared for their power:
> Fit for Adicia there to build her wicked bower.

Meanwhile Prince Arthur and Sir Artegal, after having solaced themselves for a space in the Soldan's palace, resolve to leave both it and the wealth therein contained in charge of the damsel Samient for her mistress Queen Mercilla, and to proceed on their way; but Samient induces them first to accompany her to that renowned princess, whose abode is not far distant. On their road thither she informs them that the neighbourhood is infested by "a wicked villain bold and stout," who lives not far off in a rocky cavern, whither he brings home all his pillage, and there stows it away beyond the possibility of recapture.

> Thereto both his own wily wit, she said,
> And eke the fastness of his dwelling place,
> Both unassailable, gave him great aid:
> For he so crafty was to forge and face,
> So light of hand, and nimble of his pace,
> So smooth of tongue, and subtile in his tale,
> That could deceive one looking in his face;
> Therefore by name Malengin they him call,
> Well knowen by his feats, and famous over all.
>
> Through these his sleights he many doth confound:
> And eke the rock, in which he wonts to dwell,
> Is wondrous strong and hewn far under ground,
> A dreadful depth, how deep no man can tell;
> But some do say it goeth down to hell;
> And, all within, it full of windings is
> And hidden ways, that scarce an hound by smell
> Can follow out those false footsteps of his,
> Ne none can back return that once are gone amiss.

He is called Guile in the argument at the head of the Canto. When the knights have heard this account, they eagerly request Samient to conduct them at once to the villain's dwelling-place: they will not, they declare, move one footstep farther on their road to the court of Queen Mercilla till they have abated that nuisance. She accordingly brings them within sight of the rock, and then they arrange that the maid shall first advance alone to near the mouth of the den, and there sit down,

> Wailing, and raising pitiful uproar,
> As if she did some great calamity deplore;

that the noise may bring out the caitiff. This device has the expected effect: Malengin soon shows himself, and an uncouth sight he is, with his deep-set hollow eyes, his long shaggy locks rolling down over his shoulders, his garments of the strangest cut and material, and all worn and in tatters;

> And in his hand a huge long staff he held,
> Whose top was armed with many an iron hook,
> Fit to catch hold of all that he could weld,
> Or in the compass of his clutches took;
> And ever round about he cast his look:
> Als[a] at his back a great wide net he bore,
> With which he seldom fished at the brook,
> But used to fish for fools on the dry shore,
> Of which he in fair weather wont to take great store.

The damsel is considerably alarmed when she finds the monster at her side, and calls aloud for help;

> But, when the villain saw her so afraid,
> He gan with guileful words her to persuade
> To banish fear; and with Sardonian smile
> Laughing on her, his false intent to shade,
> Gan forth to lay his bait her to beguile,
> That from herself unwares he might her steal the while.

> Like as the fowler on his guileful pipe
> Charms to the birds full many a pleasant lay,

---

[a] Also.

> That they the whiles may take less heedy keep
> How he his nets doth for their ruin lay,
> So did the villain to her prate and play,
> And many pleasant tricks before her show,
> To turn her eyes from his intent away:
> For he in sleights and juggling feats did flow,
> And of legerdemain the mysteries did know.
>
> To which whilst she lent her intentive mind,
> He suddenly his net upon her threw,
> That overspread her like a puff of wind;
> And snatching her soon up, ere well she knew
> Ran with her fast away unto his mew,
> Crying for help aloud.

But when he comes to the entrance of the cave, and there sees the two knights, he throws down his burthen and takes to flight.

> But Artegal him after did pursue;
> The whiles the prince there kept the entrance still:
> Up to the rock he ran, and thereon flew
> Like a wild goat, leaping from hill to hill,
> And dancing on the craggy cliffs at will;
> That deadly danger seemed in all men's sight
> To tempt such steps, where footing was so ill:
> Ne ought availed for the armed knight
> To think to follow him that was so swift and light.

In this emergency the never-failing Talus is called in, and, pursuing him with steps as adventurous as his own, and still more agile, soon forces him to come down again to the plain. Nor does he do more than protract his fate for a very brief space by a series of expedients to which he now has recourse, ingenious enough to have puzzled and baffled any other than the iron man:—

> Into a fox himself he first did turn;
> But he him hunted like a fox full fast:
> Then to a bush himself he did transform;
> But he the bush did beat, till that at last
> Into a bird it changed, and from him passed.
> Flying from tree to tree, from wand to wand:
> But he then stones at it so long did cast,

That like a stone it fell upon the land;
But he then took it up, and held fast in his hand.

So he it brought with him unto the knights,
And to his lord Sir Artegal it lent,
Warning him hold it fast for fear of sleights:
Who whilst in hand it griping hard he hent,[b]
Into a hedgehog all unwares it went,
And pricked him so that he away it threw;
Then gan it run away incontinent,
Being returned to his former hue;
But Talus soon him overtook, and backward drew.

But, whenas he would to a snake again
Have turned himself, he with his iron flail
Gan drive at him with so huge might and main,
That all his bones as small as sandy grail[c]
He broke, and did his bowels disentrail,
Crying in vain for help, when help was past;
So did deceit the self-deceiver fail:
There they him left a carrion outcast
For beasts and fowls to feed upon for their repast.

The two knights now proceed "with that gentle maid" on their road to the court of her royal mistress;—

To which when she approached, thus she said;
"Lo now, right noble knights, arrived ye be
Nigh to the place which ye desired to see:
There shall ye see my sovereign lady queen,
Most sacred wight, most debonaire and free,
That ever yet upon this earth was seen,
Or that with diadem hath ever crowned been."

Arriving at the palace, they find it to be

Of pompous show, much more than she had told,
With many towers and tarras[d] mounted high,
And all their tops bright glistering with gold,
That seemed to outshine the dimmed sky,
And with their brightness dazed the strange beholder's eye.

A magnificent porch stands " open wide to all men day

[b] Held, grasped.   [c] Gravel.   [d] Terraces.

and night," yet guarded by a gigantic figure, to keep out Guile and Malice and other such mischief-makers too apt to intrude into princes' courts:—

> His name was Awe; by whom they passing in
> Went up the hall, that was a large wide room,
> All full of people making troublous din
> And wondrous noise, as if that there were some[e]
> Which unto them was dealing righteous doom:
> By whom they passing through the thickest press,
> The marshal of the hall to them did come,
> His name hight Order; who, commanding peace,
> Them guided through the throng, that did their clamours cease.
>
> They ceased their clamours upon them to gaze;
> Whom seeing all in armour bright as day,
> Strange there to see, it did them much amaze,
> And with unwonted terror half affray:
> For never saw they there the like array;
> Ne ever was the name of war there spoken,
> But joyous peace and quietness alway
> Dealing just judgments, that mote not be broken
> For any bribes, or threats of any to be wroken.

As they enter they see, at the screen in the hall, one with his tongue nailed to a post, having been adjudged by law to suffer that punishment for foul blasphemy committed by him against the queen,

> Both with bold speeches which he blazed had,
> And with lewd poems which he did compile;
> For the bold title of a poet bad
> He on himself had ta'en, and railing rhymes had sprad.[f]

Over his head is written "the purport of his sin in cyphers strange:" *Bonfont* (or Fountain of Good) the name had originally been, but it has been altered into *Malfont* (Fountain of Evil). Passing on they are brought at length into the presence of that gracious queen;

> Who sate on high, that she might all men see
> And might of all men royally be seen,

---

[e] Some one.   [f] Spread.

Upon a throne of gold full bright and sheen
Adorned all with gems of endless price,
As either might for wealth have gotten been,
Or could be framed by workman's rare device;
And all embossed with lions and with flourdelice.

All over her a cloth of state was spread,
Not of rich tissue, nor of cloth of gold,
Nor of ought else that may be richest read,
But like a cloud, as likest may be told,
That her broad-spreading wings did wide unfold:
Whose skirts were bordered with bright sunny beams,
Glistring like gold among the plights [g] enrolled,
And here and there shooting forth silver streams,
Mongst which crept little angels through the glittering gleams.

Seemed those little angels did uphold
The cloth of state, and on their purpled wings
Did bear the pendants through their nimbless[h] bold;
Besides, a thousand more of such as sings
Hymns to high God, and carols heavenly things,
Encompassed the throne on which she sate;
She, angel-like, the heir of ancient kings
And mighty conquerors, in royal state;
Whilst kings and kesars at her feet did them prostrate.

In her hand she holds a sceptre, pledge of the peace and clemency " with which high God had blessed her happy land;" at her feet lies her sword, the steel rusted from long rest;

Yet when as foes enforced, or friends sought aid,
She could it sternly draw that all the world dismayed.

And round about before her feet there sate
A bevy of fair virgins clad in white,
That goodly seemed to adorn her royal state.

These are the Litæ (or Prayers), the lovely daughters of high Jove by the righteous Themis:

——————————— Those, they say,
Upon Love's judgment-seat wait day and night;
And, when in wrath he threats the world's decay,
They do his anger calm and cruel vengeance stay.

---

[g] Plaits, folds.   [h] Nimbleness.

> They also do, by his divine permission,
> Upon the thrones of mortal princes tend,
> And often treat for pardon and remission
> To suppliants, through frailty which offend;
> Those did upon Mercilla's throne attend,
> Just Dice, wise Eunomie, mild Eirene;
> And them amongst, her glory to commend,
> Sate goodly Temperance in garments clean,
> And sacred Reverence yborn of heavenly strene.[1]

Underneath the queen's feet lies a huge lion, so tightly bound with a strong iron chain that he cannot move; all he can do when his savage choler rises is to utter a rebellious murmur or slight growl.

On the two knights approaching her with lowly reverence, Mercilla also, inclining her head,

> A cheerful countenance on them let fall,
> Yet tempered with some majesty imperial.

It chances that at the moment she is engaged in the administration of justice; and the commencement of the trial of a great and weighty case has been suspended by their entrance. After they have been presented the hearing of this important cause is resumed; and, that they may the better understand the proceedings, she places them on the throne beside her, the one on her right hand and the other on her left.

> Then was there brought, as prisoner to the bar,
> A lady of great countenance and place,
> But that she it with foul abuse did mar;
> Yet did appear rare beauty in her face,
> But blotted with condition vile and base,
> That all her other honour did obscure,
> And titles of nobility deface:
> Yet, in that wretched semblant, she did sure
> The people's great compassion unto her allure.

This proves to be no other than our old acquaintance, the witch Duessa; but the charges brought against her, and all the other circumstances, clearly point at Mary of Scotland. First there rises up "a person of deep reach

---

[1] Descent.

and rare insight," named Zeal, who, with powerful eloquence, begins to accuse the lady of many heinous crimes, and with sharp reasons rings her such a peal that even many who had been allured to pity her have their compassion changed to abhorrence and loathing while they listen to his oration. She is not now, he states, brought into question on account of the many knights she has in former times beguiled and abused, but for treason more recently wrought by her against the dread Mercilla:

> For she whilome (as ye mote yet right well
> Remember) had her counsels false conspired
> With faithless Blandamour and Paridel,
> (Both two her paramours, both by her hired,
> And both with hope of shadows vain inspired),
> And with them practised, how for to deprive
> Mercilla of her crown, by her aspired,
> That she might it unto herself derive,
> And triumph in their blood whom she to death did drive.

Paridel, it has been already stated, represents the Earl of Westmoreland; his friend Blandamour—designated in the First Canto of the Fourth Book "the hotspur youth," as if in allusion to the well-known surname of young Harry Percy in the time of Henry the Fourth—is clearly from this passage to be taken to stand for the Earl of Northumberland, the other leader of the northern insurrection of 1569. But through the grace of heaven, Zeal goes on to say, that wicked plot had failed, and its contrivers had met with the reward meet for their crimes: and here was the false Duessa, " now untitled Queen" (this expression is very remarkable and conclusive), brought also to receive the judgment she deserved. After Zeal has enforced his argument with much more reasoning to the same effect, many other grave persons also appear to plead and give evidence against the prisoner:—

> First was a sage old sire, that had to name
> The Kingdom's Care, with a white silver head,
> That many high regards and reasons gainst her read.

This, no doubt, is Burghley.

> Then gan Authority her to oppose
> With peremptory power, that made all mute;
> And then the Law of Nations gainst her rose,
> And reasons brought, that no man could refute;
> Next gan Religion gainst her to impute
> High God's behest, and power of holy laws;
> Then gan the People's Cry and Commons' Suit
> Importune care of their own public cause;
> And lastly Justice charged her with breach of laws.
>
> But then, for her, on the contrary part,
> Rose many advocates for her to plead:
> First there came Pity with full tender heart,
> And with her joined Regard of Womanhead;
> And then came Danger threatening hidden dread
> And high alliance unto foreign power;
> Then came Nobility of Birth, that bred
> Great ruth through her misfortunes' tragic stour;
> And lastly Grief did plead, and many tears forth pour.

Here we are told that the Briton prince was for a moment touched with compassion for the fallen queen,

> And wox inclined much unto her part,
> Through the sad terror of so dreadful fate,
> And wretched ruin of so high estate.

It has been supposed that Spenser designed Prince Arthur, in part at least, for a representation of his patron the Earl of Leicester; and Leicester was at one time thought to be inclined to support the party of the Queen of Scots. When Zeal, however, perceives the prince thus relenting in the prisoner's favour, he brings forward new evidence and new charges. First he calls Duessa's old accomplice Ate, who, " glad of spoil and ruinous decay," readily makes a full statement of " all her trains and all her treasons:"—

> Then brought he forth with grisly grim aspect
> Abhorred Murder, who with bloody knife
> Yet dropping fresh in hand did her detect,
> And there with guilty bloodshed charged rife:
> Then brought he forth Sedition, breeding strife
> In troublous wits and mutinous uproar:
> Then brought he forth Incontinence of life
> Even foul Adultery, her face before,
> And lewd Impiety, that her accused sore.

The result is that the Prince's compassion is quite extinguished; Artegal, for his part, with his strong instinct of justice, has been firmly set against her from the first; so that she is unanimously held to be guilty. Zeal then urges her punishment, and loudly calls upon the mild Mercilla for judgment. But she, although she cannot conceal from herself that the prisoner deserves to die, is too much affected with pity to let just vengeance light on her; she rather, we are informed,

> ——————— let, instead thereof, to fall
> Few pearling drops from her fair lamps of light;
> The which she covering with her purple pall
> Would have the passion hid, and up arose withal.

Canto X. (39 stanzas).—This new Canto the poet opens as follows:—

> Some clerks do doubt in their deviceful art
> Whether this heavenly thing whereof I treat,
> To weeten Mercy, be of Justice part,
> Or drawn forth from her by divine extreat;§
> This well I wote, that sure she is as great,
> And meriteth to have as high a place,
> Sith in the Almighty's everlasting seat
> She first was bred, and born of heavenly race;
> From thence poured down on men by influence of grace.
>
> For, if that virtue be of so great might
> Which from just verdict will for nothing start,
> But, to preserve inviolated right,
> Oft spills the principal to save the part;
> So much more then is that of power and art
> That seeks to save the subject of her skill,
> Yet never doth from doom of right depart;
> As it is greater praise to save than spill,
> And better to reform than to cut off the ill.

These lines are introductory to a further celebration of the clemency of Mercilla in declining to take the life of Duessa

> Till strong constraint did her thereto enforce;
> And yet even then rueing her wilful fall

---

§ Extract.

With more than needful natural remorse,
And yielding the last honour to her wretched corse.

While Arthur and Artegal, delighted and filled with admiration, both by what they see of her general government, and by the particular courtesies and favours of which they are themselves the objects, still tarry at Mercilla's court, there arrive two youths from a foreign country to implore her succour for their mother, a widow, who is kept in great dolour and fear by a strong tyrant, by whom her land has been invaded, and the greater number of her children slain:—

> Her name was Belge; who, in former age
> A lady of great worth and wealth had been,
> And mother of a fruitful heritage,
> Even seventeen goodly sons; which who had seen
> In their first flower, before this fatal teen
> Them overtook and their fair blossoms blasted,
> More happy mother would her surely ween
> Than famous Niobe, before she tasted
> Latona's children's wrath that all her issue wasted.

But now, of all that numerous brood, the tyrant had left her only five, having devoured the other twelve, and sacrificed their blood to his idols. Belge, with her seventeen sons, is obviously the country of the Netherlands, anciently the habitation of the Belgæ; of the seventeen provinces of which five, namely, Holland, Zealand, Utrecht, Guelderland, and Friesland, declared themselves independent in 1579 by the celebrated Union of Utrecht (afterwards joined in 1580 by Overyssel, and in 1594 by Groningen). The tyrant by whom Belge is oppressed is, of course, Philip II. of Spain. "Soothly," we are told,

> ——————— he was one of matchless might,
> Of horrible aspect and dreadful mood,
> And had three bodies in one waste empight,
> And the arms and legs of three to succour him in fight.

The allusion here may be to Philip's triple dominion over Spain, the Netherlands, and Portugal. But his father, it is added, had also " three bodies' power in one

combined," and this, we may presume, must refer to the
union in the Emperor Charles V. of the three sovereign-
ties of Spain, the Netherlands, and Germany. It is
strange that these striking points in the allegory should
have been overlooked by the commentators. His three
bodies and his dominion of Spain together naturally lead
the poet to identify Charles with the old giant Geryon.
The tyrant under whom the widow Belge suffered was,
he further tells us, of the race of the giants, being the
son of that same Geryon who had formerly oppressed
Spain, and by whom all strangers arriving in that coun-
try used to be given as food to his kine—" the fairest
kine alive, but of the fiercest kind." For they were all,
it is said, purple coloured, and were under the charge of
a cruel and murderous herdsman called Eurytion, who
never slept either by day or by night, but walked about
tending them continually with his two-headed dog
Orthrus, the monstrous progeny of Typhaon and the
foul Echidna: " but Hercules them all did overcome in
fight." Geryon's son, named Geryoneo, after his father
fell " under Alcides' club," straightway fled from that
sad land, and

—— came to this, where Belge then did dwell
And flourish in all wealth and happiness,
Being then new made widow, as befell,
After her noble husband's late decease;
Which gave beginning to her woe and wretchedness.

This Upton interprets as describing the state of Belge
" when the Spaniards had subverted the liberties of the
States after the assassination of the Prince of Orange."
But the words evidently do not refer to any assassina-
tion, any more than they do to the time (1584) when
the Prince of Orange was assassinated. Belge's noble
husband must be Charles the Bold, the last Duke of
Burgundy, slain in 1477, the marriage of whose daughter
with Maximilian of Austria brought the Netherlands into
the possession of that foreign house. The poet goes on to
relate that Geryoneo (here to be understood as meaning
the House of Austria generally) in the first instance

offered himself and was accepted by Belge as her champion to defend her against all foreign foes; that for a long time he executed that office faithfully, so that at last she committed everything to his hands, " and gave him sovereign power to do whatever he thought good or fit;" and that then he began

> To stir up strife and many a tragic stour;
> Giving her dearest children one by one
> Unto a dreadful monster to devour,
> And setting up an idol of his own,
> The image of his monstrous parent Geryon.

The dreadful monster is plainly, as pointed out by the commentators, the Inquisition, set up in the Netherlands by Philip under the government of the Duke of Alva: but the last line is evidently to be further explained as designating the Popish religion by a reference to the triple crown of the Roman pontiff. The two youths whom the widow sends to Mercilla may perhaps have a special reference, as has been suggested, to the Marquis of Hauree and Adolph Metkerk, who were deputed to Elizabeth by the United States in 1577; but it is not necessary to consider the matter so literally; they are called by the poet Belge's two eldest sons, the most natural ambassadors for her to employ in her circumstances. When they present their suit Prince Arthur chances to be present, and seeing that none of the other knights seems inclined to offer himself, he steps forward, " admired of all the rest in presence there," and entreats the Queen to grant him the adventure of going against Geryoneo. Here at least we seem to have the Briton Prince manifestly representing the Earl of Leicester, whose appointment in 1585 as Captain-General of the forces in the Netherlands, and his conduct in that post throughout the two following years, make so principal a passage of his history. Arthur sets out on his expedition the very next morning, with " those two gentle youths" as his guides, and soon arrives

> Within the land where dwelt that lady sad;
> Whereof that tyrant had her now deprived,

And into moors and marshes banished had,
Out of the pleasant soil and cities glad,
In which she wont to harbour happily:

words pointing to the geographical situation of the insurgent provinces as compared with that of the others which remained in subjection to Spain. Belge is in such a state of grief and distraction that the sight of the armed knight at first alarms her; but on seeing her sons she knows that he is come to help her, and, falling on their necks as they kneel before her, and bursting into tears, "Ah, my sweet boys," she says,

—————— "now I gin new life to feel;
And feeble spirits, that gan faint and reel,
Now rise again at this your joyous sight.
Already seems that fortune's headlong wheel
Begins to turn, and sun to shine more bright
Than it was wont, through comfort of this noble knight."

Arthur would have her leave her present miserable abode and go with him to some place where they might have rest and refreshment.

"Ay me!" said she, "and whither shall I go?
Are not all places full of foreign powers?
My palaces possessed of my foe,
My cities sacked, and their sky-threatening towers
Razed and made smooth fields now full of flowers?
Only these marishes and miry bogs,
In which the fearful ewfts[1] do build their bowers,
Yield me an hostry[m] mongst the croaking frogs,
And harbour here in safety from those ravenous dogs."

"Nathless," said he, "dear lady, with me go;
Some place shall us receive and harbour yield;
If not, we will it force, maugre your foe,
And purchase it to us with spear and shield:
And, if all fail, yet farewell[n] open field!
The earth to all her creatures lodging lends."
With such his cheerful speeches he doth wield

---

[1] Efts, or newts.   [m] Hostelry, or inn.
[n] Well betide, welcome.

Her mind so well, that to his will she bends;
And, binding up her locks and weeds, forth with him
wends.

They journey on till they come to a city, apparently Antwerp (where the Duke of Alva built a citadel) "the which whilome that lady's own had been," but which has now been taken from her by her foe, who has shut up its haven and ruined the trade of its merchants, and has also set upon its neck a strong castle by which it is completely commanded and kept in subjection. He has also made it "bear the yoke of Inquisition,"

And forced it the honour that is due
To God to do unto his idol most untrue.

To him he hath before this castle green
Built a fair chapel, and an altar framed
Of costly ivory full rich beseen,
On which that cursed idol, far proclaimed,
He hath set up, and him his god hath named;
Offering to him in sinful sacrifice
The flesh of men, to God's own likeness framed,
And pouring forth their blood in brutish wise,
That any iron eyes, to see, it would agrize.°

And, for more horror and more cruelty,
Under that cursed idol's altar-stone
An hideous monster doth in darkness lie,
Whose dreadful shape was never seen of none
That lives on earth; but unto those alone
The which unto him sacrificed be:
Those he devours, they say, both flesh and bone;
What else they have is all the tyrant's fee:
So that no whit of them remaining one may see.

Finally, the tyrant has placed in the conquered city a strong garrison commanded by a seneschal of the most merciless temper and of eminent military skill. Belge would have the prince to shun the place, but her dissuasions have no effect on him; he rides straight up to the wall of the castle, and desires the warder to call the seneschal forth. The latter at once accepts the challenge; they encounter " in the middle plain;" the seneschal's spear can find no entrance into the prince's

° Horrify.

shield, "so pure the metal was and well refined;" but Arthur's makes to itself ready passage not only through his adversary's shield, but also "through his habergeon and eke his horse." But as he marches up to try if he can find entrance into the castle, after having thus slain its master, three knights all armed to point issue forth, and ride against him all at once. He receives their three spears on his shield as firmly as if he were a bulwark, not swerving in his saddle the least aside; and not only so, but transfixes the middle one on his own spear and hurls him lifeless to the ground. The other two immediately turn and take to flight; but Arthur, pursuing them, overtakes them as they reach the gate of the fort, and slays the one on the threshold, the other at the screen (or inner door). All the other persons that are in the castle then make their escape by a postern gate; and the victorious Briton prince conducts Belge and her two sons into the place,

> Where all that night themselves they cherished,
> And from her baleful mind all care he banished.

Canto XI. (65 stanzas).—When news is brought to Geryoneo that the Lady Belge has found a champion, and that his seneschal has been slain, he instantly arms himself, and, setting out with his retinue, comes and marches up and down before the gate of the castle where Prince Arthur is, and with much vaunting and menace calls upon him to deliver him his own. The prince does not keep him waiting long, but, coming forth to him, "full nobly mounted in right warlike wise," asks if he be the same who has done the Lady Belge all that wrong?

> He boldly answered him, he there did stand
> That would his doings justify with his own hand.
>
> With that so furiously at him he flew,
> As if he would have over-run him straight;
> And with his huge great iron axe gan hew
> So hideously upon his armour bright,
> As he to pieces would have chopped it quite;
> That the bold prince was forced foot to give
> To his first rage, and yield to his despite;
> The whilst at him so dreadfully he drive,
> That seemed a marble rock asunder could have rive.

His three sets of hands and arms give Geryoneo, of course, a considerable advantage, enabling him, as he sees occasion, to shift his weapon from hand to hand and from side to side, and to strike his enemy in front, in flank, and from the rear, as he chooses. After he has several times performed this operation, however, the prince, as he is trying it again, meets him with a counterstroke so swift as to smite the uplifted arm off altogether. The infuriated monster then grasps his axe in all his five remaining hands at once, and, heaving them on high, comes down with what he intends for an annihilating blow; but it luckily falls short of the prince, and only wounds his horse's head. The giant, seeing his adversary now reduced to fight on foot, is stated to have thereat

—— laughed so loud, that all his teeth wide bare
One might have seen enranged disorderly,
Like to a rank of piles that pitched are awry.

Another tremendous stroke of the axe is only prevented from cleaving Arthur in twain by his dexterous interposition of his adamantine shield before it has come quite down upon him. In return, however, he deals the giant such a blow, or rather furious succession of blows, that two more of his arms drop from him.

With that all mad and furious he grew,
Like a fell mastiff through enraging heat,
And cursed, and banned, and blasphemies forth threw
Against his gods, and fire to them did threat,
And hell unto himself with horror great:
Thenceforth he cared no more which way he strook,
Nor where it light; but gan to chafe and sweat,
And gnashed his teeth, and his head at him shook,
And sternly him beheld with grim and ghastly look.

In this mad and reckless condition he soon gives "the child" an opportunity of sending his sword, by a remarkably fortunate thrust, not only through one of his bodies but through all three; and he rolls on the ground a senseless lump,

—— biting the earth for very Death's disdain;
Who, with a cloud of night him covering, bore
Down to the house of dole, his days there to deplore.

When this is seen by the Lady Belge, who with her two sons has been all the while looking on from the castle, as have " all the people both of town and land" from the city wall, she runs down, and, prostrating herself with her boys before her victorious champion's feet, " in all that people's sight"—

Mongst joys mixing some tears, mongst weal some woe,

—returns him fervent thanks, and would have him accept for his own the realm his valour has saved; but, taking her up by the lily hand the magnanimous prince assures her that it is the justice of her cause that has fought for her that day, and that for any service he has rendered he accounts the consciousness of having rendered it sufficient reward. She then requests of him that he will not lay down his victorious arms till he has completed his good work, and informs him that there stands in the neighbouring church a famous idol devised and set up by the late giant, to which he was wont to offer up her children and her people in daily sacrifice, consuming them by fire with all the tortures he could invent; and that

⸺ underneath this idol there doth lie
An hideous monster, that doth it defend,
And feeds on all the carcases that die
In sacrifice unto that cursed fiend:
Whose ugly shape none ever saw, nor kenned,
That ever scaped.

The prince, on hearing this, again takes his arms and shield, and proceeds to the church.

There he that idol saw of massy gold
Most richly made, but there no monster did behold.

Upon the image with his naked blade
Three times, as in defiance, there he strook;
And the third time, out of an hidden shade
There forth issued from under the altar's smook
A dreadful fiend with foul deformed look,
That stretched itself as it had long lain still;
And her long tail and feathers strongly shook,
That all the temple did with terror fill;
Yet him nought terrified, that feared nothing ill.

An huge great beast it was, when it in length
Was stretched forth, that nigh filled all the place,
And seemed to be of infinite great strength ;
Horrible, hideous, and of hellish race,
Born of the brooding of Echidna base,
Or other like infernal fury's kind :
For of a maid she had the outward face,
To hide the horror which did lurk behind,
The better to beguile whom she so fond did find.

Thereto the body of a dog she had,
Full of fell ravin ᴾ and fierce greediness ;
A lion's claws, with power and rigour clad,
To rend and tear whatso she can oppress ;
A dragon's tail, whose sting without redress
Full deadly wounds whereso it is empight ;ᑫ
And eagle's wings, for scope and speediness,
That nothing may escape her reaching might,
Whereto she ever list to make her hardy flight.

Much like in foulness and deformity
Unto that monster,ʳ whom the Theban knight,
The father of that fatal progeny,
Made kill herself for very heart's despite
That he had read her riddle, which no wight
Could ever loose, but suffered deadly dool ˢ :
So also did this monster use like sleight
To many a one which came unto her school,
Whom she did put to death deceived like a fool.

The monster, even at her first coming forth, is dismayed at the sight of the prince's blazing shield, and would have turned back to hide herself again in her lair if he had not prevented her. She then flies at the shield, and, fiercely seizing hold of it, tries either to rend it to pieces or to rive it out of his hand. Finding it in vain to seek to make her relax her gripe, he takes his sword and with one powerful stroke smites off from her feet her lion's claws.

With that aloud she gan to bray and yell,
And foul blasphemous speeches forth did cast,

ᴾ Ravenousness.   ᑫ Infixed.
ʳ The Sphinx.   ˢ Sorrow.

 And bitter curses, horrible to tell;
That even the temple, wherein she was placed,
Did quake to hear, and nigh asunder brast;
Thot with her huge long tail she at him strook,
That made him stagger and stand half aghast
With trembling joints, as he for terror shook;
Who nought was terrified, but greater courage took.

 As when the mast of some well-timbered hulk
Is with the blast of some outrageous storm
Blown down, it shakes the bottom of the bulk,
And makes her ribs to crack as they were torn;
Whilst still she stands as stonished and forlorn;
So was he stunned with stroke of her huge tail:
But, ere that it she back again had borne,
He with his sword it strook, that without fail
He jointed it, and marred the swinging of her flail.

The monster now screams out louder than ever, and, rearing herself on her ample wings, throws herself with the whole weight of her body upon him; but he has had time to interpose his shield between her and his head, and while she is trying to crush him he thrusts his sword into her entrails, and ends the battle.

 Then all the people which beheld that day
Gan shout aloud, that unto heaven it rung;
And all the damsels of that town in ray [u]
Came dancing forth, and joyous carols sung:
So him they led through all their streets along
Crowned with girlands of immortal bays;
And all the vulgar did about them throng
To see the man, whose everlasting praise
They all were bound to all posterities to raise.

The story now returns to "noble Artegal," who has also left the court of Mercilla, and proceeded on his original enterprise, the deliverance of Irena, and the chastisement of her oppressor Grantorto. He has passed over much way and through many perils, accompanied, as usual, only by his faithful attendant Talus, when he meets an aged man journeying alone, and recognises him to be an old knight named Sir Sergis, by whom Irena

   [t] Then.   [u] Array.

had been attended when he first saw her at Fairy Court. Sir Sergis informs him that Irena still lives, but that she is bound in prison, having been surprised and taken captive by Grantorto, when, at the time that Artegal had promised to meet and fight with the tyrant for trial of her right "at the Salvage Island's side," she had gone thither, in full confidence that her champion would make his appearance. And now Grantorto is about to take her life, having fixed a day by which, if no champion shall present himself to justify her against him in battle, and to prove her innocent of the crimes with which he charges her, she must die. With his tender sense of justice and honour, Sir Artegal, sorely grieved, reproaches himself that he should have been the cause of drawing the fair lady into all this trouble and peril; "But witness unto me," he adds,

> ———— ———— ye heavens! that know
> How clear I am from blame of this upbraid:
> For ye into like thraldom me did throw,
> And kept from complishing the faith which I did owe.

Having been informed by Sir Sergis that ten days are all the time allowed her to provide a champion,

> "Now turn again," Sir Artegal then said;
> "For, if I live till those ten days have end,
> Assure yourself, sir knight, she shall have aid,
> Though I this dearest life for her do spend."

As they ride along, however, they are drawn aside, pressed as they are for time, by a new adventure. They perceive a little way before them a confused rout of people; and, when they approach nearer, they see a knight pursued to and fro by a rude multitude who are trying to overthrow and capture him; while at some distance another body of them have got "amid their rake-hell hands," and are carrying off, a lady, who is crying bitterly and stretching out her hands to him for aid. The knight battles with his numerous assailants with the highest courage and energy, dealing among them blows on blows, "gainst which the pallid death finds no defence;" but they are too many for all his efforts to drive them off;

> And now they do so sharply him assay,
> That they his shield in pieces battered have,
> And forced him to throw it quite away,
> Fro danger's dread his doubtful life to save ;
> All be that it most safety to him gave,
> And much did magnify his noble name :
> For, from the day that he thus did it leave,
> Amongst all knights he blotted was with blame,
> And counted but a recreant knight with endless shame.

Artegal and Sir Sergis now ride up to his assistance ; but they too fail to make any impression upon so great a multitude, and are forced to recede,

> ———————— until that iron man
> With his huge flail began to lay about ;
> From whose stern presence they diffused ran,
> Life scattered chaff, the which the wind away doth fan.

The delivered knight now informs them that he is named Burbon, and had been well known and of great repute till this misfortune fell upon him, which, he says, all his "former praise hath blemished sore ;" and that the lady is Flourdelis, his own true love, although she has forsaken him—"whether," he adds,

> ———————— "withheld from me by wrongful might,
> Or with her own good will, I cannot read aright.
>
> But sure to me her faith she first did plight
> To be my love, and take me for her lord ;
> Till that a tyrant, which Grantorto hight,
> With golden gifts and many a guileful word
> Enticed her to him for to accord.
> O, who may not with gifts and words be tempted !
> Sith which she hath me ever since abhorred,
> And to my foe hath guilefully consented :
> Ay me, that ever guile in women was invented !"

Every reader sees that Burbon is Henry Bourbon of Navarre, or Henry IV. of France, that Flourdelis is the French crown, that the rude multitude are his rebellious Roman Catholic subjects, and that by his throwing away his shield is meant his change of religion, or recantation of Protestantism, in the year 1593. Spenser very distinctly intimates his own strong feeling upon this transaction. Artegal is made immediately to ask Burbon why in his danger and terror he should have thrown away his own good shield?

> "That is the greatest shame and foulest scorn,
> Which unto any knight behappen may,
> To lose the badge that should his deeds display."

And, when Burbon, "blushing half for shame," has made the best excuse that he can, he still rejoins,

> ——————————— "Certes, sir knight,
> Hard is the case the which ye do complain;
> Yet not so hard (for nought so hard may light
> That it to such a strait mote you constrain)
> As to abandon that which doth contain
> Your honour's style, that is, your warlike shield.
> All peril ought be less, and less all pain,
> Than loss of fame in disaventrous field:
> Die, rather than do ought that mote dishonour yield!"

Burbon answers that when time shall serve he may possibly resume again his former shield, and argues that "to temporize is not from truth to swerve."

> "Fie on such forgery," said Artegal,
> "Under one hood to shadow faces twain:
> Knights ought be true, and truth is one in all."

He consents however to give him his aid in endeavouring to rescue the lady from the crew of peasants in whose hands she still is; and, chiefly through Talus and his iron flail, this is, with no great difficulty accomplished:—

> The rascal many soon they overthrew;
> But the two knights themselves their captains did subdue.

When, however, they get possession of the lady they find her "neither glad nor sorry for their sight." "Yet," it is added,

> —— wondrous fair she was, and richly clad,
> In royal robes and many jewels dight;
> But that those villains through their usage bad
> Them foully rent and shamefully defaced had.

When Burbon catches her by "her ragged weed," and would embrace her, she starts back in disdain and anger, bids him avaunt, nor will be allured by all he can either say or offer her; till Artegal addresses her on her extraordinary and unbecoming conduct:—"What foul disgrace," he says,

> —————————————— " is this
> To so fair lady, as ye seem in sight,
> To blot your beauty, that unblemished is,
> With so foul blame as breach of faith once plight,
> Or change of love for any world's delight?
>
> . . . . .
>
> Dearer is love than life, and fame than gold,
> But dearer than them both your faith once plighted hold.

" Much," we are told,

> —— was the lady in her gentle mind
> Abashed at his rebuke, that bit her near;
> Ne ought to answer thereunto did find:
> But, hanging down her head with heavy cheer,
> Stood long amazed as she amated [v] were.

Burbon at length, without more ado, clasping her in his arms, takes her up upon his steed, and rides off with her, she apparently making no opposition.

All this while Talus, who, it may be observed, never stops of his own accord when he has got fairly engaged at his favourite work, has been pursuing, scattering, and slaughtering "the rascal many" in his usual tremendous style; but Artegal at last calls him off, and they resume, along with Sergis, their journey to the sea-coast.

Canto XII. (43 stanzas).—Spenser shows great art in managing his transitions from line to line or stage to stage of his various and involved narrative. He thus winds his way now from Artegal's last to his next adventure:—

> O sacred hunger of ambitious minds,
> And impotent desire of men to reign!
> Whom neither dread of God, that devils binds,
> Nor laws of men, that commonweals contain,
> Nor bands of nature, that wild beasts restrain,
> Can keep from outrage and from doing wrong,
> Where they may hope a kingdom to obtain:
> No faith so firm, no trust can be so strong,
> No love so lasting then, that may endure long.

---

[v] Frightened.

> Witness may Burbon be; whom all the bands,
> Which may a knight assure, had surely bound,
> Until the love of lordship and of lands
> Made him become most faithless and unsound.

And witness of the same thing, he adds, let Geryoneo be, by whom we have seen the fair Belge oppressed; and so, finally, be likewise Grantorto, who is now to occupy our attention.

When Artegal and his companions arrive at the seacoast they find there by good chance a ship ready to put to sea; and, wind and weather serving, a day's sail carries them across to the opposite shore. Their landing is opposed by a numerous military force; but that is quickly disposed of: as soon as the water became shallow enough for wading,

> Talus into the sea did forth issue
> Though darts from shore and stones they at him threw;
> And wading through the waves with stedfast sway,
> Maugre the might of all those troops in view,
> Did win the shore; whence he them chased away
> And made to fly like doves, whom the eagle doth affray.

Artegal and Sergis now land, and set forward for a town which they see at a little distance. Meanwhile the fugitives have carried the news of their arrival to Grantorto, who thereupon has put himself at the head of all his remaining forces, and come forth, with the hope of being able to attack them before they have left the shore; the tyrant and his host, on meeting the two knights, charge them with great fierceness;

> But Talus sternly did upon them set,
> And brushed and battered them without remorse,
> That on the ground he left full many a corse;
> Ne any able was him to withstand,
> But he them overthrew both man and horse,
> That they lay scattered over all the land,
> As thick as doth the seed after the sower's hand.

As usual, the iron man goes on scattering and killing till he is stopped by Artegal; who then, a truce having been agreed to, sends a herald to Grantorto desiring him to appoint a day when they may try the right of fair Irena's cause in single combat. Grantorto, very glad to have an end put to the slaughter of his people before they are every man of them slain, appoints the following morning. Sir Artegal pitches his tent for the night on the open plain, and is well supplied with all needful accommodations by the exertions of old Sergis among persons whom he knows to be secret friends of Irena, although the tyrant has strictly commanded that none should dare to afford him any entertainment. Upton takes Sergis to be Sir Francis Walsingham, for what reason does not appear: he is more probably some adviser by whom Lord Grey was assisted while he held the government of Ireland.

All this while no one has brought the tidings of Artegal's arrival to Irena; and when the morning comes, she believes that her life's last hour has come. She rises and attires herself in garments fit for such a day, and is brought forth, with heavy countenance and heavier heart, to receive, as she imagines, the doom that she must die. But, when, on coming to the place, she sees Sir Artegal "in battalious array waiting his foe," new life springs up within her:—

> Like as a tender rose in open plain,
> That with untimely drought nigh withered was,
> And hung the head, soon as few drops of rain
> Thereon distil and dew her dainty face,
> Gins to look up, and with fresh wonted grace
> Dispreads the glory of her leaves gay;
> Such was Irena's countenance, such her case,
> When Artegal she saw in that array,
> There waiting for the tyrant till it was fair day.

He appears at length and marches into the field with haughty and fearless gait;

> All armed in a coat of iron plate
> Of great defence to ward the deadly fear,
> And on his head a steel-cap he did wear
> Of colour rusty-brown, but sure and strong;
> And in his hand an huge pole-axe did bear,
> Whose steel was iron-studded, but not long,
> With which he wont to fight, to justify his wrong.

Of stature huge and hideous he was,
Like to a giant for his monstrous height,
And did in strength most sorts of men surpass,
Ne ever any found his match in might;
Thereto he had great skill in single fight:
His face was ugly and his countenance stern,
That could have frayed one with the very sight,
And gaped like a gulf when he did gern;[w]
That whether man or monster one could scarce discern.

Grantorto is very evidently the genius of the Irish rebellion of 1580—an allegorical representation of the spirit of Popery as animating the insurgent or native party. In his *View of the State of Ireland* Spenser describes the Galloglass, or Irish foot-soldier, as "armed in a long shirt of mail down to the calf of his leg, with a long broad axe in his hand," much as Grantorto is pictured here. Although he is also, as we have seen, made to be the seducer of France from Henry of Navarre, it does not seem to be necessary to adopt Upton's notion that we have here again King Philip of Spain, as we certainly have in Geryoneo, and as we probably also have in the Soldan.

Artegal suffers severely at first from the storm of blows with which the tyrant assails him, and, although he adroitly shuns as many of them as he can, and often stoops to escape them—

No shame to stoop, one's head more high to rear;
And, much to gain, a little for to yield:
So stoutest knights doen oftentimes in field—

yet the heavy and nimbly wielded iron axe, cleaving his armour, gashes his flesh in numerous places. He at last manages, however, when the felon has raised his arm for a more than usually ponderous stroke, to plunge his sword into his side, when a torrent of blood gushes out from the wound, and Grantorto brays and yells tremendously. At the same time he catches the intended blow of the battle-axe on his shield, from which the giant then strives in vain to extricate his weapon, dragging about the knight in all directions as he tugs at it;

[w] Grin in rage.

till at last Artegal gives him up his shield, and, flying at his head with his good sword, Chrysaor (the poet has forgotten that it was long ago broken to pieces by Queen Radigund), first comes down upon him with a blow that makes all his huge frame stagger, and, then following that up with a rapid succession of others, at last compels him to bite the earth ;—

> Whom when he saw prostrated on the plain,
> He lightly reft his head to ease him of his pain.

The people all shout for joy ; and, falling at fair Irena's feet, adore her "as their true liege and princess natural ;"—

> And eke her champion's glory sounded over all.

Artegal then, leading her "unto the palace where their kings did reign," there establishes her in the peaceful possession of her kingdom. After this he proceeds to punish with severity all such as had either openly or secretly taken part with the late tyrant ; the effect of which was that soon there was not an individual in the country who, so long as this good knight continued in the administration of Irena's affairs, durst once have disobeyed her.

> During which time that he did there remain,
> His study was true justice how to deal,
> And day and night employed his busy pain
> How to reform that ragged commonweal:
> And that same iron man, which could reveal
> All hidden crimes, through all that realm be sent
> To search out those that used to rob and steal,
> Or did rebel gainst lawful government;
> On whom he did inflict most grievous punishment.

This is exactly the same account that Spenser gives of the government of his patron Lord Grey in his prose tract on the State of Ireland. It is known, however, that the severity of the Lord Deputy, which the poet so warmly admires and defends, exposed him after his return to England to great obloquy. This sufficiently explains the remarkable passage that follows. Artegal, we are told, was "through occasion" called away to Fairy Court before he could thoroughly accomplish his plans of reform ; so

>   that of necessity
> His course of justice he was forced to stay,
> And Talus to revoke from the right way,
> In which he was that realm for to redress:
> But envy's cloud still dimmeth virtue's ray!
> So, having freed Irena from distress,
> He took his leave of her there left in heaviness.

He has scarcely arrived in that other land from which he had crossed over to the kingdom of Irena when he meets, sitting together by the wayside, two foul, ill-favoured hags, in ragged and tattered garments, further painted at full length in this powerful style:—

> The one of them, that elder did appear,
> With her dull eyes did seem to look askew,
> That her mis-shape much helped; and her foul hair
> Hung loose and loathsomely; thereto her hue
> Was wan and lean, that all her teeth arew [x]
> And all her bones might through her cheeks be read;
> Her lips were, like raw leather, pale and blue:
> And, as she spake, therewith she slavered;
> Yet spake she seldom; but thought more, the less she said:
>
> Her hands were foul and dirty, never washed
> In all her life, with long nails over-raught
> Like puttock's [y] claws; with the one of which she scratched
> Her cursed head, although it itched naught;
> The other held a snake with venom fraught,
> On which she fed and gnawed hungrily,
> As if that long she had not eaten aught;
> That round about her jaws one might descry
> The bloody gore and poison dropping loathsomely.
>
> Her name was Envy, knowen well thereby:
> Whose nature is to grieve and grudge at all
> That ever she sees done praiseworthily;
> Whose sight to her is greatest cross may fall,
> And vexeth so, that makes her eat her gall:
> For, when she wanteth other thing to eat,
> She feeds on her own maw unnatural,
> And of her own foul entrails makes her meat:
> Meat fit for such a monster's monsterous dieat;

---

[x] In a row.   [y] Kites.   [z] That may fall.

And, if she happed of any good to hear,
That had to any happily[a] betid,
Then would she inly fret, and grieve, and tear
Her flesh for fellness, which she inward hid;
But if she heard of ill that any did,
Or harm that any had, then would she make
Great cheer, like one unto a banquet bid;
And in another's loss great pleasure take,
As she had got thereby and gained a great stake.

This, it will be observed, is feminine Envy. The description may be compared with that of Lucifera's male counsellor of the same name in the Fourth Canto of the First Book. The second hag is now brought forward into the same magic light:—

The other nothing better was than she:
Agreeing in bad will and cankered kind,
But in bad manner they did disagree:
For whatso Envy good or bad did find
She did conceal, and murder her own mind;
But this, whatever evil she conceived,
Did spread abroad and throw in the open wind:
Yet this in all her words might be perceived,
That all she sought was men's good name to have bereaved.

For, whatsoever good by any said
Or done she heard, she would straightways invent
How to deprave or slanderously upbraid,
Or to misconstrue of a man's intent,
And turn to ill the thing that well was meant:
Therefore she used often to resort
To common haunts, and companies frequent,
To hark what any one did good report,
To blot the same with blame, or wrest in wicked sort:

And, if that any ill she heard of any,
She would it eke, and make much worse by telling,
And take great joy to publish it to many:
That every matter worse was for her melling:
Her name was hight Detraction, and her dwelling
Was near to Envy, even her neighbour next;
A wicked hag, and Envy self excelling
In mischief; for herself she only vexed:
But this same both herself and others eke perplexed.

---

[a] Haply.

Her face was ugly, and her mouth distort,
Foaming with poison round about her gills,
In which her cursed tongue, full sharp and short,
Appeared like aspe's sting, that closely kills,
Or cruelly does wound whomso she wills;
A distaff in her other hand she had,
Upon the which she little spins, but spills;
And fains to weave false tales and leasings bad,
To throw amongst the good which others had disprad.

The two have now combined against Sir Artegal, and, as his mortal foes, lie in wait to do him what mischief they can, all for having delivered Irena from their snares.

Besides, unto themselves they gotten had
A monster which the Blatant Beast men call,
A dreadful fiend of gods and men ydrad,
Whom they by sleights allured and to their purpose lad.

Of the Blatant Beast, of whom we shall hear more in the next Book, it will be sufficient to say for the present that it may be understood to typify what in modern times is commonly designated, by a more respectful form of words, Public Opinion.

When Sir Artegal comes up, the two hags fall to howling like two shepherd's curs when a wolf has got among their flocks;

And Envy first, as she that first him eyed,
Towards him runs, and, with rude flaring locks,
About her ears does beat her breast and forehead knocks.

Then from her mouth the gobbet[b] she does take,
The which whylere she was so greedily
Devouring, even that half-gnawen snake,
And at him throws it most despitefully:
The cursed serpent, though she hungrily
Erst chawed thereon, yet was not all so dead,
But that some life remained secretly;
And, as he passed afore withouten dread,
Bit him behind, that long the mark was to be read.

[In other words, Grey long experienced the effects of the malice with which he was now attacked.]

Then the other hag, the account proceeds, coming be-

VOL. II.   [b] Mouthful.   T

hind him, began to revile him and rail upon him, charging him with having, both by abuse of his power and by unmanly guile, not only tarnished his own honour, but stained that bright sword, intrusted to him to be used as the sword of justice, in much innocent blood. Grantorto, too, she asserted, he had treacherously surprised, and foully put to death. These were the very charges brought against Grey for the manner in which he had suppressed the Earl of Desmond's rebellion.

> Thereto the Blatant Beast, by them set on,
> At him began aloud to bark and bay
> With bitter rage and fell contention;
> That all the woods and rocks nigh to that way
> Began to quake and tremble with dismay;
> And all the air rebellowed again;
> So dreadfully his hundred tongues did bray:
> And evermore those hags themselves did pain,
> To sharpen him, and their own cursed tongues did strain.
>
> And, still among, most bitter words they spake,
> Most shameful, most unrighteous, most untrue,
> That they the mildest man alive would make
> Forget his patience, and yield vengeance due
> To her, that so false slanders at him threw:
> And, more to make them pierce and wound more deep,
> She with the sting which in her vile tongue grew
> Did sharpen them, and in fresh poison steep:
> Yet he passed on, and seemed of them to take no keep.
>
> But Talus, hearing her so lewdly rail
> And speak so ill of him that well deserved,
> Would her have chastised with his iron flail,
> If her Sir Artegal had not preserved,
> And him forbidden, who his hest observed:
> So much the more at him still did she scold,
> And stones did cast; yet he for nought would swerve
> From his right course, but still the way did hold
> To Fairy Court; where what him fell shall else be told.

And so ends the Canto and the Book.

END OF VOL. II.

www.ingramcontent.com/pod-product-compliance
Lightning Source LLC
Chambersburg PA
CBHW032144230426
43672CB00011B/2444